Katie would like to dedicate the book

With thanks to all my family and friends for their love and support. To George the dog for keeping me company on our many morning walks and keeping my feet warm under my desk on cold winter mornings. To my parents who are a continued source of inspiration and without whom I would not be the person I am today. To my sister Jenny for your humorous mocking of my constant misuse of the English language – if there are any mistakes in here I blame Nigel. And finally, to Ben for your endless love and support, for which I cannot thank you enough.

Nigel would like to dedicate the book

To those who allow me to enter Nigel world: Catherine, Eliot and Toby. On a personal note I would like to wish West Ham United well at the Olympic Stadium, and hope that Plymouth Argyle get promotion. To Albert and Thelma for always being there. I raise a glass to Roger. Obviously, I will blame Katie for all mistakes.

A Practical Guide to Event Promotion

This *Practical Guide to Event Promotion* offers the reader a short and succinct overview of the range of marketing communication materials from print to social marketing that can be used to promote an event successfully to the correct target markets. It includes invaluable advice on how to identify the type of communication tools most applicable to the kind of event that is being promoted and its target market; how to use and implement these effectively; useful tips on things to avoid; as well as suggested time frames to use before, during and after the event. Examples of best practice and insights from events marketers are integrated throughout. Although full of practical information, a strong theoretical base underpins the advice included on how event managers can apply communication and persuasion theory to key audiences.

This book will be a useful resource for Events Management students putting on an event as part of their course and for assessments, and those wanting to convert general theory into practical skills they will use in the workplace.

Nigel Jackson is Reader in Persuasion and Communication at the Plymouth School of Tourism and Hospitality, Plymouth University, UK. He has published over 30 peer-reviewed journal articles and the textbook *Promoting and Marketing Events* (2013). His research specialises in political communication and persuasion.

Katie Angliss is a Lecturer in Events Management at the Plymouth School of Tourism and Hospitality, Plymouth University, UK. Her research interest is in how organisations use events to enhance their corporate reputation. Prior to this Katie worked in corporate Public Relations (PR).

A Practical Guide to Event Promotion

Nigel Jackson and Katie Angliss

Routledge
Taylor & Francis Group

LONDON AND NEW YORK

First published 2018
by Routledge
2 Park Square, Milton Park, Abingdon, Oxon OX14 4RN

and by Routledge
711 Third Avenue, New York, NY 10017

Routledge is an imprint of the Taylor & Francis Group, an informa business

British Library Cataloguing-in-Publication Data
A catalogue record for this book is available from the British Library

Library of Congress Cataloging-in-Publication Data
A catalog record for this book has been requested

ISBN: 978-1-138-91533-6 (hbk)
ISBN: 978-1-138-91534-3 (pbk)
ISBN: 978-1-315-69028-5 (ebk)

Typeset in Sabon and Frutiger
by Keystroke, Neville Lodge, Tettenhall, Wolverhampton

Printed and bound in Great Britain by
TJ International Ltd, Padstow, Cornwall

Contents

Contents

List of figures

List of tables

List of boxes

Preface

This book has been several years in gestation and has three main sources, the first two are general background and the third is the catalyst for us setting out to put fingers to the keyboard. As an academic study events management is still in its early stages; in childhood, possibly approaching adolescence. Initially, textbooks and journal articles drew from other disciplines, but gradually event-related books have been created. Shortly after *Promoting and Marketing Events* was published in 2013 a number of other related articles and books were also published. However, these have nearly all been primarily introductory to the basic ideas; there was little taking us to the next level of how to do it. Then, having identified a gap, we considered our own practical experience in marketing, PR and corporate events and realised that we had both learnt many lessons over the years and imparted them to others, both formally through training but also informally. Without the third factor, though, the idea would probably have laid on the backburner. A few years ago we changed the nature of an assignment for our second-year module, adding a more practical aspect. We initially produced a short guide and extensive reading list, and then ran classes to help build up skill sets. Nonetheless, we realised that something more detailed was missing, and it is from this simple fact that this book was born. We have the experience and knowledge to fill the gap of a text-book that offers practical tips and hints, but within a wider conceptual underpinning.

While practitioners will be able to dip in and out to gain some interesting insights, this is clearly a textbook aimed at events management, marketing and PR students. Therefore, we offer a range of examples, case studies and advice (driven by our own or others' experiences). At various points we also suggest scenario-based tasks, usually derived from an amalgam of actual experience, so that students can start to pull together their learning. Although we teach in a UK university, most of the theoretical underpinning can be applied universally. We use a range of different examples from around the world to give a flavour both of what is common and what is country-specific. Clearly, you need to apply the customs, cultures, laws and experiences of whatever country you live in. Since one of the authors has spent most of their life outside the UK this has reminded us that the world is not Eurocentric. We hope that whether you are a student, lecturer, commentator or practitioner this book is of value to you.

Acknowledgements

Obviously any errors are entirely our own, but there are a number of people without whose help this book would not have come to fruition whom we want to thank. Clearly the support and love, not forgetting regular sustenance, of both of our families have provided the right environment. All of the students on *Promoting Events* have helped to stimulate our thoughts with their enthusiasm, ideas and comments about communicating events in general. We would also like to record thanks to colleagues at Plymouth University who have offered their comments. Discussions on communication and persuasion theory with Darren Lilleker of Bournemouth University helped to shape some of our ideas in Chapters 2 and 3. We owe a big thank you to John Hibdige who at several points has offered us and our students his insight on the logistics of putting on events, especially the technical components. Jennifer Steyn was very helpful in sourcing an international aspect to event marketing. We also appreciate the visual marketing images provided by Simone Aronje-Adetoye, the Managing Director of the Limpopo Youth Orchestra, and the invite provided by Fern Cargill from the University of South Australia.

In addition we would like to say thank you to the anonymous referees whose comments helped to shape how students and lecturers might use the book. We owe a debt of gratitude to the editorial team at Routledge, Philippa Mullins and Emma Travis who saw something in our original idea and have helped a rough idea to be published. We have been touched by the enthusiasm of those who have been interviewed to provide the case studies, or to check examples. We are particularly grateful for their time to offer us their experience, ideas and to check our copy, because without them this book would have lacked some insight.

We would also like to acknowledge the following for the use of illustrations: with thanks to the International Olympic Committee for permission to reproduce an edited version of their Factfile available on their official website (www.olympic.org); permission to reprint Figure 3.6 from Jennifer Steyn and Lensflaire CC; permission to reprint Figure 4.2 from Jane Devonshire, Tindle Newspaper Group; permission to reprint Figure 4.3 from Simone Aronje-Adetoye, Limpopo Youth Orchestra; permission to reprint Figure 5.1 from South Australia University; permission to reprint Figure 12.1 Big Festival Weekend 2015, Plymouth, image courtesy of Plymouth University; permissions from The Appointment Group for their images on websites.

Chapter 1

Introduction

Introduction

American Founding Father Benjamin Franklin (1706–1790) said: 'If you would not be forgotten, as soon as you are dead and rotten, either write things worth reading, or do things worth the writing' (*Poor Richard's Almanac* 1738). This neatly sums up the communication process for the events manager, who by putting on events is doing something, and by writing (or talking) about it they are at the same time promoting what they are doing. Within this context of 'saying and doing something' this chapter will set the scene for explaining the meaning and importance of routes to market for event managers. We then assess marketing communication literature to highlight the development of practical promotional materials. Finally, the structure of the book will be set out, and in particular why and how we combine apparently disparate channels together. At the end of the chapter students will be able to:

- Select relevant techniques for appropriate routes to market;
- Assess which promotional tools may best apply for your event;
- Understand your tools better by knowing their historical development;
- Recognise the importance of using an integrated communications strategy.

Routes to market

You can have the most amazing event, but if your target audience has not heard about it, then no one will turn up. Routes to market are all the activities an event undertakes to reach their audiences, and to get them to attend. Typically, an event will combine key components of the marketing mix, such as the processes and distribution, with the promotions mix to identify specific tools and techniques. We can draw a simple analogy with you deciding to visit your friend who lives 300 miles away. Will you go directly to them or stop off on the way to visit a tourism site or another friend? Will you go by plane, train, car or hitchhike? How long will it take you and how much will it cost? Will they be able to pick you up at the airport or train station? The decisions you make here are whether to travel directly or not, which transport method provides best value for money and possibly what might suit your friend. There is not necessarily a bad route, but some routes are better for you than others.

It is worth noting that if you have only one or two events, especially if they are fairly small or limited to a narrow target market, selecting your routes to market will probably not be that difficult. However, as management consultants Booz and Co (2010) identify, selecting the correct routes is a trickier task if you are rapidly growing, have a range of markets and operate across geographical areas.

Accenture (2014) have taken this basic idea of routes to market and suggested that organisations develop market 'archtypes'. These 'archtypes' recognise that in a global economy grouping markets with similar commercial environments, consumer types and capabilities allows an organisation to develop fit-for-purpose strategies for each different audience. They are therefore looking for patterns in one market, which can be replicated in others, so that they are grouped together in part by routes to market.

Figure 1.1 outlines the core four components which help you decide what might be the combination of activity for your best route to market for each event: direction; channel; tool; and customer.

Direction assesses whether you will reach the customer directly or indirectly via an intermediary. Most events will sell direct, so the customer phones up or visits the event website to pay for their tickets. However, without trying to be too pedantic, e-commerce could be direct or indirect; the former would be the case if the event is running the online sales themselves but the latter if they were using the services of an e-ticketing agency. Direction can also refer to whether the communication is designed to be just one-way, to inform and persuade the message receiver to attend, or two-way to deliberately engage in dialogue.

The channel is the means by which you will seek to reach your target attendees. We shall discuss these in more detail in Chapter 3, but for now it is worth noting that the most common promotional channels are:

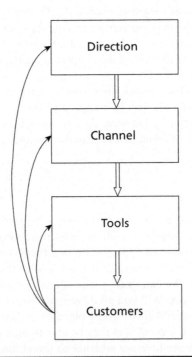

Figure 1.1 Selecting the best route to market

- Advertising
- Personal selling
- Public relations
- The internet
- Sponsorship
- Sales promotion
- Direct marketing
- Trade shows and exhibitions.

As Figure 1.2 shows, the first two channels, advertising and personal selling, are collectively referred to as above the line because a commission is paid. The other channels are below the line because although they obviously incur a cost it is not in the form of a commission. Though we must note that it is possible that commission is payable for an e-ticketing agency. As we shall see throughout this book it is unlikely, and indeed unwise, for an event to choose just one channel.

Very closely linked to channel is our third component, the exact tools to be used. Just selecting, for example, public relations and the internet as our channel does not alone provide enough insight into what precisely we will do and when. So, if we look at public relations, we may well decide to send out press releases and consult with key stakeholders such as local residents. Thus, before we announce our event via the media, we would have paved the way by talking to local politicians and resident organisations, and if need be made changes to our event. Similarly, if we decide to use the internet, we could use the event website, or communicate via social networks such as Twitter, Facebook, Hyves, Orkut and QZone. Selecting both the channel and tools decides precisely how an event will seek to reach its customers, and Table 1.1 explains what influences the thinking behind why a tool might be chosen.

There is an assumption that when thinking about their customers an event will consider the value proposition they are offering. This is essentially the value the customer will ascribe to the experience from attending an event. In essence, the event needs to construct a message that offers an attractive experience to the potential event attendee. Having sorted out their offer, the event communicator needs to identify to whom they will make it. Such targeting would typically be based on segmenting your audience, so are certain personal characteristics such as gender, age, where they live and income relevant to you? Or is there a behavioural pattern, such as past attendees, that makes some targets more likely than others?

In addition to the four factors that create an overall framework outlined in Figure 1.1, further variables may have an impact on the precise nature of the routes chosen. Table 1.2 outlines other variables which may be taken into account relating to the nature of, or context, that affects the message receiver rather than the construction of the message.

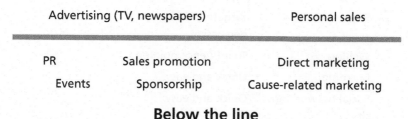

Figure 1.2 Above and below the line

Table 1.1 Selecting the right channel and tool

Channel	Tools	Why selected	Type of events
Advertising	Newspaper	Read by target audience.	Community-based but also larger regional events.
	Radio	Size of audience.	Larger regional events.
	Television	Size of audience.	Larger regional and national events.
	Online ad	Reaches people beyond a geographic location.	One that can be accessed online.
	Trade	Reaches suppliers and buyers in an industry.	Trade shows, award ceremonies, networking events.
Personal selling	Event organiser	Limited budget.	Events with a small budget.
	Sales team	Need to stand out in a competitive market/high-value tickets.	Business to business events/ luxury events.
	Contract out	Limited skills.	Big events, especially in entertainments.
Public relations	Media relations	Cheap and easy.	Any event, but especially those with smaller budgets or community-based.
	Issues management	Avoids crises.	
	Community relations	To gain support.	Any event that might affect residents or political bodies.
The internet	Website	Cheap, wide distribution, complexity of message.	Community-based. All events.
	Email	Cheap, targeted and interactive.	
	E-newsletter	Targeted, cheap and persuasive.	
	Weblog	To influence opinion.	
	Microblog	Quick and easy.	
	Social networking site	Quick and easy.	

Channel	Tools	Why selected	Type of events
Sales promotion	Price discounts	To generate immediate sales.	Ticket-based.
	Product enhancements	To generate immediate sales and enhance event experience.	Ticket-based.
Sponsorship	Event sponsorship (main or ancillary)	To sell products.	More likely to be bigger events with many spectators.
Direct marketing	Direct mail	To support a brand.	Any event.
		To encourage attendance.	
		Get across complex messages.	
Trade shows and exhibitions	Exhibition stand	To reach either key industry buyers or individual customers.	They are events in their own right.
	Sponsorship of meetings, material or awards	To reach either key industry buyers or individual customers.	

Table 1.2 Factors that affect the route to market

Factor	Options
Country	Different cultural factors
Type of business	Public or private
Nature of audience	Internal, members or external
Type of customer	B2B or B2C*
Nature of communication	

* Business to Business or Business to Consumer.

1.1 Exercise scenario

You have been asked to help promote a 10km fun run for a local children's hospice in your city (population 150,000 people). The local authority has already agreed to the necessary road closures, and a local running club will organise it. This is the first time the event has occurred, and you are hoping for 1,000 runners who will need to pay a small fee and generate sponsorship for the charity. It is also hoped there will be up to 5,000 spectators. You have no marketing budget. It is now January and the event is taking place in October. So how do you choose and use the appropriate routes to market?

Remembering that you have no money our advice is to break this down by addressing the following:

- Who are the different audiences?
- How do you best reach, both collectively and individually, those who might be persuaded to run?
- How would you reach potential spectators to get them to turn up?
- Who might be your possible sponsors and how might you best reach them?
- What are the contacts and routes to market that sponsors and others involved in the event have that you might be able to use?
- How will you assess whether you have chosen the correct routes?

The development of promotional materials

We suggest that our current use of promotional tools is shaped by a range of factors, which include:

1 How political rulers maintain their power or are challenged by others. Rulers typically seek to control the channels of information that citizens receive, whereas the latter are more likely to seek to use new sources of information and bypass such control.
2 How individuals and groups within society share their experiences.
3 The development of public opinion so that citizens have some say on the wider issues that affect their experiences.
4 Technological developments that introduce new ways of communicating and so shape society.

While there are often linkages between all four we shall focus primarily on how technological change has created the communications world in which you operate. We suggest that the tools open to you are the result of three particular technological revolutions:

- The printing press
- Broadcasting
- The internet.

The written word

Although the oral tradition was dominant for millennia, and indeed is still celebrated, for example with the Orkney Storytelling Festival (www.orkneystorytellingfestival.co.uk), our concern is with mass communication tools. Ancient societies had used the written word to offer instructions and news, but these were essentially hand-produced one at a time. Written communication was transformed when Johannes Gutenberg invented the printing press around 1439, which enabled the mass production of books and eventually the creation of newspapers and pamphlets.

One of the first newspapers was the *Notizie Scritte* posted by the Venetian government in 1556 which cost a Gazetta. Many of the newspapers that British readers will be familiar with were created in the eighteenth and nineteenth centuries, for example *The Observer* (1791) and *The Manchester Guardian* (1821). Since the early twentieth century, the style of UK newspapers differed depending on their audiences. The tabloids (or red tops) such as *The Sun* and *The Mirror* focus on a more working-class audience, with a more sensational approach to news. Their daily diet is light news, crime, sex, celebrity, sport and unusual human stories. The broadsheets such as *The Daily Telegraph* and *The Times* are targeted at middle and professional classes. Their content is focused on serious news, international events, political and economic events, and in terms of 'planned events' tend towards the 'high-brow' such as drama and classical music. However, the divide is blurring with the broadsheets carrying more sport and celebrity news, and several of them are no longer printed in the 'broadsheet' format.

Emergence of broadcasting

Although television may now be the dominant broadcast channel, it was radio that was the first broadcasting tool. After Heinrich Hertz discovered radio waves in 1888, in 1894 Guglielmo Marconi experimented with transmitting and detecting radio waves. Initially radio was considered as a means of communicating between ships and ship-to-shore. It was only in 1920 that the Marconi company made the link with entertainment when they broadcast from their Chelmsford works. In the 1930s to the 1950s radio was the dominant broadcast media. It may be an apocryphal story, but it is suggested that when CBS aired in news bulletin format H.G. Wells's *War of the Worlds* in October 1938, it led some listeners to believe that an actual Martian invasion was in progress. If this story is true, and we have some doubts, it is an interesting example of the power of this medium.

Although John Logie Baird gave the first public demonstration of television in 1925, it did not take off until the 1950s. A series of events such as the coronation of Queen Elizabeth II in 1953 and the assassination of US President John Kennedy in 1963 encouraged more and more people to turn to television. By the 1960s in many parts of the developed world television had taken over from radio. However, what is common to both technologies, as Curran and Seaton (1997) suggest, is that their use and growth were as much a social construct as a technical one.

The internet

The launch by the Russians of Sputnik 1 in 1957, followed in 1962 by the Bay of Pigs crisis, led US military planners to ask how the US armed forces and the government would communicate during a nuclear war (Abbate 1999). The ability of one computer to 'talk' to another was considered the answer. The 1960s saw the development by military scientists of the Advanced Research Projects Agency Network (ARPANET), launched in 1969. The military had been the driving force behind this nascent computer network, but during the 1970s and 1980s the academic community was increasingly involved. There was also a computer network operating outside ARPANET, established around the US counterculture movement (Castells 1996). In 1970 email was developed which enabled person-to-person communication.

By the 1980s the development of software and various protocols meant that the internet, in effect, existed as we now know it. However, it was still the preserve of a small community of experts. It took Tim Berners-Lee to invent the World Wide Web in 1989, and later the creation in 1993 of a freely available browser, Mosaic, to transform this communication medium. It then became increasingly open to wider social, commercial and political usage.

After the creation of the World Wide Web the developments came fast and furious. In 1997, Ian Ring produced the first blog, SixDegrees.com, which was believed to be the first social network. Friendster followed in 2002, LinkedIn in 2003, Facebook in 2004 and Twitter in 2006. Such rapid technological developments have changed how we communicate.

Book structure

The structure of this book is predicated on two beliefs about the management of the communication process. First, that the tools used should be integrated with each other and not used at random and independently. For example, the message pushed out in a direct mail letter should be repeated in some way on the website, or a media relations campaign might precede an advertising campaign in order to raise awareness. Second, communication should not be viewed as a one-off hit, rather, irrespective of the individual event it should aim to help build relationships with the target audience.

This book will address the practical detail of producing event communication material, but within an academic underpinning. The book is divided into four different sections, Part I effectively sets up the rest of the book. Part II looks at how event managers can use a variety of written and printed materials, often the bread-and-butter of event promotion. Part III turns attention to the application of recent technological change in how the internet is now used to support, and as an alternative to, printed materials. Our last section addresses a range of primarily visual techniques.

In terms of the detail, the two chapters in the first section 'Theoretical underpinning' assess how event managers can apply communication and persuasion theory to key audiences, and then identifies the types of communication tools that can be used. The four chapters in Part II 'Printed material' cover some of the channels that event managers first learn to use. These include how to write a range of advertisements, a direct mail campaign, media relations tools and how to use merchandising either to generate additional income or to provide a long-term promotional keepsake. The three chapters in Part III 'Online media' address how event managers can create and use their website, social networking sites and email and e-newsletters. Part IV 'Multimedia' will cover more visual/image-based means of communicating. These include how to create and use a video, how to use photography to promote events and make your exhibition stand more attractive so that traffic can be driven to it. This book will help Events Management students wanting to convert general theory into practical skills they will use in the workplace. It will empower event practitioners either to create their own effective communications channels, or to be better able to manage others doing this on their behalf by understanding the dos and don'ts and the meaning of the language used.

We offer one minor health warning. We have deliberately provided a range of website urls which can help to illustrate our points. At the time of writing they were all accessible; however, the nature of events is such that some may not still be available when you open them. Indeed, at early stages of this book we identified a number of sites we later had to delete. We apologise if this is an issue for you, but you should be able to find other similar sites to help your depth of understanding.

The history of sponsoring the Olympics

Sponsorship in various forms has supported the Olympic Movement since the first modern Olympic Games in Athens in 1896. The use of sponsorship has gradually evolved from each Olympic cycle to the next, including both summer and winter Olympics. Below are outlined some of the key milestones in the history of sponsorship in the modern Olympic Games.

1896 **Athens** – Companies provide revenue through advertising during the Olympic Games.

1912 **Stockholm** – Approximately ten Swedish companies purchase sole rights to take photographs and sell memorabilia of the Olympic Games.

1920 **Antwerp** – The official Olympic Games programme contains a great deal of corporate advertising.

1924 **Paris** – Advertising signage appears within view from the Olympic Games venues for the first and only time in history.

1928 **Amsterdam** – Current TOP Partner Coca-Cola begins the longest continuous Olympic partnership. Concessionaires are granted rights to operate restaurants on stadium grounds.

Advertising continues in the official Olympic Games programme. The IOC stipulates that posters and billboards may not be displayed on the stadium grounds and buildings.

1932 **Lake Placid** – The OCOG [Organising Committees for the Olympic Games] solicits businesses to provide free merchandising and advertising tie-ins. Many major department stores in the eastern US feature the Olympic Games marks in window displays, and many national businesses use the Games as an advertising theme.

1952 **Helsinki** – The first Olympic Games to launch an international marketing programme.

Companies from 11 countries make contributions of goods and services ranging from food for the athletes to flowers for medallists.

1960 **Rome** – An extensive sponsor/supplier programme includes 46 companies that provide technical support and products such as perfume, chocolate, toothpaste and soap.

1964   **Tokyo** – 250 companies develop marketing relationships with the Games. Seiko creates quartz-timing technology, providing the most accurate timing system to date.

1976   **Montreal** – With 628 sponsors and suppliers, domestic sponsorship generates US$7 million for the OCOG.

1984   **Los Angeles** – For the first time, the domestic sponsorship programme is divided into three categories. Each category is granted designated rights and product category exclusivity.

The marketing programme is limited to the host country and US companies.

1988   **Calgary** – The IOC creates The Olympic Partners (TOP) worldwide sponsorship programme, in coordination with the 1988 Seoul OCOGs in Seoul and Calgary, as well as 159 NOCs. TOP is based on the 1984 Los Angeles model of product category exclusivity.

1992   **Albertville** – TOP grows from nine to 12 partners in the programme's second generation.

1994   **Lillehammer** – Broadcast and marketing programmes generate more than US$500 million, breaking almost every major marketing record for an Olympic Winter Games.

1996   **Atlanta** – The Games are funded entirely via private sources.

2000   **Sydney** – Sets a new standard for brand protection through education, legislation and advertising controls.

2004   **Athens** – In the smallest country to host the Olympic Games to date, Athens 2004 achieved its sponsorship revenue target two years before the Games and ultimately generated revenue from national and torch relay sponsorship that was 50% higher than initial estimates.

2006   **Turin Torino** – The programme accounted for 6.14% of the total sponsorship spending in the market, which was significantly higher than previous Olympic Winter Games sponsorship programmes and represented nearly 1% of the total advertising spend in the Italian market, 35 times greater than that of Salt Lake 2002.

Source: Olympic Marketing Fact File 2014 online at www.olympic.org/Documents/IOC_Marketing/OLYMPIC_MARKETING_FACT_%20FILE_2014.pdf.

With thanks to the International Olympic Committee for permission to reproduce an edited version of their Fact File available on their official website (www.olympic.org).

Your task

1 Was the early growth of sponsorship a direct result of a deliberate strategy from the International Olympic Commission (IOC), or do you feel that the early running was made by the commercial operations seeking an opportunity?
2 Sponsorship is now obviously important to the IOC. What are the benefits, what could go wrong and what are the consequences of both?
3 This case study shows a series of developments in sponsorship. What might be the source of such innovative change?
4 What would the summer and winter Olympics and Paralympics look like if there was no sponsorship? Is sponsorship now a core part of all mega-events?

Discussion questions

1 How would you decide which routes to market to utilise?
2 In a world of ever-changing technology how will you decide whether and when to discard older methods and adopt newer ones?
3 Event communicators will usually test techniques to see what delivery, timing or content works best. With such frequent testing of tools how would you disaggregate which one(s) is having the desired effect?
4 What do you believe will be the next three big tools in events communication, and why?

Further information

Books

Bartels, R. (1976) *The History of Marketing Thought*, 2nd edn, Columbus, OH: Grid Publishing.
Garrett, A. and Wilson, H. (2005) *IBM's Route to Market Strategy*, Cranfield University School of Management.
Gechev, R. (2012) Event Marketing in N. Ferdinand and P. Kitchen (eds) *Events Management: an international approach*, London: Sage.

Article

Jindal, R., Reinartz, W., Krafft, M. and Hoyer, W. (2007) 'Determinants of the variety of routes to market', *International Journal of Research in Marketing*, 24 (1): 17–25.

Websites

http://paramarketing.com/routes-to-market/ – management consultants that offer advice on how to reach your routes to market.
www.promotionalproductswork.org/collegiate-corner/history-of-promotional-products – the history of promotional products in the US.

PART I

THEORETICAL UNDERPINNING

This section sets up the book by looking at key theoretical context and concepts.

Chapter 2

Communicating with your audiences

Introduction

The previous chapter highlighted some of the historical trends that shape how and why event managers communicate with their key audiences. This chapter will provide a conceptual context as to how we communicate, leading towards a more detailed understanding in Chapter 3 on the exact tools you will use. We will start by outlining what communications means, and the problems that it might solve. We will then introduce some key communication and persuasion models to provide a conceptual underpinning. In particular, we will assess how to construct powerful messages. By the end of the chapter students will be able to:

- Understand the core components of successful communications;
- Apply research on how we read and understand different written messages;
- Assess how events managers can persuade;
- Create a persuasive message.

What is communications?

As event managers you are part of the communication business. You have to communicate all the time, for example to your staff, customers, partners and participants. Moreover, you do this before, during and after the event, in a variety of locations and using a range of tools. This might include a written flyer, a team briefing and making public announcements. While each communication tool will have, as we shall see, rules peculiar to it, in this chapter we shall outline some of the wider ideas that shape how you communicate. If you understand the different ways in which people communicate and respond to communication, you are more likely to be able to be an effective communicator achieving your goals.

As an event manager you will need to know who to communicate with, how to communicate with them, and the message to be delivered. In addition, you need to be aware that events themselves are considered communication tools. Thus Getz (2008: 151) suggests that events are 'artifacts' which have a precise, and often personal, meaning to the recipient. For example, the celebration of births, weddings, divorces and funerals denote symbolic significance in our lives. So while mostly you will be concerned with encouraging attendance or to use an event to

15

2.1 Defining communication

Communication is the means by which information and opinion about an event are transferred from one person to another. It may be in the form of words, pictures, aurally or it may combine all of these. Communication is used to inform event stakeholders, change their attitudes and ultimately to encourage a change in behaviour, i.e. attend the event. Communication can be both deliberate and unintended.

promote something, events can also hold ritualistic meaning. What this means is that communication, and an events role in this, cannot be separated from a society's culture. For example, Quinceañera (or Baile de Bebutantes in Brazil), the coming of age ceremony for 15-year-old girls in many South American countries, is essentially a personal milestone, often with religious significance (within the Catholic Church) that is celebrated with a fiesta.

Moreover, as our cultures evolve the meaning of events changes. For example, in fifteenth-century England most community events were linked to the farming year or Protestant festivals. As we have become an urban, industrialised and non-secular society such festivals have either ceased to exist, or their purpose has changed so that they are typically economic tools to bring in tourists. For example, modern-day Mardi Gras, closely associated with the city of New Orleans, the state of Louisiana and parts of South America, has its origins first in ancient Rome and then the Catholic Church in the middle ages, when it was a celebration allowed just before the fasting required by Lent (www.novareinna.com/festive/mardi.html). We suggest that there exists a link between communications and culture, and that communication plays a key role in how the latter changes.

So why communicate?

Table 2.1 outlines the types of event-based problems communication can help you with. You will note that these are organised into four categories: encourage attendance; safety; logistics; and management. We can further divide this by two more factors, namely, whether the problem being addressed is prior to/after or during the event.

Thus to increase attendance, communication is primarily about reaching potential attendees and persuading them to attend. Safety messages are likely to be to a wider audience that could include staff, participants and attendees, and could be as much about not doing something as encouraging an action. Communications within logistics can be used to find more efficient ways of communicating with venues, suppliers and participants. As a management function, communication seeks to impart key information, enhance morale and secure agreement to the purpose and nature of the event.

Types of communication

Although communication is ubiquitous, and without it your event will not function effectively, the concept is not one-dimensional. Rather, there is a complexity of different layers to what communication is, and how you could use it.

We can differentiate by type of communication:

Table 2.1 The use of communication to address event problems

Factor	Problem	Application/solution
Encourage attendance	Do not know who is attending?	Let targets know what is happening and why they should attend.
	Not enough are attending.	Offer an incentive for them to attend.
Safety	Ensure safety and legal compliance.	Clear instructions.
Logistics	Reduce costs.	Find an efficient means of dealing with suppliers.
Management	How to get everyone to know what is happening.	Open regular and clear structures for interaction.
	To get consistency in actions.	Agreed single message.

- Synchronous (real time)
- Asynchronous (not present)
- One-to-one
- One-to-many
- Many-to-many
- Private
- Public.

For example, typically at an event your communication will be synchronous because you are communicating with performers, staff and attendees. However, your marketing communication, such as a website, may be asynchronous since someone could read about the details of your event while you are asleep.

How information is comprehended

It is all too easy for the creator of a message to focus only on what they want to say, but we also need to understand how our audiences absorb any written information we offer them. This will have an impact on how we design our materials, and there is some science that can help. We shall look at two models that have been applied to a variety of offline text, and in Chapter 8 we shall look at one suggested to explain online viewer behaviour.

The Gutenberg diagram

The first of our models to help explain how we 'read' printed material is the Gutenberg diagram (Gutenberg was the creator of the printing press and this approach is named after him). This describes a general pattern of how our eyes move when looking at evenly distributed, homogenous information. It is suggested that the eye moves diagonally straight from

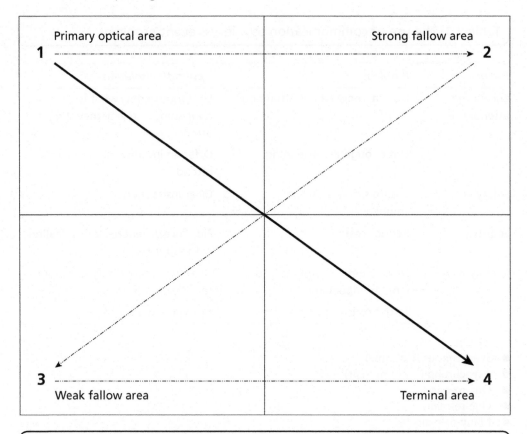

1   Primary optical area   Strong fallow area   2

3   Weak fallow area   Terminal area   4

Figure 2.1 The Gutenberg diagram

the top left to the bottom right, and so the focus is on these two points of a page. The pattern applies to text-heavy content, such as a newspaper, books and advertisements. It is associated with Edmund Arnold (1913–2007), an American newspaper designer who created the diagram as a means of giving understanding of a newspaper page. He suggested that each page should be divided into four quadrants, starting with the primary optical area (POA) on the top left where the eye (in left-to-right languages) naturally started. The eye then moves to the top right, referred to as the strong fallow area, then diagonally down to the weak fallow area in the bottom left. Finally, it moves to the bottom right or terminal area.

The pattern suggests that the eye will sweep across and down the page in a series of horizontal movements called axes of orientation. Each sweep starts a little further from the left edge and moves a little closer to the right edge. The overall movement is for the eye to travel from the primary area to the terminal area, and this path is referred to as reading gravity.

Within the Gutenberg diagram the strong and weak fallow areas fall outside this reading gravity path and so receive less attention unless there is a visual image designed to change the balance. Although the Gutenberg diagram should not be viewed as an absolute law to follow, it does suggest that left to themselves our readers will focus on two main areas: top left and bottom right (for left-to-right languages). In order to get readers to take more note of the two fallow areas (top right and bottom left) you will need to think about how your design can draw attention to them, perhaps through images. A typical use of this model would place the logo or a heading in the top left, an image or some important content in the middle, and a call to action or contact information in the bottom right.

The Z-pattern

The Gutenberg diagram can work well in designing documents which are text heavy and/or are evenly distributed, but may be of less value for your flyers and brochures. For such material a popular alternative is the Z-pattern. This describes how readers in left-to-right languages will start in the top left, move horizontally to the top right and then diagonally to the bottom left before finishing with another horizontal movement to the bottom right. Where in the Gutenberg diagram there are effectively two points that the reader focuses on, the top left and bottom right, with the Z-pattern there are four, so that the reader takes greater note of the top right and bottom left as well. For both approaches the start and the finish is the same; it is the journey between that is different.

Figure 2.2 shows the Z direction the reader follows. This starts with 1 at the top left and then the eye moves horizontally right to 2. Typically, this is where you would expect to see key content such as a heading or logos. It is then suggested that the eye moves diagonally downwards to point 3, and then from there horizontally again to step 4. This last point is of crucial importance as it is where we would normally expect to put the call to action. Thus it is step 4, which is where the reader leaves the page/poster/flyer or whatever, that is suggested as a place that might tell the reader to do something. This could be to visit a website or social media site, buy a ticket or whatever. When we are looking at promotional materials this call to action is vital, having set up the problem and then offered a solution it is important not to leave it up to the recipient to decide what to do.

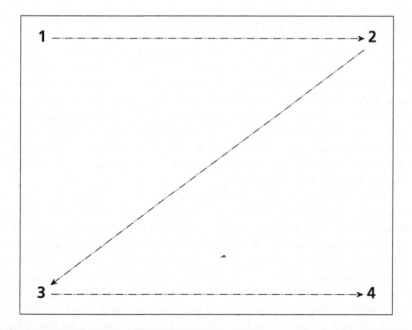

Figure 2.2 The Z-pattern

The basic Z-pattern is very simple, and may not completely replicate how everyone reads. A perhaps more sophisticated version is the Zigzag. This suggests that we still use a Z-pattern, but actually it is completed in a much shorter span, so there are several in a page and not one. So instead of looking at the page in one big single Z movement, the Zigzag suggests that there are a number of Z-movements. Accepting this version requires a slight revision to how this impacts on the design and content of your material. The start in step 1 will not always have equal weighting and step 4 will not always have a call to action, though it might include a conclusion/summation to the specific point (as opposed to the whole page) being made. However, the beginning and end of the page will still follow the same points of the Z-pattern concerning the important material at the start and the call to action at the end of the page.

We should note that the Gutenberg diagram and Z-pattern are not rigid models, rather they are suggestions to help our design. Most people probably apply different models to different communication tools, so a person might use the Gutenberg diagram when reading a letter and the Z-pattern for an advert. However, we suspect that some people are naturally more likely to view all their material via one or the other. Certainly we have found that some students use one or other model to types of communication we would not normally expect them to apply. What this suggests is that you should recognise such differences and not necessarily always rigidly stick to one model for a particular type of communication.

How we communicate

Communication is not a single process, it combines a range of methods with which to reach our audiences, often repeating or reinforcing a message in different ways, or using the direction that best suits a particular audience. Effective communication is dependent on how to reach the audience, and also how well-crafted the message is.

Mediated versus unmediated communication

There are essentially two key ways in which an event manager can communicate; either directly using unmediated communication or indirectly using mediated communication. Each uses its own channels and tools, so direct communication from the sender of a message to a recipient might include a direct mail letter, Facebook post and a meeting. An indirect approach might include media relations, advertising and events, the last of which influences by creating an atmosphere. The internet can be a type of direct communication in the form of email, or an indirect communication type such as pop-up adverts. The wise event manager will use either or both direct and indirect communication as the circumstances require, but we need to understand that they work in different ways.

The history of media use indicates that there have in the past been clear differences with one approach dominating. However, the existence and widespread use of the internet, which can be both, has challenged this simplistic model. Pippa Norris (2000) provides a means of classifying the use of communication in historical periods. As Table 2.2 shows, in the nineteenth and twentieth centuries direct personal communication dominated in the west. Such communication was based on networking and the oratorical skills of the message sender. Of course the mediated communication in the form of newspapers did exist, but Norris suggests that personal communication was key. What tended to happen was that the burgeoning press initially followed an agenda set by unmediated communication, for example, the 1880 British general election is widely believed to have been won by William Gladstone through the Midlothian campaign. Gladstone conducted a series of public meetings in a small part of

---

Table 2.2 Norris's communication eras

Era	Communications used	Timescale
Pre-modern	Personal meetings, public meetings and personal contacts.	1850s to 1930s
Modern	Mass communications, first radio, and then television.	Dominated from 1930s (radio) and 1960s (television).
Post-modern	A wider range of communication channels used, of a more personalised nature, such as email and direct mail.	In some westernised countries has started to challenge the dominance of modern communications since the 1990s.

Scotland which obviously only a limited part of the electorate could actually attend, but they were widely reported to the rest of the country by the press. The move from the pre-modern to the modern communication era is driven by technological changes such as the use of cinema newsreels from the 1920s, which became a shared occasion for how people received their news, and they were entertained as well. However, this second era really takes off with the emergence and then dominance of radio from the 1930s, so, for example, families in America crowded around their radio sets to hear their President speak to them, Bob Hope tell jokes and Glenn Miller's latest songs. This was then followed up in the 1950s and 1960s by television, which was kick-started in the UK by the coronation of Queen Elizabeth II in 1953, when people bought television sets so that they could watch it. Indeed, while only 8,251 actually attended the coronation in Westminster Abbey it is estimated some 27 million watched it on television and a further 11 million listened on the radio (www.royal.gov.uk/LatestNewsandDiary/Pre ssreleases/2003/50factsaboutTheQueensCoronation.aspx0). In developed western countries by the 1970s mass communication, especially television, dominated in terms of how people received their entertainment and news. However, Norris suggests that this dominance has been challenged in some westernised countries since the 1990s by applying a wider range of communication, mixing both mediated and unmediated. So, first of all this included the use of direct mail and has now been driven by the internet which can be used for both broadcast and narrowcasting. If your event is being held in non-western or non-developed countries, society may be at different stages of their adoption of modern and post-modern communication channels.

The power of direct communications is that they enable you to pass on the message that you want to convey to the precise audience you have chosen. It can also often encourage feedback and dialogue from the recipient as well. For example, some local councils in the UK create neighbourhood committee meetings where local residents can question their local representatives, and get their views across. These often lead to Action Plans or they influence council policy. However, the weakness of this approach is that the audience might not believe you. So if you get a message straight from an event saying how good it is, you might not always believe them, thinking 'Well, they would say that.' However, if an event has third-party endorsement, then you are more likely to believe what the source says, be it good or bad. For example, if you read an article about an event and it states how good it is you are more likely to think 'Well, they have no vested interest, so it must be good, I might go.' Third-party endorsement is the potential power that mediated communication can have.

It can be argued that we now exist in a mediated society, where our sense of what is real is created by which media we access. For example, sport in particular is more frequently experienced via television and radio than actually attendance. Thus, Nielsen reported that 111.5 million Americans watched Super Bowl XLVIII in 2014 on television, whereas just over 82,000 spectators (Sporting Charts) watched at the MetLife Stadium, East Rutherford, New Jersey. In addition, it was watched live in many countries around the world. It is not just sports, some cultural events attract live television coverage, many more people watch the BBC's live coverage of the four-day Chelsea Flower Show than attend.

Indeed, we now see that the media is not just an interested and neutral observer of events, but its needs now affect the delivery of some major events. For example, Eurovision (a song contest) since its creation in 1956 has been a physical event, but the wider television audience is far more important to its continued success (www.eurovision.tv). Indeed, there are now two tiers of contestants depending on the size and role of the television companies. Thus, since 2008 usually over 30 competitors have to take part in two semi-finals to get selected for the final, whereas the competitors from France, Germany, Italy, Spain and the UK are guaranteed a final berth. The Big Five are the sponsoring nations whose television companies believe it is worthwhile having such a close relationship. Television also has an impact on sport and probably played a key role in the development of Twenty20 cricket in 2003. Twenty20 is a much shortened version of the game and so more attractive to television audiences who can watch a whole match in about three hours, rather than up to five days.

One judgement call then is to know when to use mediated or unmediated communications. For example, Zaller and Hunt (1994) found that during the 1992 US Presidential election, candidate billionaire Ross Perot was highly effective when he spoke to electors directly through unmediated communication channels, such as events. His problem was in using indirect mediated communication, primarily the press and broadcast media. For Perot then, events were effective because he could persuade people of his views in depth. Yet in print and broadcast media he did not necessarily receive a fair hearing compared with the two main candidates who simply got more coverage. The implication is that direct communication may be a more level playing field for the outsider or small player, whereas mediated communication is dominated by the market leaders and the well-known.

Persuasive communication

Having decided how and what you will communicate, it is possible to be more persuasive in your message's effect. We shall look at a range of theories and hints and tips which you might apply. Writing over 2,000 years ago the Greek philosopher Aristotle provides a very clear framework we can use. When considering the art of effective rhetoric (persuasion) Aristotle identified three important components:

- Ethos – the speaker
- Logos – the message
- Pathos – the audience.

Ethos means that we look at the credibility of the source, and pathos assesses the audience. We shall focus only on logos and how we can make our message more persuasive as this is what is central to communicating. Persuasive communication requires possibly changing the receiver's attitudes and seeking to change their behaviour. So you might want the receiver to think better of your event/organisation, but you will certainly want them to do something as a result of receiving your message, such as visiting your website, telling a friend or buying a ticket.

Perloff (2008) suggests that there are three message factors you can improve:

1 Message structures – how the message is prepared and organised.
2 Content of the message – the appeals and arguments.
3 Language – how words and symbols are used.

If we look at the structure of messages, there are two aspects to consider. First, research suggests that the message sender should recognise an opposition viewpoint and then refute it (Allen 1998, O'Keefe 1999), and second, to make sure that you conclude by telling the audience what they should do (O'Keefe 1997). While both of these points primarily refer to speeches, the principals could relate to written communication as well.

We argue that central to persuasion is to appeal to the head (rational) and the heart (emotion). Wood (2009) suggests that attendees are rational decision makers, while Schmitt (1999) suggests that people are driven by emotion. Thaler and Sunstein (2009), in their book *Nudge*, suggest that most of us are like the fictional cartoon character Homer Simpson and make spontaneous decisions based on emotion. Very few, they suggest, make highly rational decisions like Spock in the American television sci-fi series *Star Trek*. In terms of the content of your message, we suggest that you make use, as appropriate, of a mixture of evidence-based content (rational) and case histories (emotional). With evidence-based you offer, for example, facts and quantitative statistics. Case studies and testimonials are a more qualitative approach based on someone's experience, so it is a personal story. We would suggest that in most instances combining both is likely to be the most effective for you.

The third of our factors, language, is quite complex and often based on subtle nuances, but is essentially how you say it, not just what you say. When we look at language delivered orally, speed of speech can have some effect, so a slightly quicker rate suggests that the speaker knows their stuff, though obviously too quick and the audience cannot take it in. Perhaps of more importance, and often used by politicians, is the use of intense language by using metaphors, graphic words and emotionally charged words. Shocktober (www.halloween attractions.co.uk/shocktoberfest) a month-long Halloween event deliberately evokes images, so as an attraction it refers to itself as a 'Scream Park' and has rides such as 'Hell-ements Inferno'.

Language is not just about words, but can also include semiotics and non-verbal language. Semiotics, most commonly associated with ideas developed independently by Charles Peirce (1839–1914) and Ferdinand de Saussure (1857–1913), explains how languages work by focusing on signs, symbols and images. We obviously see such signs in the form of branding and logos which we recognise, but they can also have a direct event application. For example, directing crowds at events, so we know that the colour red means danger and are less likely to go into a part of a venue with such warning signs up. We deal with semiotics in more depth in Chapter 4 where it is associated with advertising.

Non-verbal communication may support the message, for example, if you are briefing your team about safety issues your tone or pitch of voice may change to get across the seriousness of the topic you are dealing with. If you are addressing a campaign you may use your hand movements and speed of voice to convey emotion and encourage a call to action. One of the best examples of this has been the American civil rights movement leader Martin Luther King (1929–1968). On 28 August 1963 at the Lincoln Memorial in Washington DC King made one of the most famous speeches in history, 'I Have a Dream', given to some 250,000 people attending a civil rights march (https://archive.org/details/MLKDream). Clearly the words are very evocative, but they were supported by his change in speed of voice, tone and hand and head movements.

2.2 Exercise scenario

You have been asked to produce a flyer for a one-day conference on the implications of recent legal changes. Your client, the event organiser, is a well-known company of lawyers, Daft, Taft and Laugh. They are looking primarily to enhance their reputation with other professionals such as accountants, finance advisers, business owners and senior managers. The event is free of charge, and will last from 10am until 2.30pm, with lunch provided. There will be four sessions, each with experienced senior personnel outlining the implications of recent and proposed legal changes in taxation, copyright and intellectual property, employment rights and company ownership. The venue is the best hotel in town, and there will be up to 100 attendees. All attendees need to RSVP.

You will need to consider:

1 What is the appropriate layout for this venue, event and audience for the flyer in terms of size, colour, weight, paper type, folds and number of pages?
2 How important are symbols such as logos and branding, and where will they be and how prominent?
3 How much written content will there be, as opposed to visuals?
4 What are the most important parts of each page to get across your messages? For example, where will your calls to action be?
5 What is the style of your key messages, should they be weighted towards factual and statistical information, real-life vignettes/case studies or emotional calls?
6 For this audience what are the most important messages to convey and why?

A consideration of persuasion will allow you to select and construct the correct tool(s) to meet the needs of your specific audience, event and your organisation.

Simons (2001) suggests that non-verbal communication can be expressed via at least four different channels:

1 Vocalics – The auditory channel – rate, volume, voice, articulation.
2 Kinesics – The visual channel – posture, fidgeting, body movements, gestures, eye behaviour, facial expressions.
3 Proxemics – How space and spatial relationships communicate – cultures vary in zones of comfort.
4 Haptics – The tactile channel – touch.

You will note that each of these channels fits well with most events – we might use sound to enhance the experience, and the vast majority of events are visual, physically venues seek to engage the audience with the event. The only problematic channel is haptics, given that most of the time spectators cannot touch participants.

Julius Solaris (2014) in his event manager blog (www.eventmanagerblog.com/influence-persuasion-events) highlights 25 ways in which you can influence the attendees at your events. His practical ideas are derived from his understanding of Dale Carnegie's *How to Win Friends and Influence People* and Robert Cialdini's *Influence: Science and Practice*. Solaris recognises that an understanding of psychology can change attendee experience, and help you to get them to do what you want at the event. For example, how do you persuade all the paying attendees at an event (or a part of the venue) to take part in a card stunt where they hold up cards in sequence to make an image? Thus at the opening ceremony of London 2012 spectators had LED lights which were used to create images, patterns and text in the spectator areas. For the audience, they are not just being passive; rather, it enhances their experience through participation.

One approach to persuasion that may well be very appropriate to events is the idea of evoking social norms; we tend not to go against something which we believe everyone else does. For example, Cialdini (1999) found that the most effective placard message in a hotel room to get guests to reuse towels was that 'the majority of guests in this room reuse towels'. For example, if you want to encourage attendees to your festival to put litter in bins you need to have enough bins. Once they are full, people are more likely to consider it is okay to litter, and as more do it, the bigger your problem will become as it becomes a social norm.

CASE STUDY EXERCISE

Frost and Laing (2013) looked at how the websites of five Slow Movement festivals sought to apply persuasive techniques to encourage both attendance, and also to change behaviour in terms of web visitors' lifestyle.

1   They suggest that the Slow Movement Festival websites sought to be persuasive using evocative language to create images. In which way might metaphors, imagery and the like persuade you? What examples can you think of from event materials you have seen?

2   How important do you think a 'champion' or key spokesperson is to persuasive communication for an event? Why do you think they might be important (i.e. what is the psychology behind why the audience may respond positively)? Has any spokesperson for an event made you less or more likely to listen to their message?

3   In what way might Frost and Laing's idea of the importance of stressing the perceptions of authenticity concerning an event be relevant? Would you expect an event to be authentic? If so, what types of events? Does creating/stressing authenticity help to create a distinctive message about the event?

Discussion questions

1   For any event you are promoting, can you identify the three most important communication issues you face, and if so, what are your solutions to each?
2   What lessons have you learnt from the Gutenberg diagram and the Z-pattern? In what way will you look differently at, and understand, the printed materials you read and produce? How can understanding how we read help you to be a more persuasive communicator?
3   When you are producing a message, say in the form of a tweet, flyer or merchandise, how important is it to establish your credibility? And if it is, how would you achieve this?
4   Are some communication tools inherently more persuasive than others, and if so which and why? As events make more and more use of technology, how might this affect your construction of persuasive messages?

Further information

Books

Berger, C., Roloff, M. and Roskos-Ewoldsen, D. (2009) *The Handbook of Communication Science*, London: Sage.

Duck, S. and McMahan, D. (2009) *The Basics of Communication: a relational perspective*, London: Sage.

Kaptein, M. (2015) *Persuasion Profiling: how the internet knows what makes you tick*, Amsterdam: Business Contact.

McQuail, D. (2006) *McQuail's Mass Communication Theory*, 5th edn, London: Sage.

Maslen, A. (2015) *Persuasive Copywriting: using psychology of influence, engage and sell*, London: Kogan Page.

Article

Henderson, S. and Musgrave, J. (2014) 'Changing audience behaviour: festival goers and throwaway tents', *International Journal of Event and Festival Management*, 5 (3): 247–262.

Chapter 3

Events and communication channels

Introduction

This chapter will assess how events use a range of communication tools. We will start by explaining how events use communications, then we set up a typology for explaining communication usage by events, which will highlight whether the type of event industry, organisation or event purpose is likely to have any influence on which channels should be used and how. We will introduce the rest of the book by briefly introducing here the types of communication tools available to an event. Then we will identify, from the types of communication tools that events rely on, how they use them and we will critique such use. We will also try to identify those channels that events appear less likely to use, to explain why and whether they are missing a trick or not. At the end we will assess some important design factors which will shape how you use each communication channel. By the end of the chapter students will be able to:

- Understand the importance of communication to events managers;
- Recognise the meaning and application of your communications toolbox;
- Assess the value of different of tools;
- Apply basic design rules.

What is communication?

In Chapter 2 we defined and set up communication, where we explained direct and indirect communication. However, communication may be slightly more complex than just being simply direct or indirect; Figure 3.1 suggests there can be different lengths to the communication chain. Direct communication would normally be considered short, but indirect can be of different lengths. A medium chain would have only one gatekeeper, perhaps a parent, the media or employer. The long chain might use one gatekeeper; say, the media, as a means to get to another, such as parents, in order to get to the final intended recipients, children in this case.

We can also identify differences in communication direction. The first obvious difference is whether communication is designed to be one-way (monologue) or two-way (dialogue). With one-way communication the message is designed to inform the receiver, so this might be to tell them that an event is happening. Two-way communication allows for some form of feedback

Theoretical underpinning

Unmediated communication (Direct)   **Mediated communication (Indirect)**

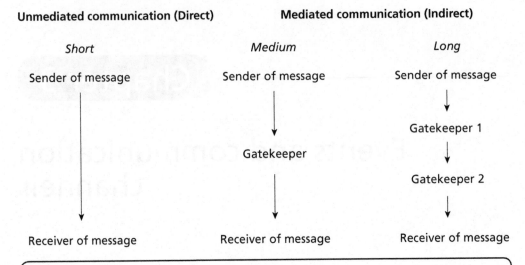

Figure 3.1 The nature of the communication chain

so that the receiver of the message can offer a response, be it in writing, orally or through body language. For example, many training courses and conferences have formal evaluation sheets that ask delegates for their experience of the event. The second aspect is whether communication is vertical, horizontal or both. Vertical communication is up and down between different levels of an organisation. It can be one-way, typically top-down, or it can less commonly also be bottom-up. This is necessary when clear, unambiguous information must be communicated between different levels of an event. Horizontal communication tends to be between the same levels within an event, such as different event departments or spectators, and so inherently implies two-way communication. It is appropriate when ideas need to be developed between different organisers, or when event attendees share their experiences. For example, the followers of many professional sports clubs add to their experience by engaging with online

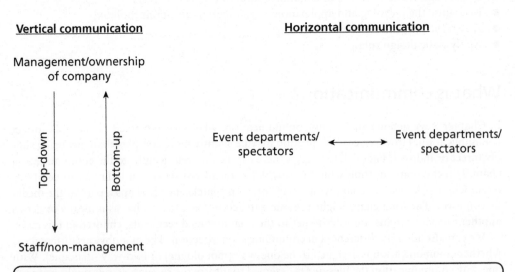

Figure 3.2 Vertical and horizontal communication

forums, such as supporters of the English football club Liverpool using the online forum on www.redandwhitekop.com to discuss their team. Vertical and horizontal communications are not necessarily in competition with each other, they can complement one another by meeting different audience needs.

Communication typology

As we highlighted in Chapter 1, event marketers use a range of communication tools as routes to market. To understand what is the appropriate tool to use it is important for the event manager to have a worldview of communications, which provides principles by which they should act. For example, if your approach is one of transactional marketing then you are primarily interested in just making a sale. Such an approach would encourage you to use one-off tools that offer a persuasive message, typically using advertising via mass communication channels or 'hard-sell' sales. This is the traditional four Ps approach to marketing: price; place; product; and promotion (McCarthy 1964). Alternatively, you might take a relationship marketing approach (Gronroos 1994) where the emphasis is on developing a long-term relationship based on trust, regular communication and dialogue with your audiences. This approach is more likely to rely on unmediated communication such as direct mail. As a result, Getz (2008) suggests there is a close fit to events with the seven Ps which adds processes; people; and physical evidence to the original four. A third approach, increasingly associated with events, is experiential marketing (Schmitt 1999) whereby 'experiences' are created to encourage a relationship between the product and the consumer. Such an approach seeks to create positive feelings through a memorable experience rather than offering rational arguments alone. Understanding your philosophical approach will help you select the most appropriate tools to use.

Communication is not just about you, and what you want to say and achieve, but also the receiver of the message. A theory from education learning styles can be adapted to help us. Fleming (1995) suggested that people learn in different ways, and he identified four different styles:

- Visual – see it
- Auditory – hear it
- Read/write – the written word
- Kinaesthetic – do it/touch it.

VARK, as this theory is known, provides us with an insight as to how audiences will view your messages, and the tools used to reach them. This theory suggests that people 'tune out' certain styles of communicating. Those who take in information visually are more likely to understand your message if there are images such as pictures, diagrams and movement. So if someone says to you 'I see what you are saying', they are likely to prefer visual images. Where auditory is the most appropriate, they are more likely to listen to what a person has to say, or the use of other sound techniques such as ambient music. Such people, for example, might prefer a verbal briefing to reading a document to get information. If a person says 'I hear what you are saying', then they probably prefer auditory communications. Those in the third category, read, are most likely to look at and digest detail in the written format such as a letter or the words rather than the images on a poster. You might be interested to know that probably many of your lecturers are likely to be read-dominant. For those who are kinaesthetic what helps is being able to touch or experience something, such as virtual tours or videos of past events. We might suggest that those who are kinaesthetic might be particularly interested in experiential marketing. In all likelihood, most of us have one dominant and one secondary learning style. The lesson VARK offers us is that audiences take in information in different ways, and so it is wise to address more than one of these approaches when sending out a message.

Charities often appear to inherently realise these different ways in which we take in information, and offer a range of ways of getting their message across. For example, say you are offering to host a coffee morning fundraiser for a charity, typically, the charity will send you a sponsorship pack which will probably include some flyers about the charity, possibly some merchandise, a sad or motivational story and a link to a website where you can access more information, especially pictures and video.

In real life you are unlikely to rely solely on one route to market, rather you will use a suite of channels, some concurrently (at the same time) and others consecutively (one after the other). You need to be aware of how each channel fits with the others you are intending to use. One of the key reasons for this is that your target audience will access information in different ways. Thus, one person might get their prime information via a newsletter, another through a few websites and others look at flyers. Obviously you need to balance this against the cost of producing more marketing communications, but remember that one shot is rarely enough.

The use of a range of tools reminds us that to maximise their effect we should take an integrative communications approach. What this means is that you should not consider any single communication on its own, rather all your communications should be viewed as inter-related. So, returning to our coffee morning example, the messages sent to those hosting the event will be different when being recruited (why do it), and when signed up (how to do it). Similarly, the message to attendees of the coffee morning will be slightly different from those sent to people who are hosting. The other important aspect to integrated communications is not only that the messages of the different channels should support each other, but very often you might want to let your audience know from where they can get further information, for example driving traffic to your online presence.

When you are constructing your material be mindful of what you want the reader, viewer or listener to do as a result – what is referred to in sales speak as 'the ask' (we looked at this in the previous chapter with the Gutenberg diagram and Z-pattern). You may be providing your audience with information about an event, but having received and understood the message what do you want them to do now? It might be to attend, buy a ticket, follow your Twitter account or whatever, but always make sure you have thought through what action you want from the message receiver.

We suggest a typology, Figure 3.3, for assessing which tools to use, based on the type of event industry, the organisation using it and the purpose of the event. The first column merely codifies some of the types of event industries, we have identified six but you could expand this list. The second column identifies three main types of organisation under which events are organised, thus we choose the event industry in column one, and then assess how it is structured/managed in column two. This we suggest has an impact on how an event will use communication tools. We note that any of our three types of event organisation could have a Transactional, Relational or Experiential purpose. However, we suggest that the type of purpose used by each different organisation may lead to different ways in which communication tools will be used, and the type of events they will be used for. If we look at transactional, all three types of organisations want attendees to do something immediately. If we look at relational, there are some differences. The government probably has a campaign, such as eating healthier foods, for which they want an event to lead to longer-term individual behavioural change. Communities and charities are probably targeting the sort of people they want to run their event. Commercial operations with long-running events want people to attend year after

Event industry	Organisation	Purpose

Sports
Campaigning
Entertainment
Corporate
Cultural
Hospitality/tourism

Government/public
- Transactional (elections, public awareness)
- Relational (change behaviour, mobilise)
- Experiential (gain attention, launch ideas)

Community/charity
- Transactional (fayre, fundraise)
- Relational (get volunteers, mobilise)
- Experiential (change behaviour)

For profit
- Transactional (get spectators, one-offs)
- Relational (customer loyalty)
- Experiential (gain attention, sponsorship)

Figure 3.3 Typology for using communication tools

year. We suggest that experiential approaches are more likely either to gain attention to an event or cause, or by generating greater interaction to lead to long-term behavioural change. We suspect that those events concerned with getting a message across are probably more likely to use communications to support relational and experiential approaches. Whereas those concerned purely with income generation are more likely to apply communication to supporting transactional and relational approaches.

Communication tools

Table 3.1 outlines the key characteristics of the tools you are likely to use, which we cover in more depth in subsequent chapters. If we look at the application, nearly all of the tools seek to inform, typically with details such as when and where an event will be. Many also seek to persuade, which is to take inform to the next stage and actually get us to want to attend. A few are used to sell directly or to encourage interaction. Indeed, we tend to find that print material such as flyers are more likely only to seek to inform and persuade, whereas the digital tools, such as websites, may fulfil a much wider range of purposes. There are two obvious conclusions when looking at this table. First, that most events need to use a range of tools, each with slightly different applications. Second, while some of these tools are used by all events, some are more likely to be used by different types, based on, for example, size, audience and nature of the event.

When considering which tools to use we need to answer key questions:

- What is my budget?
- Who is my audience – what are their needs and how best to reach them?
- What is the purpose of my communication – inform, secure sales, or enhance experience?
- What are our skills, aptitudes and access to support networks?
- What is our timescale?
- What are the mechanics of producing the material – easy and quick or slow and expensive?
- What is the event?

Table 3.1 Event communication tools

Tool	Application	Advantages	Disadvantages	Events
Posters	To inform.	Cheap to produce. Easy to distribute.	Can be difficult to stand out. Getting the right spot. Requires design skills.	Virtually all, but especially good for where the audience is geographically close to the venue.
Flyers/leaflets	To inform.	Cheap to produce. Easy to distribute in numbers.	Very common so we can 'tune out'. Some design skills required – easy to get it wrong.	Virtually all events, but especially those with smaller budgets.
Brochures	To inform. To persuade.	Get across very complex information. Can be used over time so not linked to one event. Can be delivered via the internet.	Can be expensive. Probably requires outside design/printing expertise. Postal delivery can be expensive. Have to have a good, reliable target list of the right people.	Organisations that have a rolling programme of events. High-price bespoke events aimed at a small specialist audience such as a training course.
Adverts	To inform. To persuade. To reinforce existing views.	Get across a single message clearly. Can be visual and stand out.	Cost. How to stand out from competitors? Requires expertise to use well. Will it reach our target audience?	Larger events with a reasonable budget.
Direct mail	To inform. To persuade.	We choose who gets it. Can get across complex messages. Easily measurable.	How to get/manage the mailing list. Can be expensive.	Any event can send a direct mail to past customers, but it is especially likely in B2B events.

Tool	Application	Advantages	Disadvantages	Events
Press releases	To inform.	Quick, easy and cheap to produce.	Must have news to impart. Requires a bit of skill to write and deliver. How to measure its effect?	All events. The clever ones have a rolling programme of a series of releases.
Stunts	To pique interest.	Is highly visual. Can be cheap to organise.	To get attention it has to be good – it is hard to get the creative process right.	Probably those with little or no budget. Those with a campaigning message.
Feature articles	To inform. To persuade.	Allows you to establish credibility/ expertise. Can get across complex ideas.	It is a skill. Requires a lot of thought and effort.	Those with a communications team with the relevant skills and resources.
Website	To inform. To persuade. To sell. To entertain.	Highly adaptable. Quick to update. Cheap to produce. Complex information can be presented.	Requires resources and skills to use well. How to drive traffic to it?	All permanent events that return year after year.
Blog	To inform. To engage.	To get across a complex message. To establish credibility. To build a network.	Takes time and skills. Only a few blogs ever get much interest.	Those with permanent staff or participants willing to blog their experiences.
Social networking site	To inform. To engage.	Quick, cheap and easy to use. Creates communities.	Can be abused – trolls. Needs to be regularly monitored. Cannot ignore complaints.	All events.

Table 3.1 continued

Tool	Application	Advantages	Disadvantages	Events
E-direct mail	To inform. To persuade.	Cheap to produce and deliver. Gets across complex messages. Can attach other multimedia.	Securing and managing email list. Legal considerations.	Any event can send a direct mail to past customers, but it is especially likely in B2B events.
E-newsletter	To inform. To persuade. Build relationships.	Can add value for the receiver. Encourages dialogue. Can get across complex messages.	Less popular than five years ago. Requires resources and skills to use well.	More likely to be events with a specialist audience.
Merchandising	To provide a memory. To provide value.	Generates income. Good for brand reinforcement. Reaches those not at an event.	Cost. Choosing the right merchandise. Storage.	Those with a budget and a purpose – unlikely to be small events.
Audio Visual	To inform. To heighten the experience.	Creates atmosphere. Reaches two of the VARK learning styles. Creates some tangibility.	Cost. Skills required.	Probably all events have some AV requirement.
Photography	To inform. To pique interest. To create memories.	Very powerful influencing tool. Can be central to the event atmosphere. Presents some tangibility. Branding.	Needs professional skills. Cost.	All events, but budget shapes the exact use.
Pop-up banners	To inform.	Reinforce key messages.	Cost. Creating messages that can be reused at other events.	Likely to be exhibition-based events.

The use of communication tools by events

We have presented a wide range of communication tools, and you will probably have noticed from your own experience that events tend to use some much more than others. Thus, we suggest that flyers or leaflets and posters are very common event marketing tools, which is why we have grouped them together. Advertising is common to those events with large budgets such as mega-events and major events, especially in the music and sports markets where there is a lot of competition. An adjunct of advertising, advertorials are fairly common for hospitality, but fairly rare for events. Public relations is common to nearly all events, but probably takes on greater importance for smaller events and/or those who cannot afford advertising. The internet is now a core communication channel for the vast majority of events, though not all use social networking sites because of the time the interactive aspect can take to manage. Merchandising is used heavily in certain event fields, primarily music and to a lesser extent performance-based events, such as comedy, but it can also be found in charity events where fundraisers may be given visible keepsakes such as T-shirts.

There are a variety of factors that shape which tools an event should use. As we suggested earlier your use of these tools will be influenced by whether you want to use images, words or sound, or a combination. The nature of the event is also key; Preston (2012) looks at the different approaches to marketing, depending on the type of event, such as music festivals, corporate events and social functions.

To help draw up an order of priority of tools for your event we suggest you consider:

1   Your budget – how much have you got? Then seek quotes for how much each tool should cost and then assess what you can afford.
2   Your audience – what are the channels they prefer to be reached by?
3   Your aptitudes – what skills and experience have you got?
4   Your event – what is the nature and size of your event?

CASE STUDY

Limpopo Youth Orchestra

The Limpopo Youth Orchestra (LYO) is a South African non-profit company (http://lyo.co.za/lyo/). It is a religious youth orchestra that integrates classic orchestra instruments with indigenous African instruments, with the aim of enhancing confidence and life opportunities of rural, disabled and urban children and youth. They hold regular concerts in their home province of Limpopo, but also frequently travel throughout Southern Africa as well as Europe.

The LYO uses a range of promotional materials for their concerts, including posters, flyers, social media and YouTube. When asked why they use each of these materials, Simone Aronje-Adetoye, Managing Director of the LYO said: 'We use posters and flyers to create awareness of our performances and attract audiences to attend. These are distributed dependent on our target audience and where the concert is taking place, as we target those in close proximity to these. Flyers are also used to raise awareness of children who may want to join the orchestra, which are sent to schools in the area. When designing these, we want our message to be clear that we are an orchestra, and so like to use photos of our members holding instruments. They have to be striking, using bright colours, so that people are encouraged to take a closer look at them. Font also plays an important role in design, as this helps to emphasise the key information.

We use videos of our performances that we send to churches to be played for congregations. This helps to raise awareness of upcoming concerts. Our main source of marketing is social media, specifically Facebook (www.facebook.com/Limpopo-Youth-Orchestra-110063772354195/), as it allows us to reach more audiences, and for them to engage in what we do. We like to include photos and videos of our performances on our Facebook page, as this is also a way that we can attract possible donors – it was also how we were found and invited to perform at the Christ Church Cathedral in Dublin in 2013.

When creating a promotional campaign our main considerations are:

- Target audience – whom are we trying to target?
- Venue – will it be convenient for our guests to attend?
- Date and time – we first check whether there are other major events happening in our town that may clash with ours.
- Posters/flyers are normally designed four weeks before the event and get displayed/distributed approximately three weeks before the event.
- We advertise by posting our videos and posters on Facebook as well as on Twitter. We also have a strong parent body that helps us advertise through their Facebook pages and by word of mouth. Then our members also advertise at their various schools and encourage their teachers and schoolmates to support them.'

The elements of design

While you may well be best advised to employ a professional designer to produce your materials, a basic understanding of some key design features may help you manage this process. In this section we shall look at typography, colour and layout.

Typography

Typography includes font, font size and style; it is how we present our words and messages irrespective of the tool being used. Overall, typography is used to set the tone of your material. In short, typography is your communication tool's body language. The two main types of font are serif and sans-serif. Serif font provides a decorative flourish or curl at the end of letters and symbols, while sans-serif is without any flourishes. The typography you select can help to create the 'atmosphere', and set the tone of your publication.

If we look at the letters below in Figure 3.4 we can see the difference between the two fonts.

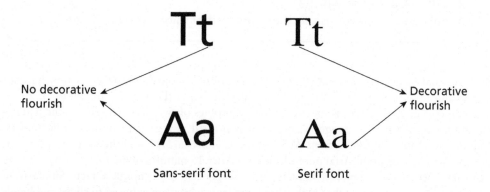

Figure 3.4 Differentiating fonts

Table 3.2 Popular examples of typography

Serif font types	Sans-serif font types
Bookman Light	Arial
Cambria	Calibri
Century	Century Gothic
Garamond	**Franklin Gothic Heavy**
Goudy Old Style	Gill Sans MT
Georgia	Helvetica
Palatino	Lucida Sans
Times New Roman	Tahoma
	Verdana

Table 3.2 outlines some of the most common typographies that you will encounter.

When choosing the appropriate font and size, think of your message, your audience and type or style of event.

Your task

1 If your event was aimed at older people or wanted to be considered class-ical what sort of fonts might you use?
2 Alternatively, if your audience was young and you wanted the feel to be 'cool' what fonts might you use?

3 Would you use different types of fonts for main text as opposed to the headlines, and if so which?
4 Would you only ever use serif or sans-serif or might you mix them up?

One area that has gained interest recently has been 'funky fonts', and whether they have an impact and if so to which types of audience. Psychologists (Diemand-Yauman et al. 2010) asked 28 college students to memorise biological profiles of two fictional species, the pangerish and the norgletti. The pangerish profile was printed in a grey 12-point Comic Sans or Bodoni font (**this is in Comic Sans MS** and this is in Bodoni MT); and the norgletti profile in an easier-to-read, 16-point Arial pure-black font. After 15 minutes of distraction, the students recalled 87 per cent of the pangerish facts versus 73 per cent of the norgletti facts. Similarly, in a semester-long study at an Ohio high school, students who were exposed to slides and handouts using less legible typefaces performed better on tests than students exposed to materials presented in more readable type.

Daniel Oppenheimer one of the authors of Diemand-Yauman et al. (2010) explains the results 'The reason that the unusual fonts are effective is that it causes us to think more deeply about the material. But we are capable of thinking deeply without being subjected to unusual fonts. Think of it this way, you can't skim material in a hard-to-read font, so putting text in a hard-to-read font will force you to read more carefully' (Oppenheimer 2012).

The thinking behind this is the idea of fluency, that something is easy to follow. This works well when the information does not require much attention. However, if you want to jolt people, breaking up that fluency can improve recall. This is precisely what Dieman-Yauman et al. (2010) found with their use of funky fonts. Do note, however, that this is a risky strategy; most advertisers try to create a fluency in their messages – to make them easier to read.

When we look at font size there are a number of factors that shape which is most appropriate. This page is written in 9.5-point font size and Sabon font. If you write an essay it will probably be in 12-point font size, often in something like Arial. Our students were surprised when we asked them what they thought the size of the main headings and key bullet points of our PowerPoint slides were. Most guessed 14 and 12, whereas they were actually 44 and 32 respectively. The lesson here is that when you are producing promotional materials such as flyers and posters the font size will need to be much larger than what you use in normal written communication.

The size of font you need to use will be dependent on:

● The material you create;
● Your audience's needs to be able to read it.

Thus, posters and banners need a big font so that people can see them and read the words, whereas brochures and a flyer may well be smaller because your audience is more likely to read from close up. While website fonts can often be customised, text in a web page is typically a minimum of 16 points and headings can be anything from 24 points on small browsers, increasing to 48 for large.

Using colour

If we are looking at visual designs such as posters, flyers and websites, then colour plays an important role. Mackay (2015) argues that colour works through understanding the psychology of the user, and does this in two key ways:

1 It intrinsically embodies meaning.
2 It extrinsically provides meaning through referential meaning: the thing we immediately think of when we see a colour.

The literature suggests that our responses to colour may be based on primal instincts. Thus Elliot et al. (2007) believe that colour associations are derived from long-held responses to colour. Early humans may have used colour as a way of interpreting and responding to their environment (Byrne and Hilbert 2003). In a sense, this argument is based on the idea that, irrespective of external stimuli such as societal norms, our brains are wired to perceive colour in particular ways.

Therefore, when trying to interpret the impact of colour we are trying to understand how our brains cognitively respond to different colours. For example, it has long been held that full colour is more likely to gain our attention than black and white (Schaie and Heiss 1964). In addition, some colours, such as red, are more likely to lead to action, whereas others, such as blue, are more likely to encourage relaxation. Thus, if you are producing a poster that wishes to encourage a person to attend an activity-based event, then hot colours may be more appropriate. Whereas if the intended atmosphere is one of calmness, then cool colours may be more appropriate.

Whitfield and Wiltshire (1990) identify six principles for understanding the effect of colour:

1 Colour has meaning.
2 The meaning is either innate or learned.
3 The perception of colour leads to evaluation of it.
4 The colour evaluation can lead to behaviour change.
5 Colour normally influences automatically.
6 Context can shape the use and meaning of colour.

Collectively these six principles suggest that colour can be used in your material to persuade your audience to attend your event, if you understand the psychology behind their use.

We can also see that some combinations of colours work and others do not. Dark letters against a light background work. Or light colours against a dark background work because the colours contrast. Think, for example, of the use of black and white. However, we do suggest avoiding red-green combinations because a large fraction of the human population is red-green colour-blind.

Layout

The purpose of page layout is to create a sense of the rhythm, tone and feel you wish to present in your promotional material. The layout directs the reader to the key messages you want them to see. Therefore, before you start to construct your document design you need to consider your concept: what is it you wish to get across?

In terms of the printed page we can either use portrait or landscape. Portrait is vertical and is common to most books, brochures and flyers. Landscape is horizontal and provides a slightly different way of presenting your material.

Probably the most common starting point for any page layout is some form of grid system, whereby you divide up each page into blocks. Grid systems are often associated with Josef Müller-Brockmann who sought from the 1960s to create order and structure for designers through simplicity. Schneider (2013) suggests that this simplicity approach was especially important in the creation of posters to music events and museum exhibitions. In particular, these used the abstract geometric shapes this style was known for.

The idea of a grid is that we can divide our page both vertically and horizontally so we can use images, columns, spaces and headings. This is essentially a modular system where we can put together a number of component parts.

We can create a number of grids, either using an even or odd number system, with the rule of thirds being the most popular for the new designer. This divides a page into three columns horizontally and vertically so there are nine equally sized boxes (Figure 3.5). The idea is that any image or material feels less static than it would if it was merely centred in the page. The boxes allow you to present the images and text, which encourages the reader to focus on what you want them to. The idea of the rule of three is to make the page more interesting to read, and usually the main thing you want the reader to focus on is where the grids intersect each other.

Figure 3.5 The rule of three

Figure 3.6 Rule of three wedding picture

Photograph of Jennifer and Jaco Steyn on their wedding day, with image demonstrating the rule of three

Credit: Image courtesy of Jennifer Steyn and Lensflaire CC

This wedding picture deliberately uses the rule of three in terms of where the happy couple is placed and the background to them.

How to gain attention

Page layout is designed to get the reader to focus on those messages you prioritise. This can be achieved in a number of ways:

1 The use of headlines is to lead the reader into the story, so you must grab their attention. To achieve this you should consider larger type, bold font and five to eight words that sum up your message. In larger and more text-heavy documents subheadings might help too. A page or a part of it can be framed by borders, where you might use bold and/or a thicker line. This is telling the reader 'here is something worth looking at'.
2 Related to borders are boxes, where key text is presented. In this book we use these typically to address important definitions.
3 Quotes can often be pulled out, sometimes in boxes or sometimes not. They are attractive because they offer a human angle, and design-wise if they are a different size and font type they can offer another feature to focus on.
4 You will be familiar with bullet points and they provide a useful way of presenting a lot of detail quickly, and in a way that is easy to digest.

5   Images in the form of pictures or diagrams often act as a rallying point for the eye, and typically contain important information.

You will note that the effect of these design tools is to break up text as the reader looks at it, and each of the features is designed to say 'look at me please'. This causes the reader to focus harder to take in the information. However, we caution against too much 'chaos' so that there is no consistent theme or there is too much chopping and changing. For example, use two or at most three font changes per page.

If you are creating a document that will be bound and stapled, you need to create a gutter, which is a space between the pages.

White space

White space is simply the absence of text or images. There is an old adage of 'sometimes less is more', so do not be afraid of white space. In terms of the overall feel you will need to decide how light or dense your page is going to be; the lighter, then inherently the greater white space you need. White provides contrast, so always have white space around borders, boxes, each section or heading, images and the like. Without white space these features just blur together and the messages are lost. Typically, you would have more white space at the bottom of the page than the top (here is where a lot of key information will be).

Discussion questions

1   With greater use of new technologies and the growing fragmentation of audiences (so they can be tailored more), what are likely to be the key communication functions for the event promoter in the next few years?
2   With a very limited budget and precise knowledge of your audience how could you use VARK to communicate your events' key messages effectively?
3   We have identified a wide number of communication tools, and with technological change this number will increase. Would you be better off mastering five or six and sticking to these, or should you keep testing and trying as many as possible, and accept the occasional failures?
4   Font, colour and layout are clearly important, but how will you use these to support, rather than detract from, your key event messages?

Further information

Books

Dawson, P., Foster, J. and Seddon, T. (2012) *Graphic Design Rules: 365 essential design dos and don'ts*, London: Frances Lincoln.

Dorst, K., Kaldor, L., Klippan, L. and Watson, R. (2016) *Designing for the Common Good*, Amsterdam: BIS.

Egan, J. (2007) *Marketing Communications*, London: Thomson Learning.

Graver, A. and Jura, B. (2012) *Best Practices for Graphic Designers: grids and page layouts*, Gloucester, MA: Rockport.

Perkins, P. (2008) *The Art and Science of Communication: tools for effective communication in the workplace*, Hoboken, NJ: Wiley.

Article

Duncan, T. and Moriarty, S. (1998) 'A communication-based marketing model for managing relationships', *Journal of Marketing*, 62 (2): 1–13.

Websites

www.fonts.com/content/learning/fontology/level-1/type-anatomy/type-classifications
www.designishistory.com/1450/type-classification/
www.noupe.com/essentials/icons-fonts/a-crash-course-in-typography-the-basics-of-type.html

PART II

PRINTED MATERIAL

This section addresses the main types of printed materials you are likely to use.

Chapter 4

Advertising

Introduction

We start with advertising because in one form or another this is often the prime means of communication for events. Paid-for advertising, such as in newspapers, is an indirect form of promotion in that the event manager does not know exactly who will access the message. Whereas other forms of advertising, such as promotional materials, can be direct; the event manager may know precisely whom they are handing them to. We start by assessing which types of events (and budgets) such advertising is applicable to. Then we consider how to use paid-for printed advertisements, such as those in newspapers, magazines, radio and television. We will then look at an underused approach, advertorials, which try to look like an independent article, even though they are paid for. Our third use of advertisement tools is promotional materials such as posters, flyers, leaflets and banners. These are probably the most popular forms of advertising for small to medium-sized events. The chapter will finish by assessing the application to events of these tools individually and collectively. By the end of the chapter students will be able to:

- Choose the correct advertising tool for your event's needs and budget;
- Understand how to produce a printed advertisement;
- Select when and how to use an advertorial;
- Construct a flyer/poster/leaflet;
- Produce a banner.

How advertising works

Advertising is a general term that is sometimes misunderstood as it covers both paid-for and other channels. If we are looking at a paid-for advert in say a newspaper, we shall use the precise term of an advertisement; for other forms, such as posters, we shall refer to advertising as a slightly looser term. For both we can shorten them to advert.

In this chapter we shall focus on the practicalities of advertising, but before we do so we shall briefly outline one theory, semiotics, which can help to explain how your advertising works. Understanding semiotics may help you to create advertisements that do what you

47

want. Adverts are usually short, sharp and to the point, and they may use a combination of words and images. In short, they need to stand out, and quickly and easily be understood. The way the receiver tends to process the message is by using shortcuts to minimise the amount of cognitive thinking required.

The theory of semiotics, mostly associated with Charles Peirce (1839–1914) and Ferdinand de Saussure (1857–1913), focuses on what we give meaning to. As a result, semiotics is the study of signs. By applying Saussure's approach Figure 4.1 shows there are essentially three components to the theory: the sign itself, the signifier, and the signified. The sign provides meaning and is comprised of two components: the signified and the signifier. The signifier is the form in which the sign is presented, such as words, a logo or a picture. The signified is how the sign is interpreted by the receiver, what cognitively this means to them.

Semiotics is around us all the time and this is precisely what advertisers tap into. There is no inherent reason why the letters e, v, e, n, t, s have any particular meaning but within the English language when combined they are given meaning; moreover, it is one that is not necessarily absolute; it is interpretable. So if you are a history student when you put the letters together you are probably thinking about a historically significant event, such as a war, revolution or a famous speech. However, as an events management student your interpretation was probably very different; you might have thought about music festivals, logistics or your future career. Therefore, when you are constructing your advert you need to work out what you want to say, how you will say it and then assess how your audience might interpret that message.

With adverts you are probably less likely to use words alone, rather, other things are given meaning by us and you will need to think what they might be for your advert. One of the most common is a logo, so McDonald's uses the golden arches and if you see this you will instantly recognise it, realise the advert is from McDonald's and then make your own interpretation of what this means for you. A logo is essentially a symbol; we find, create and adapt symbols around us all the time. Probably the best adverts you can remember have used some form of symbolism.

A sign could be a logo, image, atmosphere or anything that can be interpreted to give meaning. Signs help to reinforce the proposed meaning, making it easier for viewers of the sign to understand the message.

Colours can also provide meaning, so if you see a red and a blue tap you should be able to work out which is hot and which is cold. In different cultures colours may have different

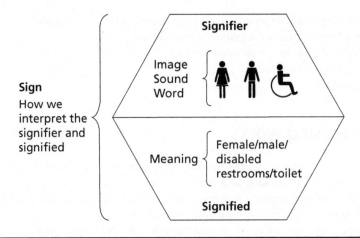

Figure 4.1 Semiotics

meanings, so De Bortoli and Maroto (2001) note that orange in Asia is viewed as a positive, spiritually enhancing colour, whereas in the US it is more likely to be associated with road hazards and traffic delays. They also note that some colours can be associated with certain events, so that Kabuki stagehands, mourners at a funeral and a mime troupe are likely to wear black.

Therefore, the logo, colours and images used in your advert can all help to trigger the desired thought process in the receiver. You should not ignore symbols and signs as they have meaning to your audience.

Why events might use advertising

4.1 Definition box

What is an advertisement?

An advertisement is a means of reaching your desired audience by renting someone else's channel of communication to reach their audiences. It allows you to control the exact message (though not the response) and so incurs a fee.

With an advertisement you are renting the space, and you hope that the right number of people look at or listen to and react to your advert. It is a very inexact science, so the US grocer John Wanamaker (1838–1922) is believed to be the source of the statement 'Half of the money I spend on advertising is wasted; the trouble is, I don't know which half' (cited in Luo and Donthu, 2005). What this means is that because most advertising uses mass communications media such as newspapers, magazines and television, it is a broadcast medium that may reach a lot of people, but you cannot easily identify exactly which ones will receive and act upon the message.

Advertisements can be used in a number of formats and publications, including magazines, newspapers and websites. Adverts are designed to capture the target audience's attention within seconds, and if it fails to do this, the advert is considered pointless.

Sometimes advertisements can become an event themselves. During the UK general election campaigns political parties sometimes hire a billboard for a very short time, hold a press conference or stunt in front of it to get across a point or launch a policy and then that is it. The advert might only be up an hour, and as the journalists leave to file their copy and the politicians move on to the next event, the advert is pulled down and replaced, typically by a commercial one. But it has its fifteen minutes of fame, and may appear as the backdrop to the news.

In essence, most events want the right people to know that it is happening, when, where and what they have to do. Advertisements provide a popular means of this for events, but it is not automatic that you should use them nor indeed which ones. This depends for example, on the nature of your event, your audience, the cost and your budget. Table 4.1 considers the factors you need to take into account when deciding whether to use advertising, and if so which type.

Table 4.1 might suggest that the disadvantages outweigh the advantages, especially for television and radio, but this is not the case. Rather, we identify the importance of knowing your audience, your budget and the nature of each advertising channel to decide what is right for you.

Printed material

Table 4.1 The pros and cons of advertising

Type of advertisement	Advantages	Disadvantages	Type of event used at
Television	Wide reach. Geographic targeting.	Cost – by far the most expensive. Will your audience be watching? Recall of television ads can be low.	Mega-events such as sporting events. Some charity fundraising events.
Radio	Wide reach. Geographic targeting. The audience can be doing something else but still receive your message.	Reach is usually smaller than TV. Cost (though cheaper than TV). Absence of visual cues. Will your audience be listening?	Music events, such as MTV's Big Crash, Radio 1 Big Weekend. Regional charity events – such as Cancer Research UK's Race for Life.
National newspapers	Wide reach. Profile by socio-economic factors. Range of advert sizes available to fit budget. Can have an online version.	Not all countries have national newspapers. Cost. Can be ignored. Hard to stand out. Newspapers in decline at expense of the internet.	Mega-events. Large entertainment-based events such as music, comedy and sports. Exhibitions such as the Chelsea Flower Show.
Local/regional newspapers	More affordable. Geographic targeting. Can have an online version.	Cost (while lower than national) is for small events still considerable. Hard to stand out. Newspapers in decline at expense of the internet.	Local/regional events, so from very small village fêtes through to entertainment tours at regionally large venues. Local sports team fixtures.
Free newspapers	Very localised.	A cost but the audience is small. Many people throw them away. Tend to be weekly.	Good for small and community-based events.

Type of advertisement	Advantages	Disadvantages	Type of event used at
Magazines	Targeted – reaches those likely to be interested in your type of event.	Lead time to produce copy is months ahead. Cost. Will it reach your audience?	More likely to be specialist.
Advertorials	The reader thinks it is a third-party endorsement.	Ethical concerns. Probably more costly than an advert alone.	Very localised, typically hospitality-based.
Flyers/leaflets/ posters	Cheap and quick to produce. Can be targeted geographically easily and sometimes to specialised audiences as well. Variety of means of delivering.	How to stand out from the crowd? Many technical decisions to get right. How to deliver them? What if you break the law when delivering them?	Probably all events, but especially those on smaller budgets.
Banners*	Highly visual. Good for geographically-based events.	Cost. Where best to put them? Limited information.	Geographically-based events.

* We are referring here to banners put up outside events, not pop-up banners such as those found at exhibition stands.

Buying media

We assume that you are considering buying print advertising. Broadcast follows similar processes but is much more complex. Before you start the creative process of producing an advert it is necessary to think about how you will physically do it, and the possible costs. We suggest that this can be broken down into stages:

1 Be clear on the details of the event you are trying to promote.
2 What is your budget and how much can you afford?
3 Identify who your target audience is, and which publications they are likely to read.
4 Select the type of advertisement and publication. So what size do you want? Then work out which specific publications you are interested in, and note that the price will vary depending on the type of publication: a daily newspaper will be a lot more expensive than a trade publication. You may also find that the price varies, depending on where on the page, and where in the publication it is. The premium positions are the inside front cover, inside back cover and back cover – which cost more than other pages.

> ### Table 4.2 What affects the price you pay?
>
> Size – business card size, quarter-page, half-page and full page.
>
> Number – a one-off ad works at more pro rata, if you run an advert in several editions of the publication the rate per issue is usually lower.
>
> Type of publication – national newspapers charge more than a regional, as does a national consumer magazine as opposed to a specialist interest magazine.
>
> Where on the page – remember the two parts of the Z-pattern – top left and bottom right.
>
> Colour – is the ad in full colour, two-colour or black and white?

5 Decide how to buy. If you are looking to place only one or a few adverts you can probably manage this yourself by contacting the advertising sales team of the chosen publications. They will tell you what they need, by when and the price. Remember that most sales teams earn commission so do see if negotiation is possible, and you may find that at the end of the month discounts may be on offer as they try to meet sales targets. However, if you are going to have a big campaign, you might be better served outsourcing a specialist media buyer that many marketing communication agencies have. Apart from using a professional who knows what they are doing, they can often get discounts that you cannot, so it may even end up being cheaper.

Printed advertisements

The Institute of Practitioners in Advertising (IPA) (www.ipa.co.uk), the UK trade body representing marketing, communication and advertising agencies, identifies three components to advertising, that we can adapt to an events context:

1 An event manager identifies a problem (typically the need to publicise the event and/or sell tickets).
2 The event manager identifies the target consumers to whom the event is aimed.
3 The event manager creates a relevant and distinctive way of reaching the audience in creative and media terms.

The IPA suggests that technological change in the form of digital media channels and social media is developing so rapidly that advertising is changing fast to respond to these changes.

Advertisements come in a variety of formats depending on your audience and, in particular, the size of your budget. Television advertisements are expensive to produce and to hire the space. While some mega-events may use them, such as the FIFA World Cup and the Academy Awards (Oscars), they are way beyond the budget of all but a very few events. Therefore, we shall not cover television advertising. Although cheaper than television, radio advertising is also expensive and beyond the means of most events. If you do happen to have enough funds for broadcast advertising, your role will be very limited, rather you will probably be buying in specialist marketing communication and creative support to select the advertising space and produce the advertisement. However, some form of printed advertisement is common to many events.

As noted above, advertisements can be used in a number of formats, such as paid-for and promotional material. In this section we shall deal with the former. One of the reasons why advertising can be difficult to define is that there are essentially two different types: corporate and product-based. Corporate advertising does not seek to increase sales directly, rather it seeks to change, support or enhance the reputation of a company or event. It is not uncommon for major multinationals or those with a particular philosophical approach. For example, Toms Shoes donates a pair of shoes to an African child for every pair they sell, and most of their advertising focuses on this (www.google.co.uk/search?q=toms+shoes+advert&num=20&biw=2560&bih=947&source=lnms&tbm=isch&sa=X&ei=UKaWVePgJsSt7AbD9oWIAw&ved=0CAcQ_AUoAQ). However, this is fairly rare for events. The BBC advertises their Radio 1 Big Weekend, the purpose of which is ultimately to enhance the reputation of the station. Product-based advertising focuses on trying to increase sales by persuading the audience to purchase a ticket for your event (though it can be used for non-ticket events to increase attendance). While most of the principles are shared, we shall focus on product-based printed advertisements as these are the most likely option that you will be using.

How to create a printed advert

When creating advertising campaigns for events and festivals Allen et al. (2011) suggest that it is necessary to:

- Provide tangible clues to counteract the intangible nature of the event, by showing images of the event in action or by using a logo;
- Seek continuity over time by using recognisable symbols, spokespersons, trademarks or music;
- Only promise what it is realistically possible to deliver;
- Make the service tangible by showing people members of the target audience enjoying the event.

In addition, we suggest that when you are constructing your advert you consider:

- How will I grab the reader's attention straight away – do I need a strong visual, gimmick or short, large-font size message?
- What style appeals to my audience – funky, simple, conventional or wacky?
- Impart the most important content – you can probably really only get across one key message with most ads, such as why they should attend.
- Avoid being too busy – concentrate on the core message.
- Use colours that are appropriate to your audience.

Advertorials

Advertorials, sometimes referred to as native advertising, open up some ethical questions in that they can be criticised for effectively being a trick. They are written as an article in a journalistic style to appear that they are produced by an independent third party, when in fact they are paid for. As noted by Cameron and Ju-Pak (2000), it is a growing trend as marketers look at more effective ways of spending their advertising budget. Typically, an advertorial is for a whole page, or sometimes a half-page. Countries have different regulations on their use, but typically somewhere (usually at the top of the page) it needs to be clear that it is an advertisement, often with the words 'Advertisement' or 'Advertising feature' displayed. The hope of the advertiser is that the reader will not see such a notice or heading and will assume that they are reading an article. This is because, as Robinson (2002) found, the impact is greater if it is read more like an article than an advert.

The first obvious difference between an advertisement and an advertorial is that the latter is very text heavy, just like an article, although it will probably have some pictures. Whereas an advert is probably in a box, surrounded by other ads, has few words and is probably image heavy. Thus, Jackson (2013) notes that an advertorial requires advertising space to be purchased, usually in a newspaper (so it incurs a cost just like all advertising), but it is written to read like a feature article. It is therefore a sleight of hand, hoping that the reader will think they are reading an article by an independent third party.

Advertorials are definitely a niche advertising area, typically with local newspapers, though some trade publications use them. Thus far, there have been a limited number of events that have used them. Harrison-Hill and Chalip (2005) suggested that advertorials in sports magazines could be a way of promoting events such as motor-rally sports. Jackson (2013) found that New Zealand-based agency Write Agency (www.writeagency.com) provided powerful copy describing in attractive terms the King St. Great Race Ball. He also noted that MagStar Retail used advertorials to indirectly promote an event. Asia-based Chain Media (www.chainmedia.com/advertorial) suggests that an organisation should hand out advertorials to attendees at an event.

Advertorials tend to be for things like pubs, restaurants and some tourist attractions. Thus, if your event is at a primarily hospitality or tourist venue, then an advertorial might be applicable.

Writing an advertorial

An advertorial is a soft sell, rather than a hard pitch, exactly like a feature article. The focus is on providing information that will be useful to the reader, rather than overtly seeking to persuade them to attend the event. As a result, you might want to provide some statistical information, such as number of attendees, headline acts, awards won or whatever is relevant. What you certainly want to include is case studies: successful feature articles stress the human interest and this is exactly what you need to do. For example, a story of someone who has attended your event(s) and it has had a major impact on them (note, this must have actually happened; you cannot make it up). Advertorials are typically from about 400 to 500 words up to about 1,000 words and usually have a couple of 'action pictures' supporting the text.

CASE STUDY

Using an advertorial – South Devon Steiner School

The South Devon Steiner School (www.southdevonsteinerschool.org) occasionally use advertorials to promote their Advent Fair, Summer Fair and open days. The fact that they are a non-profit organisation and have built up a good relationship with their local paper means that theirs may not be a typical advertorial experience, but it offers an insight as to how this underused channel can be utilised.

2015 Advent Fair Organiser, Yolanda Drewell, says 'The school has used advertising features for our fairs for quite a few years. The reason they work is that people are more likely to read what they perceive to be "editorial" rather than advertising, as the former is deemed to be more credible.

The newspaper is responsible for putting the feature together, and seeks advertising from the school's suppliers in order to pay for the "editorial" space. The more advertising support for a feature, the more editorial space is provided. The school is asked to buy one advert that forms the anchor advert. We have found that the staff at Tindle Newspapers are generous, and we usually end up with a full page for the cost of one anchor ad.

The newspaper editorial staff is on hand to write up the editorial for the feature, though sometimes we draft the copy, and have found either way works well.

We chose the *Totnes News* series because the geographical net was spread wide, and the readership and circulation are high.

We do not really know how well the advertising feature works for us, as we also use other forms of marketing for these events, such as email campaigns, village posters, press releases and social media. However, the reach is so broad and I believe that local newspapers are well read so we assume the features do work. We also try to use good photographs which will appeal.'

Figure 4.2 Steiner School advertorial

Example advertorial from Steiner School

Credit: Permission to reprint from Jane Devonshire, Tindle Newspaper Group

Flyer/leaflet/poster

We address these three tools together because they are either alternatives or they complement each other. They are very common forms of advertising for events; it would be a very unusual event that did not use at least one of these. One of the main reasons for this is that they are usually a lot cheaper to produce than a printed advert. Indeed, with modern desktop publishing (DTP) programs many small events can do the basic design, and sometimes print without having to buy in designers and printers (though you probably get a better quality if you do). The second reason is that with an advert you are not sure precisely who receives the message, or even if they have. With flyers, leaflets and posters you can have a bit more input into who actually sees them, perhaps by handing them out or placing them in key areas. For example, if you are organising a school fête your audience is likely to be local and so posters on the perimeter of the school, community centres and libraries are likely to be viewed by those you want to attend. For smaller events these tools, along with perhaps a press release, will be the only ones they can afford.

Flyers and leaflets are very similar, with the difference primarily being in the quality of production and sometimes their size. A flyer is sometimes known as a handbill. Typically, they are produced on one side of paper, be it A4 or A5, often in black and white and they are sometimes merely photocopied or printed straight from a computer. One of the authors was on holiday in the UK and was handed a flyer for a weekly 'duck race' (they use numbered yellow plastic ducks – the winner is the person whose duck reaches a set point on a river). In short, they are a cheap and easy way of providing information about an event, and are most likely to be for small local events such as the opening night of a new bar or club.

The design and print quality of a leaflet is usually much better, for example, being in colour and they probably contain more information. A golden rule with a leaflet is that because you are going to the expense of producing it, you print on both sides, even if the reverse only has a picture and some basic details about the event or event organisers. They tend to be A6, A5 or A4, they can be folded (some in map-like shapes). If you have the skills and software you might design them yourself, or you might buy in a designer. Leaflets are normally printed professionally.

Leaflets and flyers act as a cue, primarily this is for something near to the time of being given out, but some flyers and leaflets might provide information that could be of use later. For example, a *What's On* guide adds value in that it might also be used later when the receiver wants something to do. An organisation with several events might put them all together in a single leaflet, for example *Wild About Plymouth* produces four leaflets a year outlining their activities over the forthcoming three months. Or they may be designed to lead to immediate action – such as promoting an event taking place in the very near future. For example, Haight Street in San Francisco is well known for its flyering of all sorts of products and events on telephone poles (Rodriguez 2011). Many events such as exhibitions, music gigs and comedy performances use flyers and leaflets.

A poster is a *visual* presentation of information and should be designed as such – do not simply reproduce your flyer or leaflet in poster format. It should be understandable to the reader without verbal comment – someone might look at it while talking to another delegate or even while in the toilet. Posters may be used differently in different countries. For example, where literacy levels are low posters using images are an effective means of promoting an event.

A poster is typically one side of paper, and rarely smaller than A3, though often it is A2, A1 or AO. It is usually on heavier paper, and often glossy. It is therefore more expensive. The vast majority of posters are in colour which adds to their cost. You need to be aware of the branding of your event/sponsors, for example is there a certain colour that should be used? You also

Table 4.3 Paper size	

Size	Measurements
A0	841 × 1189mm
A1	594 × 841mm
A2	420 × 594mm
A3	297 × 420mm

need to be aware that some colours do not come out as well, be very careful for example in using yellow as it can make it difficult to read the poster if you have the wrong colour text. It is also worth noting that people who are colour blind may struggle to read posters using certain combinations, for example red text on a green background or vice versa. Visuals (typically in the form of photographs or some graphics) are key to a poster, and it is probably sensible to focus on these first before looking at the text. The text (wording and typography) should be simple, do not try to get across complex messages, and do not try to have too much information. A poster that is too busy will often not be read.

Figure 4.3
Limpopo Youth Orchestra

Example of a poster used to promote the Limpopo Youth Orchestra's Christmas concert

Credit: Image courtesy of Simone Aronje-Adetoye, Limpopo Youth Orchestra

The Limpopo Youth Orchestra uses posters, such as the one above, as a promotional technique for their performances. This poster for a Christmas concert links together the Christmas and music themes through imagery of decorations and music notes, and includes a photograph of their performers. Additionally, they use a large and clearly visible font to convey the key information of what the event is, who it is by and how much it costs. This makes it easy for their target audience to understand the intended message.

It is possible that a designer might suggest whizzy design things that you can do – just make sure they are right for your audience. For example, if your event is for over-55s, fading out a picture is unwise; it will make it difficult for them to read your text (fading out is where a picture is reproduced at less than 100 per cent and so is in the background of the page).

With posters you need to remember that there may well be different custom, practice and legislation covering their usage. Thus, many organisations may make their premises available for posters for a fee. For example, it is possible to advertise with Transport for London (www.tfl.gov.uk) on London's tube stations, buses and coach and rail stations. However, in the UK most local councils will use powers under the Town and Country Planning Act 1990 for what is referred to as illegal flyposting – in other words, putting up your poster wherever you want.

During French elections there are tight laws concerning the use of advertising (including access to billboards provided by the government) which has led to the use of posters that are referred to as affiches. These posters still have significant weight during election campaigns. Whereas in the US with different laws posters are rare and television advertising dominates (Lilleker and Jackson 2011).

How to produce a flyer/leaflet/poster

One of the first issues you need to address is to select and manage your commercial printer. Some clients may feel that printers try to resemble magicians, and some printers complain that clients cannot be clear on what they want. There is a bit of truth in both views; printing can appear a mystery at first, and if you keep changing your mind this will lead to unbudgeted extra costs.

We suggest, therefore, that the first thing you need to do is to be very clear what you want to achieve. In the first instance you need to be honest with yourself and work out what the purpose of the publication is. You then need to consider key factors which shape the printing brief:

- What size, paper and colour of print do you need?
- What are the deadlines for receiving copy, proofs, sign-off and delivery?
- What folding, stapling and other finishing is required?
- How will the printer receive your copy?
- Who will be responsible for what?

Having an idea of what you want to achieve, you need to choose your printer. General advice on almost any service is to ask for quotes from three different suppliers, though this may not always be possible. Some people like to choose one printer and keep to them, but the authors' experience is that printers have different abilities and equipment and some have access to other services, such as design. The authors tended to have three that they would work with on a regular basis, depending on the task. Always be clear in advance what will incur an extra charge, for example, 'run on' costs of printing extra copies?

Quite possibly, the most important stages are the brief you give your printer and then the proofing/sign-off stage. Do not take the proof stage lightly; make sure that you do it in a quiet space and focus on the job at hand, and give yourself time to do it. Sometimes using someone who has not been involved in the document is a good way of identifying any issues – by the time you have read it ten times you see what you want to see.

It is our experience that printers use a range of terms that can sound impenetrable, but you need to learn some of the basics. We learnt by talking to colleagues, but one easy way is to find a useful guide such as provided by Gregg Stalter at: www.bbc.co.uk/news/uk-scotland-tayside-central-36387704.

When you are looking to produce a flyer, leaflet or poster we suggest some general rules to consider:

- Have a clear message;
- Keep it simple and brief;
- Use the visuals/design to support the message;
- Consider breaking up the design with boxes, borders, testimonials and diagrams;
- Write in a positive way;
- Include the most important details, such as when, where and price of the event;
- Have a call to action – something to do;
- Do not use print that is too small;
- Always, always proofread – ideally at least a day after you have finished the text and possibly use someone not involved in the process.

> **Questions to ask when producing a poster?**
>
> - What is your main message?
> - What are the headings?
> - What are the images to be used?
> - Do you go for one big visual or a number of smaller ones?
> - What is the call to action?
> - Whose contact details need to be included?

Banners

A banner is not a single tool. A range of approaches, sizes and types are available. Some banners are used at an event to reinforce messages to attendees, such as pop-up banners. These are reuseable banners that fold away into their own base. We talk about these in more depth in Chapter 13.

Most banners, however, are designed to gain attention and hopefully attract attendees to a forthcoming event. Thus, hanging banners are usually for the sides of buildings, railings or lampposts. For example, the National Theatre uses lamppost banners to promote upcoming shows such as *War Horse* and the *Curious Incident of the Dog in the Night-Time* (www.google.co.uk/search?q=london+theatre+lamppost+banners&source=lnms&tbm=isch&sa=X&ei=8IMBVb3kAaSu7gbxlYDQAQ&ved=0CAgQ_AUoAg&biw=1366&bih=643#tbm=isch&q=national+theatre+lamppost+banners&imgdii=). A much more recent form of advertising is digital banners where there is a scrolling banner across a web page. Slightly different digital images are Gobos, which are templates that are then projected to create whatever image you want. While they can be used to promote an event on the exterior of a building, they are more commonly used at an event to create awareness of what is going on (www.google.co.uk/search?q=digital+projection+gobo&biw=1366&bih=643&source=lnms&tbm=isch&sa=X&ei=C4Y BVZ6HLMLe7Abm44DQDQ&ved=0CAcQ_AUoAg).

At their very cheapest level banners might be home-made, such as a white bed sheet with writing on, but typically they will be digitally printed on waterproof materials and often they have 'metal eyes' so they can be attached to where they will be hung up.

Banners generally have very little writing on them, as they are designed to be seen only briefly, while still providing the relevant message. This short message needs to be easy to read and understand while delivering your desired message, as many of your audience may only see it once and only for a couple of seconds.

Remember, banners can be quite expensive, so if your event will be repeated you might want to avoid a precise date and rather put 'This Saturday', or 'The last Saturday of the month', so that you can reuse the banner.

How to produce a banner?

Think about:

- What do you want to say (what is your intended message)?
- Where will it be displayed?
- How big does the banner need to be and are there any size limitations?
- Will your target audience see your banner?
- What colours will you use?
- What size font?
- Any images?
- What will it be made of?

Discussion questions

1 If you are putting on a local community event with virtually no marketing budget what forms of advertising should you use, and how? Conversely, if you are promoting a popular comedian visiting a regional entertainment venue for three nights, and it is expected that there will be advertising, what would you focus on, and why?

2 You are producing an A1 full-colour poster to promote an event aimed at children aged 5–8. Yet your actual audience is their parents, guardians and schoolteachers. What is the single, easy-to-understand message you need to get across to convince them they should bring their children?

3 Media sales teams may promise you the moon if you buy space in their publication, but how will you know if your advert has achieved what you want?

4 If you are considering producing a number of pop-up banners to accompany you at exhibitions, given that you may use them for several years, how do you select the appropriate messages that will have longevity for your brand and products?

Further information

Books

Piercy, J. (2013) *Symbols: a universal language*, London: Michael O'Mara.
Sissors, J. (2010) *Advertising Media Planning*, New York: McGraw-Hill.

Journals

Journal of Advertising
Journal of Advertising Research

Websites

For information on creating adverts:

www.hongkiat.com/blog/70-creative-advertisements-that-makes-you-look-twice/
http://recruiterbox.com/blog/5-points-to-consider-while-designing-your-first-print-advertise-
    ment/

For information on producing posters flyers and leaflets:

www.printaholic.com/15-tips-for-writing-effective-flyers/

Further detailed information on writing an advertorial can be found at:

www.write.co.nz/Resources/Writing+tips/How+to+write+a+good+advertorial.html
www.rab.com/public/about/about.cfm?section=about – the Radio Advertising Bureau represents
    America's broadcast radio industry.

Chapter 5

Direct communication

Introduction

The previous chapter focused primarily on using indirect or impersonal communication; we now turn to how events can communicate directly with their audiences. We need to note that the divide can be blurred at points, for example leaflets and flyers can be inserted within mail-shots. The weakness of advertising, apart from cost, is that it is a broadcast approach; you simply do not know if you are reaching the right people. In this chapter we will assess how to reach a named individual, group or organisation directly. The numbers reached will certainly be smaller, but they are more likely to include a higher percentage of those you specifically want to reach. We shall first introduce what direct marketing means and then we shall address the detailed means used for direct marketing campaigns. This will include the construction of the following one-to-one and one-to-many communication channels: (a) brochures, (b) direct mail, (c) invitation/tickets and (d) Short Message Service (SMS). Direct communications is rarely a one-shot, and we expect to show the linkages between these routes. By the end of this chapter students will be able to:

- Understand when to use direct marketing;
- Construct a mailing list;
- Use brochures in the appropriate circumstances;
- Write a direct mail letter;
- Design an invitation.

Reaching your audiences directly

What we are considering is direct marketing, using a range of means to reach an audience direct from the event manager. Sometimes people may equate direct mail as equal to direct marketing, but it is only one component part of it. Direct marketing refers to an event manager making direct contact with potential audiences in order to promote their event, and hope-fully persuade the receiver of the message(s) to attend. A range of tools are used including brochures, direct mail, e-direct mail (which we shall deal with in Chapter 10), invitations/tickets and SMS.

Of these tools, brochures are not widely used; rather, they are a niche for specific types of events, most likely to be used for business to business (B2B) events. For example, one of the authors was responsible for the marketing communications of a large training company, and a mailshot with a brochure to key organisational personnel was the main tool used. Direct mail (both postal and email) is common to B2B events and any business to consumer (B2C) that has built up good information on its customers over a number of years. Invitations and tickets are central to most events; they are part of the event offer. SMS is also a niche area of more relevance to those events that can get customers to sign up to receive such messages.

Direct marketing provides a number of possible advantages:

- It enables an event manager to reach the precise audience they want. This means that if you can get to the right audience it can be much more cost-effective.
- Direct marketing can enable an event manager to get across much more complex messages than advertising.
- Direct marketing can be more effective than advertising in generating feedback. This might be in the form of a voucher, encouraging people to contact you and ask for further details or, in the case of an invite, simply allow you to know who intends to attend.
- It is generally accepted that direct marketing can be fairly accurately measured. You should know to whom you sent your brochure, letter or invite, when and whether they responded (and if so in what way).

One of the strengths of direct marketing is that it encourages the event manager to test what works. You can try different messages, channels, timing and audiences to see which is the most effective.

However, there are some downsides to direct marketing. The first hurdle you will face is actually getting the data on whom to target. If you are trying to sell products such as insurance, clothes and holidays you will probably buy in a list. This is known as postcode or zip code marketing. This works on the basis of profiling; that people living in certain types of locations or houses may be interested in certain products. This approach is less common for events; rather, you are much more likely to need to collect and manage your own data, typically from past attendees or those who reply to promotional material. This involves investing, what are for an event likely to be, significant human resources to capture, store and use this data.

Let us assume that you can capture data for those interested in your event, the second big problem is one of cost. This would normally include designing the material, producing it and delivering it. If you are using the internet, say an e-direct mail, the second and third components are negligible. However, even for a printed high-quality invite, the production and postal costs can seem quite significant.

Buying a list

Buying a list is probably only of interest to the very largest consumer events who can profile their target audience, or events whose main target is business based, as with training courses, award ceremonies and conferences. As a result it is worth noting that there may be some differences if you buy in a target list if your event is B2B or B2C. If your audience is B2B, what you are likely to do is buy a list of organisations in an industry or geographical place that you are interested in. If your audience is B2C, then such lists are normally geographically based, so in the UK they are typically based on the electoral register. Having decided that you need to buy in a list, what next?

The first point is to proceed with caution, and surfing on a web search engine will find a wide range of companies who claim amazing results for their data. Yet you need to be realistic; the Direct Marketing Association's 2015 DMA Response Rate Report (www.thedma.org.uk) shows that with a house list (one you have created from your contacts) direct mail achieves a 3.7 per cent response rate, and a 1 per cent response rate for a prospect list (one you have bought in from an agency). Therefore, if you get a 1 per cent response rate you are probably doing well, so do not believe the hype, rather work out what is the right list for your event.

Some basic things to include when sourcing a list are:

1 Consider very carefully whom you want to reach.
2 Do your research. Speak to someone who has used a data list and consult any relevant trade bodies such as the Direct Marketing Association (www.dma.org.uk/), National Mail Order Association (www.nmoa.org) or the Direct Marketing Association New Zealand (www.dma.co.nz) whose websites often contain information, and ideally buy from a company that is a member of that body.
3 Prepare clear precise questions to ask the suppliers, such as how often they 'clean' data (check for duplicates, out-of-date addresses etc.).
4 Decide on your budget and keep to it, some suppliers may promise you the earth if you purchase a bigger list.
5 Work out how you will segment your data, such as gender, age and geography, so that you can tailor messages to promote your event.
6 Remember, if anything goes wrong with the list it is your event reputation that will be tarnished.
7 If you are trying to reach people from different countries be aware of the different laws and ethical standards. What might be allowed in one country might not be in another.

If you are operating in the UK, excellent and very detailed advice can be found from the Information Commissioner's Office guidance on Direct Marketing (https://ico.org.uk/media/for-organisations/documents/1555/direct-marketing-guidance.pdf).

In the UK, the 1998 Data Protection Act outlines what you can do with lists, and what protections exist for customers. A quick summary of these rights is provided by *Which?* (www.which.co.uk/consumer-rights/regulation/data-protection-act).

If you looking to direct mail to other countries there is likely to be a maze of regulations, dos and don'ts, so seek advice such as from the host direct marketing trade body.

Constructing your own mailing list

If your budget is small or your event audience is made up of primarily individual consumers, you are much more likely to construct your own mailing list based on data you can easily access and, ideally, control. Therefore, in creating your list you are most likely to look at past attendees of your event.

The very first thing to be aware of when producing a list is to understand the legal requirements in your country, and there is usually an assumption (in some countries it is the law) from most ethical direct marketers that you need the permission of the person that they are happy to receive information from you. With email direct marketing there are usually stronger laws/standards, but with other communication it is usually assumed that if someone gives you their details they are implying acceptance that you may contact them later. For example, if you have a competition at your exhibition stand at a trade or consumer show, it is not unreasonable that you might get back to those who enter using the details they provided.

The first step in creating your own list is to identify from whom, from what and how you currently collect data – to audit what data you have access to. The chances are that you are not fully utilising the sources available to you. The easiest thing to address is who could be in your list, this probably requires an assessment of who contacts you (and how). More difficult is to work out what you want to find out and how you secure this. In all likelihood this will lead to changes to your systems of data collection. For example, one of the authors changed the telephone script for what reception and the sales team asked. Typically, a human resources manager from a company would ring up enquiring about what courses the company provided, and the phone operator was instructed to ask 'How did you hear about us?', with a tick box provided. This is very useful information as it helps to assess which promotional tools are working, and such data can be recorded. An audit of what information you collect and how, should enable you to make your data collection procedures more efficient and effective

Table 5.1 highlights that you need to look at both your own staff as well as customers for usable data. Looking at sales-based data is fairly obvious, but less so are mystery shoppers and participant observation, yet events lend themselves so well to these. We tend to get caught up in 'hard' data, such as sales, but for you it is as important to understand clearly what the experience of attendees is. The use of mystery shoppers enables you to understand the interaction between staff and attendees. Participant observation is a subtle way of getting data; typically you have observers whose only role is to note the reaction of attendees. For example, at one surfing competition the observer noticed that those in the VIP area were so far away they could not really see the scoreboards and so did not know what was happening.

Keeping a list of existing and potential customers and event attendees could be done in a couple of ways. For smaller companies or individual event managers, a simple database such as a Microsoft Excel spreadsheet could be used, while many larger organisations might use

Table 5.1 Sources of data

Staff sources	Customer sources
Staff meetings	Ticket sales
Minutes of meetings	Customer questionnaires/focus groups
Mystery shoppers	Mystery shoppers
	Participant observation
	Loyalty cards
	Ticket buyers
	Inbound email
	Inbound telephone calls
	Business cards
	Competitions
	Invites
	Vouchers/offers
	Search engine optimisation (SEO)

a Customer Relationship Management (CRM) system. Using a Microsoft Excel database is generally more cost-effective and requires fewer technical skills than buying specialist CRM software, and for smaller events it is just as effective.

A useful function of Microsoft Excel is its ability to link to other Microsoft Office programs such as Microsoft Word. This enables personalised messages to be created and sent by email, or printed to be posted or used at the event itself. This function is called a Mail Merge; a step-by-step guide is available on the Microsoft support website (https://support.microsoft.com/en-gb/kb/294683). This does, however, require your database created in Microsoft Excel to be in a specific format, with separate columns assigned to each field. Some example fields/columns include:

- Title
- First name
- Last name
- Telephone
- Email address
- Address line 1
- Town/city
- Postcode.

A CRM database is a piece of software designed specifically to monitor and manage relationships you have with your stakeholders. These databases can hold detailed information, far more than simply their contact details, about your stakeholders so you can develop relationships with them, based on their engagement with you. An example of this could be you trying to increase attendance from a certain demographic of your audience members; by monitoring which events they have previously attended, you could send them information about other events that might interest them. You could also closely monitor and record any correspondence you send to them, as well as any responses they send to you.

When you decide to create your own list for direct marketing purposes you need to allocate the resources to manage it. Not only does this relate to actually sending out material, but, perhaps more importantly, regularly updating the data, to take out duplicates, out-of-date contacts and requests to be removed. If someone has asked to be removed from your list, comply quickly, because if you keep sending them material understandably they will get annoyed.

5.1 Tip box

Creating a list

Each event has a specific target audience identified according to what the event objective is – sometimes this is individuals and sometimes it can be cohorts of people, grouped together according to appropriate criteria or their profiles. Your target list needs to reflect this.

When trying to create a mailing list try not to start completely from scratch, aim to build on what you have used before, so make sure contact data is up to date and you have an idea of an individual's previous engagement with you, for whatever reason/interest. Check the list with colleagues to ensure no one is included who should not be (i.e. if you represent a larger organisation you will be expected to have accurate details and to know if someone has changed jobs or companies, or even passed away). Make sure that all the details are correct and place it in one reliable source, not several databases.

For some events it is sometimes possible to increase your mailing list through and reach out via social media, and other more open and less targeted channels.

Brochures

Where a leaflet or flyer is typically a throw-away document, a brochure is designed to be kept and used ideally more than once. A brochure is a sales tool which can be aimed not just at consumers, but also resellers and sales teams. With the first it is designed to inform and persuade, and for the last two it is a means of giving them the information to help them sell your products, but also provides an aide-mémoire they can give to consumers. So brochures aim to both inform and persuade.

Brochures involve significant investment of resources as they contain more pages and content than leaflets. Their main use is to promote products and services that are intangible, so Fill (2009: 558) suggests that 'the brochure acts as a temporary product substitute'. As a result, they aim to create awareness of a need.

The length of brochures allows them to be used to explain technical or complex products, or those with a range of options to buy. It also allows for more opportunity to use supporting images and pictures. Whereas a flyer would be two sides, a brochure is longer, typically 16 or 32 pages, or whatever you want. You should try to get benefits and not just features into the text of flyers and leaflets, but it is easier to do for brochures (you have more space). There is also an assumption that where a poster or flyer is about one event and will be used once, a brochure might be about multiple events and referred to several times.

Originally brochures were expensive because of the print and mailing costs. However, it is now very common to produce a PDF version that can be sent by email. It is worth noting though that there is still a cost and the convention is not just to send out spam to any email address, so you need to use permission marketing. This means that your e-brochure should only be sent out to people who have agreed to receive an email, typically via a tick box. Visit Scotland encourages events and tourist destinations to send them e-brochures which they then promote (www.visitscotland.com/e-brochures/). It is possible to look either for events with e-brochures in particular activities, such as food, or to look by region.

Brochures are more likely to be used by B2B events such as training courses, team building and venues that provide meetings and conferences. In addition, companies that promote event services often use brochures to promote their skills, products and experience. For example, if you are looking to source an event planning agency, many provide a brochure in the form of a PDF on their website. For example, wedding venue Danesfield House (www.danesfieldhouse. co.uk) has a 42-page brochure on its website that you can download. This is highly visual with good-quality pictures of the venue, weddings being held there, the food and the rooms. A slightly different approach is taken by a wedding planner (www.theweddingofmydreams. co.uk) where you have to register to have a catalogue sent to you by post. Common to all of these examples is that they stress the human interest; what the impact of these events or venues will be on individuals.

While most brochures are a promotional/sales tool, some are designed to enhance the experience by providing information for the customer at the event. For example, some exhibitions produce brochures for visitors, providing information about who is on what stand, seminars and the speakers.

CASE STUDY

E-brochures

Prague Eventery (http://pragueeventery.com) is a full-service event and destination management company (DMC) that provides customised services for meetings, incentives, conferences and events for global companies. They organise a bespoke programme of activities for their clients, many of whom are blue-chip companies. As part of the process of gaining new business their proposals are presented in e-brochure format. To the client it reads like a real-life brochure as the pages click over from left to right like a book or brochure; you do not keep scrolling down like a word or PDF document.

Mike Ferreira the Managing Director explains how it works: 'Whilst this might appear a gimmick, the important thing for us is to create a vehicle to effectively transfer a lot of information. Sending a proposal in something like a PDF creates obstacles, the client has to download a very big file and possibly download a programme, all of which takes time they do not have. Instead we send our clients an email with a link to a web page which they open, so that in effect we create a web page in our website which only they can access. The client can choose to download it if they wish, but they have the choice. Because we use a digital format we can offer so much more than can be provided in a PDF; for example, video or links which can be opened to show the venues and activities available. Therefore, our e-brochures are convenient, easy to access and immediate for our clients.

We do not sell packages; rather, each client's proposal will be different. Because we often deal with large events such as conferences and conventions where many hundreds of attendees are transported to Prague, there can be a lot of detail. We might, for example, have eight different hotels for accommodation, seven venues and nine restaurants. Our proposals can often be 70 pages in length, this would be a lot to download and read in PDF format, and we could not offer the visual and interactive elements.

This e-brochure format is used at different stages of the bid. After the initial proposal the client will come over for a site visit, then the proposal is reviewed and ultimately the final version is agreed. Throughout we use the same easy-to-use web-based process. The proposal can then become the basis of the itinerary given to attendees.

> The e-brochure is easy to produce for us. We had IT help setting up the pro-gramme to meet our specifications, and now we can easily use it. One of the team is able to produce and manage the e-brochure.
>
> Our use of e-brochures is different from most of our competitors who tend to rely on PDF documents, and the response is often very positive. We often get feedback such as "what a beautiful, informative and easy-to-use proposal". The e-brochure enables us to meet our clients' needs, and offer so much more in content.'

The assumption is that brochures are only used prior to the event to get people to attend, but for certain markets, such as conferences, exhibitions and meetings, post-event brochures may be an effective marketing tool. These events are ones where the customers who attend, primarily businesses or non-commercial organisations, invest significant sums, such as for travel, accommodation and equipment/materials. A post-event brochure can remind attendees what a good and commercially successful event they have just attended, at the very point when they may be considering their budget for next year.

Such post-event brochures are applying the idea of cognitive dissonance. If you look at many advertisements for high-value products, such as cars, they are not so much telling you to buy a particular car but, rather, if you have bought such a car they are reinforcing a view that you have made the correct decision. A post-event brochure is in effect creating a feel-good factor, reminding you that you attended the right event. In addition, if your event had spon-sors, this is another way in which you can promote them, and so can be part of the package you offer them.

One of the most important aspects of a brochure is the cover; why should the target open and read the brochure? It needs a title and a pictorial image which is likely to entice the receiver. The branding of the organisation or event is also important. In short, keep it simple and to the point. And remember it should be about what the consumer wants to buy, not just what you want to sell.

Direct mail

The key to direct mail is that it seeks to provide the personal touch – from a named person to a named person. There are some similarities between direct mail and brochures, as they can serve the same purpose, and marketers may choose one or the other, indeed there will often be a direct mail letter accompanying a brochure. However, direct mail can also be used for different purposes from brochures because it is cheaper to produce, and can be written quickly.

Direct mail marketing involves sending an offer, announcement, reminder or whatever to a particular person at a physical or virtual address. Direct mail could be a simple letter alone, or it could be accompanied with for example a voucher, DVD or a catalogue attached. Direct mail is frequently used to send tickets/invites, a letter explaining the details of the event with the ticket/invite attached.

One of the key advantages of direct mail is that fairly complex messages can be explained through it. Direct mail is well-suited to one-to-one communication, because it can be personalised to a target audience. It is also possible to measure its effects. Typically, direct mail is used with other media such as websites, to which it will seek to drive traffic.

The downside for direct mail is that it can have a poor reputation, in the form of unsolicited 'junk mail'. However, direct mail that you have permission to send to your contacts (i.e. your own list) should not have this limitation.

Most direct mail is used prior to the event; however, if you capture attendee details you can send a direct mail letter after the event. This could reinforce key messages, seek feedback or try to sell early bird tickets for the next event.

Invitations/tickets

Ticketing is important for events whose primary income is from the entrance fee, and the extent of ticket sales can help to determine the success or failure of an event (Allen et al. 2011). Invitations are a form of ticketing used for corporate and private events (Allen et al. 2011). Invitations and tickets are good ways of monitoring attendance for your event and keeping track of the number of people who attend. They are also ideal ways of providing your audience with further information about the event, including arrival times, dress codes and directions. Tickets and invitations provide a further avenue for the sponsors of your event to be identified, as their logos could be included.

A ticket can also be a keepsake. For example, in January 2015 the lower division football team Accrington Stanley missed out on drawing Manchester United in the FA Cup because they lost in the previous round. However, this did not stop them from printing and selling 250 tickets of a 'virtual' game against Manchester United – the game that never happened. In so doing they raised approximately £5,000. Some of their fans obviously thought that a souvenir ticket was an appropriate way to commemorate this non-event.

Table 5.2 addresses the main types of different tickets available.

Table 5.2 Different types of tickets

Type	Description
Single tickets	Most common – admits one person.
Family tickets	Typically two adults and two children, very common for tourist-based events.
Free event tickets	Attendees have to apply for a free ticket. Used to make sure numbers do not exceed capacity.
Table ticket	Common for award/s ceremonies where an organisation will buy a whole table, typically of ten or 12 seats, and includes food and drink.
Early bird	Discounts offered to generate income early in the planning process.
Concessions	Some events, especially sports, may have reduced prices for children, disabled, military or older people.

When considering how to use ticketing the event manager has a checklist of questions you need to address:

- Will you have a physical ticket or online?
- How will the guest list be constructed?
- How will money be collected?
- Do you need ticketing software?
- How will you sell tickets?
- If you use an agency what will it cost?
- If you are managing ticket sales will you incur a fee, and if so what?
- Will the ticket cover everything at the event?
- What is the key message you want on the ticket?
- Will there be self-service?
- Will there be VIP/express tickets?
- Will there be limitations – such as how many a person can buy?
- What are the terms and conditions – do you need help writing them?

An invite can be the first formal contact you have with an event, and like a ticket it can be a memorable keepsake. The style of invite is likely to reflect the event, so one for a wedding would probably be different from that of a divorce party (the former is more likely to be traditional in colour, size and style, whereas the latter might be more zany and individualistic). The nature of some events means the invitation will be very formal, such as an invitation to meet the Queen at a Garden Party at Buckingham Palace (www.royal.gov.uk/RoyalEvents andCeremonies/GardenParties/Gardenparties.aspx).

The first thing to consider with an invite is to be clear why the person is being invited, be it sponsor, VIP or winner.

Table 5.3 outlines some of the different approaches to invites, and to which types of event they might best fit.

Table 5.3 Different types of invites

Type of invite	Nature of invite
Card invite	Tends to be for parties and award/s ceremonies, usually on embossed card.
Handwritten	For very small intimate events such as a private party or exclusive dinner or cocktail party.
Electronic	An email attachment – it may look exactly the same as a card invite, but is delivered electronically.
Letter	There may be an accompanying letter to the invite card.

CASE STUDY

Using invites

The University of South Australia (www.unisa.edu.au/) organises a number of events. Fern Cargill, the Advancement Officer, explains how they make effective use of invitations to support their events, 'Within the Advancement Services Unit, we manage a range of events for alumni, donors and other key constituents with an emphasis on relationship building. These can take place on or off campus, and in Adelaide, across Australia, or in countries around the world. Events range from interstate cocktail receptions for alumni, through to ceremonies where student scholarship recipients are awarded in front of an audience of donors; from seminars showcasing the university's latest research through to an annual black tie awards night celebrating the achievements of our graduates.

We use invitations for some of our events. Event name, date, time, venue, and registration information (how to RSVP and deadline) are the key things that appear on all event invitations, as well as the university's logo/branding. In addition, we might feature information about dress code, ticket price (where applicable), details about the speaker(s), host or event proceedings, directions to the venue and parking details, as well as requesting dietary or access information from our guests (as part of the RSVP).

Guest lists are tailored depending on the nature of the event, as is the decision-making over the final list. For example, when promoting an interstate alumni function the guest list will be based on individuals who are classed as "alumni" (e.g. individuals with a qualification from our university or an antecedent institution, or individuals who worked as staff members with our university for five years or more), living within the state or location where the event is based, with an email address and who are happy to receive emails about events. This type of criteria will be mapped out by the staff member managing the event and the guest list collated by a member of the database team ready for sending.

For a more complex or significant event, a member of the Advancement team will compile recommended criteria (this might include high-level donors, corporate partners, senior staff, and so forth) which would then be approved by the Director of Advancement before being collated by a member of the database team. The Vice Chancellor's office may be asked to approve guest lists for the most prestigious of events. In addition, we have a number of recurring events which people subscribe to – for example, our Successful Ageing Seminars which are open to the public – so in those instances promotions are sent to the dedicated group that have subscribed to communication.

Information that we hold largely comes from the individuals themselves. We store an array of information from contact details, UniSA education details, employment details, dietary and access requirements where these have been communicated to us, communication preferences, history of event attendance, giving history (e.g. donations), and records of any meaningful correspondence. All constituents on our database are categorised with a "constituent code" (one or more) which helps to identify the reason for their presence on our database and segment our data.

When dealing with a database of almost 240,000 individuals and organisations keeping data up to date is always a challenge but we have a number of steps in place to help with this. For alumni, we provide regular opportunities for individuals to update their details – we send periodic emails asking them to check the information that we hold, and we also have a dedicated members' area where alumni can log in to update their details. We also update our records based on returned mail or bounced emails, and have utilised mass data cleansing exercises from time to time.

My advice to someone thinking of creating their own list and designing event invitations is that they should start by thinking about the aim(s) of the event and who needs to be in the room to achieve this. We usually start at a high level by thinking about the "categories" of people that we want to reach and the richness of data that is available to us – for example, if you need to build a guest list for a sector-specific event, can you reach people that have previously clicked on articles on that topic in your e-newsletters, or people that work in that industry, or who have attended similar events in the past? Obviously, event capacity and location will dictate the size of your guest list somewhat.

When designing the invitations think about the audience you are hoping to reach and the message(s) you are trying to convey and impact you want the invitation to have. Don't forget to cover the basics, and offer multiple methods of RSVP (phone, email, online form, etc.). Where you are planning to invite VIPs or special guests, think about whether it is appropriate for that person to get the standard invitation or if they need special treatment (a pre-invitation phone call, or handwritten note from a senior staff member).'

Figure 5.1 University of South Australia invite

Example invitation for the University of South Australia 25th Birthday Gala Dinner

Credit: Image courtesy of University of South Australia

5.2 Tip box

Using invites

When you are thinking about using invites our advice is that the first question to ask is whether the event will be invite only. If it is, this gives a degree of exclusivity which should make it attractive, but it is probably wise to have a reserve list in case it is not as popular as you had hoped. Indeed, based on past experience can you work out how many will attend? Once people have confirmed they will attend, will they then get sent a ticket or will they simply turn up and be ticked off the guest list? The former maintains the sense of quality and exclusivity, but the latter is simpler and much cheaper. Our view is that if they have been sent an invite this will probably suffice for a ticket. Having decided who will attend and what they will receive, be very clear how you will reach them. Posted invites are obviously more costly but the impact is greater, whereas email is cheaper and quicker. While obviously your budget will be important, we suggest that the answer to this conundrum is to look at the nature of the audience and your event. A high-prestige event, such as a major awards ceremony sent to major 'players' in an industry, probably should have an invite sent out by post to maintain the sense of importance of the event.

SMS

The use of a Short Message Service is where a message is sent to mobile (cell) phones. Those who receive the message have normally decided to opt in to the service, and may get updates on special offers, news or information. It is therefore based on sending the same text message to all who subscribe. As implied the messages are short, which means that the information to be imparted has to be simple and easy to convey. There is little room for preliminaries; the whole message is essentially a call to action. This could be to visit a website or more likely to remind them to attend an event. For example, the 2015 Rugby World Cup used SMS to provide updates on tickets of the matches taking place (www.rugbyworldcup.com/front-row).

The key issues with using SMS are:

● Getting the list;
● Deciding on content, including how often to send out;
● Managing the process, including whether to use an agency.

The advantage of SMS marketing is that you can get a response quickly. For example, say you have some tickets left over that you need to sell off at a discount on the day of your event, then you will soon know how effective the campaign has been. However, in direct marketing terms, SMS is only ever likely to be a marginal tool.

Karr (2014) points out that when constructing your SMS message you should:

- Grab their attention, for example, do you want a cheap ticket or how can you avoid queuing?
- Tell them who you are – unless you tell them which event or organisation you are from they will not know;
- Avoid text speak – use clear, simple language;
- Keep it short – you generally have 160 characters or less;
- The ask – tell them what to do such as how to purchase what you are offering them.

SMS is good if you have an offer such as reduced prices and new seats available or late changes in the programme, say the start is being delayed or there is a traffic accident. So they should be messages that can add value for the recipient, not just about you getting across your marketing messages.

Given that emails cost nothing to send, and texts incur a cost, it is important to understand why you might use text messaging. The answer appears to be more psychological than any inherent technical advantage. Most readers of this book will have a smartphone that receives both texts and emails; do you read all of your texts and emails? Probably not, we seem programmed to be more likely to open texts than emails, hence why SMS campaigns can be successful.

When to use direct marketing

Table 5.4 highlights the situations and types of events where each of the different direct marketing tools might be used.

Sometimes you might only use one of these tools, but in most instances we suspect that there will be a combination. The factors that determine which you use are likely to be based on your budget, the type of event, your purpose of using direct marketing, when in the event cycle you are using it and your skills.

Table 5.4 The application of different direct marketing tools

Type of direct marketing	Type of event	Advantages	Disadvantages	When to use
Brochure	Conferences. Training courses and Away Days.	Both a promotional tool and a guide at the event. Can cover a lot of information. Provides an additional channel for sponsors.	Cost. Not everyone reads them. Getting the contact details.	Lead-up to the event. During the event if providing a guide.

| Table 5.4 continued | | | | |

Type of direct marketing	Type of event	Advantages	Disadvantages	When to use
Direct mail	Conferences. Training courses. Awards ceremonies. Specialist interest such as toy fayres.	Is personalised. Should be targeting those most interested in the event. Can get across complex messages.	Getting the contact details.	Can be an event's first marketing communication – designed to get sales going.
Invite/ticket	*Tickets:* Sports. Entertainment. Venues with a fixed capacity. *Invites:* Parties and social occasions. Awards ceremonies.	Identify who and how many intend to attend. Provide a keepsake – so encourages after-event recall.	Getting the contact details. Requires a team to manage the process. Producing and printing can be expensive. Fraud/ counterfeits.	Invites often accompany any direct mail letter. Tickets sent when payment made or intent made for free events.
SMS	Any with paying attendees.	Quick to send out. Uses a ubiquitous channel.	Management of list. Cost.	To increase sales. To send out updates on urgent or time-specific information.

Discussion questions

1 We assume that most events have to create their own mailing lists, rather than buying in a list. If this is the case, how will you manage the process? Who will be doing it, what organisational and IT skills do they require, what software will you need, how will you access the data and who might be able to help?

2 As consumers we are now inundated with messages, therefore the art of producing an eye-catching mailshot combines design and authoring skills. What are the principles you will use in creating a well-crafted mailshot letter? Remember you need to get a lot of detail across in very few words.

3 When would you invest in a printed or e-brochure for an event? What type, size and audience best fits this tool?

4 Invitations incur costs in terms of drawing up a guest list, design, printing and delivery. How would you assess whether an invite has been money well spent?

Further information

Websites

A good article on direct marketing legislation worldwide is offered by Jay Cline at: https://iapp.org/news/a/2009-08-opt-in-or-out-for-global-marketing

Some good detail on writing and producing brochures can be found at these sites:

www.wikihow.com/Design-Brochures
www.kuraoka.com/how-to-write-a-brochure.html
http//marketing.about.com/od/directmarketin1/a/brochmktg.htm
www.debretts.com/british-etiquette/communication/written-etiquette/invitations

Chapter 6

Media relations

Introduction

Media relations is one of the most common tools for promoting an event. Sometimes this can appear to be tied up in mumbo-jumbo; the preserve of a limited few, but in fact this is not rocket science. The art of media relations can be fairly easily learnt, there are certain 'formulas' that can be applied. We shall focus primarily on the writing/creative skills you require. The starting point of media relations is to be able to identify what is a news story, we shall then look at how to use the most popular forms of media relations: (a) press releases; (b) feature articles; and (c) stunts. By the end of this chapter students will be able to:

- Understand how to develop news stories for an event;
- Write a press release;
- Write a feature article;
- Develop ideas for stunts.

What is news?

Before you can start thinking about allocating resources to media relations it is important to understand what is news? Possibly one of the easiest sources to help you think about this was Harold Evans who was the Editor of *The Sunday Times* from 1967 to 1981, and has an almost legendary status in British journalism. Evans stated that:

> News is people. It is people talking and doing. Committees and Cabinets and Courts are people; so are fires, accidents and planning decisions. They are only news because they involve and affect people.
>
> Cited in Byrne 2002: 28

Even though you are producing an event, what is key is human interest: what is the impact of your event on people? Thus, you might be opening a new children's playground, and the canny event manager will focus their release on how many children will benefit from it, and in what way. This is impact.

You might assume that news is what we see dominating television news programmes and the front page of the newspapers, whereas for most of us this is not the case. News is really what people are interested in, and your event can be packaged as news. It is possible to construct a simple checklist to help you to identify a story. We suggest that key elements to news are likely to be:

- Timing – how immediate the story is, for example, during an election campaign;
- Significance – how many people are affected by it, for example, a sports stadium fire or accident;
- Proximity – how close to the audience (this could be geographically or by interest), for example when the Olympic torch relay toured around the UK prior to London 2012;
- Prominence – famous or infamous people, for example a Royal wedding;
- Human interest – a person who can now do something as a result of attending your event;
- Unusual – this could be a first or just an odd story, for example in June 2015 when Dave Grohl the lead singer of the band The Foo Fighters broke his leg on stage in Sweden;
- Conflict – something is contested, such as student protests in London;
- Emotion – it matters to someone, for example charity events such as Live 8.

This does not mean that all of these will be present, but journalists are likely to pick up on stories that have at least one of these features.

Andrew Marr (2004) the BBC Political Editor noted a trend towards 'shopping' news that might benefit many event managers. He suggested that journalists were becoming more interested in gossip, products and celebrity; areas on which many event fields can provide interesting and timely news stories.

Obviously many of your news stories will be presented through a single press release 'launching' your event, but with a little creative thought it is possible to get more than one story from your event, or to create stories that are not overtly linked to your event but help to promote it. The key is for you to think what the news angles could be. Typical questions you can ask to help develop news include:

- Anniversaries – the 200th anniversary in June 2015 of the Battle of Waterloo secured significant coverage for a re-enactment involving 5,000 enthusiasts;
- Stunts – during the 2015 Copa America football competition, one of the host cities, Rancagua, remodelled its bus stops to resemble goals;
- Events – for example, many solicitors run free advice sessions on particular legal issues;
- Opening – getting a celebrity to open your shop, building or school;
- A first – to get a qualification, to use a technology, to offer a product;
- Job-creating – a major local and trade story – it says you are successful;
- Awards – has an awards body given you anything? This is something food retailers and restaurants use a lot;
- Winning a competition – winning a trade competition can be good publicity – for example the Speciality Foods Association in America run their SOFI awards;
- Charity donations – especially if this ties in with the people concerned, say a photo opportunity of an official handover of a cheque;
- Seasonal – giving advice on issues such as dieting around New Year, love around Valentine's Day (14 February) and getting into your swimming costume in the summer.

For most events you can send out several press releases before and even afterwards. For example, the World Travel Market (http://news.wtmlondon.com/press/wtm-2015/) Show at ExCeL London, 2–5 November 2015, sent out more than 30 press releases over several months. These included when tickets were available, a competition, leading speakers, announcing partnerships and a post-event assessment. This is a good example of where you can look at one event and drip, drip a range of stories leading up to it.

If you are a local community event it can be difficult to get beyond local media coverage, and to do so you have to think of something that is quirky, different or fits in with wider news stories. In the wettest summer on record in the UK, the Thruxton Flower and Produce Show in September 2012 (www.thruxtonvillage.com/flower-produce-show/) gained front page national Sunday newspaper coverage because it had introduced two new categories, Largest Slug and Heaviest Snail. It also helpfully pointed out that these entries would be kept away from the others. Given that slugs and snails are major foes of gardeners, this story piqued the interest of readers.

The purpose of a press release is to impart news that a journalist wants to use. Your first job then is to identify what is the news contained within your event? You may think that this is difficult, but all it requires is constructing a creative process to develop ideas. When one of the authors worked for a marketing communications consultancy they regularly met their clients, and nearly always were told 'We do not have any stories.' After being questioned for 45 minutes over a cup of coffee there would be eight or nine stories that could be the basis of press releases. The trick is to find a creative means of developing news. Possible ways of achieving this could be:

- Meetings;
- Mind mapping;
- Talking to people;
- Observing what your organisation/event is doing;
- Thinking like a journalist.

Once you have developed the basic news story, you need to think about the different angles to present for that event/release, and which is the strongest. To do this you should:

- Identify the facts;
- Identify what is 'new' contained within the story, such as a first (this could be to the world, your geographical area or field of events);
- Identify whether there is something unusual or different about it – for example, 'The Last Man Standing' at the Phoenix in London has a pub quiz with a difference including challenges and chaos (www.pheonixcavendishsquare.co.uk);
- Assess how important/significant it is – ask would anyone outside my event/organisation care?

There is a tendency when considering how to get media coverage to start immediately with the tools you will use. However, Hitchens (2008) rightly cautions against this and suggests that a framework is required first. He identifies techniques that help create media interest; the tools are only used once the processes are in place. Research conducted by Hitchins (2000) constructed a template for such a framework:

1 Create news vehicles such as surveys/forecasts.
2 Take advantage of opportunities of media preoccupations (hot topics).
3 Campaigns.
4 Slogans (such as headlines).
5 Talk to the particular needs of each media.

6.1 Tip box

Media relations advice

Having spoken to a number of journalists over the years, a typical conversation was this:

Q1: As a local newspaper journalist how important are events to you?

Events are crucial as this is where we network, and gather tips and information for articles.

Q2: How do you prefer to receive stories relating to events – by phone, press release, or does it not matter?

It does not matter, although press releases are helpful as we then have all the details written down in advance.

Q3: When you receive a press release, a phone call or speak to someone from an event, what are the factors which determine whether you use the story or not?

It is all about public interest. We do not just cover every and any event held, it must be newsworthy. People must want to read about the event. Usually this comes down to the reason for the event. For example, if it is a charity event we would publish it to help raise awareness for the charity. If it is a celebrity's birthday it would be more of a gossip piece.

Q4: What sort of event-based news is more attractive to you?

In a local newspaper, charity events are the most commonly covered. Unless it is political or something else community-based which people need to know about.

Q5: Once you have decided to use a story, say you have received a press release, what do you do next?

We contact the organisers to arrange a time to meet at the event, and to find out if there is anything specific we should be covering at the event (for example speeches or award handovers).

Q6: What is your advice as to how events can maximise their local media coverage?

Keep in contact with us. We are more likely to think of you again if you keep inviting us. If we are running short on news, we are then also more likely to contact you. Also make sure you supply the details the journalist needs as soon as possible. Journalists work on deadlines and it is frustrating to have to wait for details. If you take too long, the chances are that that article will be scrapped as it is then 'old news'. It is important to: get to know us; target our specialists; and do not bombard us.

Writing a press release

Press release template

PRESS RELEASE

Today's date   For immediate release

Snappy descriptive heading of up to eight words

Opening paragraph up to 35 words that addresses the who, what, where, when and why.

Next most important paragraph of 40–50 words.

Subsequent paragraph of 40–50 words

Subsequent paragraph of 40–50 words

Subsequent paragraph of 40–50 words

Subsequent paragraph of 40–50 words

Etc., etc.

ENDS

For further information: your telephone and email details – only have one person as contact otherwise it can get confusing.

Editor's Notes: assume the journalist knows nothing about you, what your event is or organisation best known for, and who is available for interview.

Assuming that we have identified a strong news story, there are a number of ways in which a release can be constructed and we offer a coherent framework (see the press release template in Tip box 6.1) that you can apply:

1 Layout

- The words 'News Release' or 'Press Release' at the top, typically centred, or you might have headed paper.
- The date (this is the day you are sending the release out, not the event).
- An embargo time (a strict limit of when the information can be used), use only rarely – most releases are 'For immediate release'. The journalist knows that they can use the release straight away.

We assume that to whom it is being sent, such as news editor, picture editor or whatever, is on the covering email by which the press release will be sent to the media outlet.

2 Structure

Press releases normally follow a simple formula:

- An attention-grabbing headline in bold or slightly bigger type (but do not try to be too clever – just sum up the story to the journalist, a subeditor will probably re-write it).
- An opening paragraph of the five Ws: who-what-when-where-why.
- A second paragraph outlining your case very briefly.
- Subsequent paragraphs either making additional but less central points, or quotes of the opinions of a spokesperson.
- Finish with the word 'ENDS' – the journalist knows that the story is now finished.
- Always have **For further information** that has contact name, telephone number(s) and email for further information. To help control the process only have one person as the contact (usually you).
- Last, include **Editor's Notes** listing background facts or the existence of photographs, people available for interview. Does not include opinion. It should always include what is in the jargon (though not in your release) referred to by some as the 'boiler plate' – a short sentence about the event/host organisation and any main sponsors/partners. In effect, this is the corporate message you want to get across.

3 General rules

Journalists receive dozens of press releases each day. To stand out your press release needs to be easy to read, and there must be a news story contained, tailored to the needs of their viewers, listeners or readers:

- The most important paragraph is the first one. In a maximum of 35 words you need to explain the 'who-what-when-where-why'. The journalist will then decide whether there is a story or whether to bin your press release.
- Occasionally you cannot fit all five Ws into 35 words, and then we would start the second paragraph with the why.
- Paragraphs should be in order of importance to the story; this is sometimes referred to as the 'inverted pyramid' (see, for example, Gordon 2011). If it adds nothing to the story, do not include it.
- Use quotes when you can, but try to make them snappy and interesting. If you have a sponsor or event partner, they would expect to be quoted (agree the release and their quote with them in advance).
- Write in a way a non-expert can understand what you are saying – avoid jargon or complex language.
- Paragraphs should only be 40–50 words in length, and do not be afraid of one-sentence paragraphs.
- Use double or 1.5 line spacing to allow journalists to make notes.
- Different countries have different norms, but as a rule, get it on one or two sides of A4.
- Typically, your release (the text) is likely to be 250–350 words. Any less and you probably will not explore the story enough, any more and the journalist may stop reading.
- If you are going to break the rules, especially the length of the first paragraph, know why you are doing so.

4 Timing

With a little practice most people can write press releases, the more difficult bit is getting it to the right person at the right time. To achieve this you must:

- Find out the deadlines of your target media.
- Do not send it too far in advance of their deadline or your embargo, but neither should you leave it to the last minute. For a daily publication, ten days should be fine; for a weekly publication, two to three weeks; and for monthlies, this would generally be sent two to three months in advance.

The opening paragraph

After identifying the story, probably the hardest part is writing the opening paragraph. Remember in 35 words you need to get across the 'who, what, where, when and why'.

Some possible examples include:

- Award-winning dietician Bill Bloggs is organising Anttown's first ever carbs-free day, with 500 people expected to throw stodgy food at huge weighing scales in front of the town hall at 7pm on Saturday 20 May.
- Four hundred people are expected to join The Shack, Fishtown, to celebrate the new crab season with their first ever Crab Day Celebration on Fishtown beach from 10am to 4pm on Sunday 1 June.
- Widget World, the leading global widget industry conference, will host a number of the world's business leaders in the field at ExCeL, London on Saturday 21 November.

Press release exercise

Competitive eating brief

The Event
Anytime University Students Union is hosting the first World Pasty Eating Championships from 8pm on Monday 29 February 2016.

The Championships is aimed at anyone who believes that they can eat a Pasty quickly. Spectators as well as competitors are welcome. Competitors need to pay an entrance fee of £2.50 (entrance free for spectators). All proceeds will go to local charities.

The Pasties, which will meet strict regulations of size and content, are being provided by a local pasty shop. There will be two competitions, one for a Large Pasty (meat, potato, swede and onion) and one for a Large Vegetarian Pasty (various vegetables). The winner, for each category, will be the competitor who is adjudged to have eaten their pasty the quickest. Two hundred spectators are expected.

Background
1 This will be the first year of this event. However, other such eating competitions based on regional specialities are growing in popularity.
2 Competitors can, if they wish, enter both the Large Pasty and Large Vegetarian Pasty eating

competition. The winners of each event will receive a pasty-shaped trophy, and will be allowed to eat a pasty a day for a month at their local pasty shop.

3 Both competitions are open to anyone who believes that they can eat a pasty in the quickest time. It is expected that some professional 'gurgitators' (fast eaters) will also attend the competition. Fast eaters need not be big or overweight, but what they can do is eat food quickly.

Lecturer notes

This is a made-up event but it is an amalgam of real events, primarily designed to get in custom at slack times for venues. It raises a number of issues for us. The first is that people have died at such events, so it is a high-risk event we would not advise you to put on. However, the scenario above highlights some interesting PR-related developments, such as the vegetarian option, reflecting interest in social and sustainable issues. Wide societal concerns may force you to look at the detail of your event in order to manage its image and reputation.

Possible news angles for this story are:

Assuming that we were writing for the local newspaper, *The Anytown Gazette*, possible news stories could be:

- First-ever world championships;
- World Championships visits Anytown;
- Professional 'gurgitators' to visit Anytown;
- Competition is for both meat and vegetarian pasties;
- Two hundred spectators expected.

The news angles are in effect the key component parts of the news story, and you will note words like 'first' and 'world' feature.

Your task

Use this brief to write a press release.

You will need to consider what an interesting heading would be, the components of the first paragraph and the order of subsequent paragraphs. The background notes above, i.e. the gurgitators, will provide journalists with some interesting insights which they can use to demonstrate that they know what they are talking about. Also consider who you will cite and what they will say.

Using quotes

You will have noted from Harold Evans that news is about people, but it is also by people. As a result, it is the norm to have a quote from someone involved in your event. Many students assume that the quotes they read in the newspapers are based on the journalist talking at the event. This may indeed be the case, but probably more common for news from events is that the quote comes from the press release. It surprises many students to learn that quotes in press releases are usually drafted by the person writing the release, though they always check the source is happy with what it is proposed they will say. It is therefore important that you select the correct person to speak publicly on behalf of the event, check that they are happy with what they are saying and that the quote you write on their behalf adds colour to the event.

Quotes add flavour, so as a rule you would not normally introduce them until at least the third paragraph, and often later than that. When drafting a quote you need to make sure that you have the right person, they are credible, and they say something that adds to the story, for example why something is happening or how this event compares to recent ones. Sometimes you might even see a quote explaining how the event will develop in the future.

When constructing a quote consider:

- Avoiding words like 'we are delighted' 'pleased' or some such phrase;
- Keep them short, two to three sentences;
- Releases should be about facts, but you could put opinion into a quote;
- Avoid jargon and make it sound as if the person is actually speaking to someone, so it should be conversational;
- Use the quote to add to the impact of the story;
- Have the most credible spokesperson that you can, such as an expert or the most senior person of the organisation;
- Talk to the person you are writing the quote for; this will help you to draft it in their style.

Examples of event press release quotes

Bill Bloggs, Chief Executive Officer for Anytown Health Day, said, 'This is the fourth year of the Health Day and it gets bigger every year, with more activities and people attending. For this year we have added a new children's area and a crèche so parents can have a bit of time to themselves.'

Amy Amyson, Sports Officer for Women and Sport, commented, 'Our campaign to get women to enjoy playing sport is working; we are seeing more women going to the gym, playing sport after work and school with their friends and joining organised clubs. This event is a key part in this process of getting women active in sport. The reason why this is working is that we understand the motivations for why women want to get involved, it is about stressing fun, family and well-being.'

John Johnson, Director General of the Business Leader's Pressure Group, observed, 'Our annual conference occurs just before the Presidential elections, and it offers the candidates their best opportunity to listen and speak to business leaders. We will be able to interpret what they say so that the wider voting public are able to understand their policies by cutting through the normal mumbo-jumbo.'

As a rule of thumb we *always* have a quote from someone and typically aim for two, and very occasionally three. You need to state their name and job status, such as event organiser – which makes clear why they are the right person to be the spokesperson. Quotes are typically only two sentences, occasionally three, in length. For an event there are often obvious people who should be quoted, such as the owner/organiser, but also there may be partner bodies and they need to have their say. If there are partner organisations, such as sponsors, check all parts of the release with them, not just their quote and boiler plate. Sometimes you might provide a quote from a participant/performer as this can give an interesting insight.

The purpose of the Editors' Notes section is to provide background about your organisation and establish your credibility, and so write this assuming that the journalist knows nothing about you. However, do not overload the journalist; keep just to the key information about your organisation and partners that you wish to convey. If you are referring to a report, then it might be sensible to reference it fully, and how it can be accessed. If at your event the key speakers, performers or whatever have agreed to be available for interview, then make this clear.

Learn from the process; see what journalists do and what your colleagues and event attendees say about any subsequent media coverage. Follow the basic rules outlined above to start with, and then gradually develop your own style. Practice and familiarity are important; the more releases you write the easier it gets. The first time it might take you all day to be satisfied with your results, but by the time you have written a few it should only take an hour or so.

CASE STUDY

The impact of reviews

For some events, such as music gigs and theatre performances, reviews from journalists are very important. Freelance journalist and reviewer Thomas Davidson (www.theupcoming.co.uk/author/thomas-davidson/) explains how the review process works:

'Events are chosen through a range of methods, depending on whether I am reviewing them for a publication or personally. For publications, review assignments are managed centrally by the publication and there is a fairly even split between the publication approaching various venues/performers/agencies etc. and vice versa. As a rule, however, publications will only secure access to events fitting their brief/style/message and will provide objective coverage and opinion.

When working personally, or creating freelance advertising coverage of events, the process is largely similar, but with a greater weighting towards venues/agencies contacting me to provide coverage of an event. In these instances, the brief may clearly explain that a review is considered as advertising content, rather than a truly objective piece of journalism.

What the event can do to try and encourage a publication to review it is largely dependent on the size/visibility of the publication, the perceived scale and prestige of the event, and whether the event fits with the publication's content/message/ theme. In a perfect situation, the event will fit neatly within a publication's general topic area and, as such, will be desirable to cover. In this instance, it is likely a matter of an event organiser reaching out to the publication in question to notify them of the event, and offering press passes/tickets etc. in return for coverage by the publication.

Where there is less alignment between the event and potential host publication, it is important for the event manager/marketing team etc. to show a publication how the event fits (or could be interpreted as fitting) with the rest of their content and creative direction.

At the other end of the spectrum, event teams that are pushy and/or repeatedly hound a publication for coverage are unlikely to garner much support or interest from the publication's staff, resulting in far less appetite to cover an event.

Having commissioned a review, editors are, above all else, looking for an objective account of an event, written in a style and tone that matches the publication and its largest consumer demographic/s. For example, writing in the pared-down easy-to-understand style of *The Economist* would not fit with the larger creative direction of *Vice*. Complicating this somewhat is the goal of making an objective account rich and engaging; creating copy that engages the reader and makes them likely to read other content by the publication. In this regard, commissioning editors are looking for unique voices that further highlight their publication's style/tone.

In theory, reviewing a regular night should be no different from a press event. That is to say that the *content* of the event itself should be no different and, in this regard, I have very little professional preference as I am primarily focused on reviewing the event itself. However, press nights frequently enable me to engage with event staff, cast/crew, production teams etc. and thus give me a greater depth of background information with which to create a compelling and immersive review. In this regard, press nights can be preferable to regular nights (and, of course, courtesy hospitality is never a bad thing).

On the other hand, attending a regular night allows engagement with other attendees, which in turn enables me to gather opinions and insights from members of the public. It can be incredibly useful, for example, to stumble across a superfan of a band who can provide priceless background information or anecdotes with which to flesh out a review.

On balance, both types of event have benefits, but they are generally secondary to the event itself, which should remain identical regardless of press attendance.

It's easy to say that journalists, myself included, remain entirely impartial when reviewing an event; but human psychology is, of course, largely predicated by our environment. With this in mind, providing a positive experience to a visiting journalist, although unlikely to overtly affect their final verdict, can go a long way towards putting them in a positive frame of mind when covering an event. This is likely to be most evident when a reviewer provides negative coverage of an event – in such cases, these negative opinions can be somewhat softened by pleasant and hassle-free engagement with a venue.

Personally, I place venues that make checking into an event as easy and pain-free as possible in high regard. Similarly, being provided with press packs/programmes etc. or access to cast/crew makes my job far easier compared to the alternative of trawling the internet for facts and figures.

Every publication I write for has different stylistic guidelines, but uniform among them is a commitment to providing impartial coverage of an event that accurately reflects what I saw and experienced. At a basic level this could be the technical skill of a band, the characterisation exhibited by actors in a stage performance, or the mechanics of a story (i.e. adherence to theatrical norms, use of storytelling devices etc.).

Going deeper than this, however, is important. As a reviewer, I hope that readers will be informed and engaged by my writing, and with this in mind I aim to go into greater detail (whilst still remaining accessible) when covering live events: Do the actors have chemistry with each other? How does the venue's design affect acoustics? Do the actors/musicians react to the audience? What is the "atmosphere" of the event? What does a new interpretation of a play or piece of music add to the experience? Does a show relate to wider cultural/political/societal themes? By asking questions like these, I am able to deliver a more informed verdict and communicate it in an engaging manner.

Generally speaking, the impact of reviews on events is largely dependent on the circulation of said review; a review published in a national broadsheet is, of course, going to have a larger impact (in terms of public opinion and ticket sales) than one published on a small community blog. The most easily quantified effect is on ticket sales, with a positive review theoretically leading to increased attendance. More broadly, reviews can shape future performances of an event, or even influence the planning of new events entirely. They can help event managers to further highlight strong points, or shore up weaker areas of an event through the feedback they provide. In a similar vein, highly influential reviews (or reviewers) can affect the zeitgeist by repeated comment on a particular theme or area.'

Writing feature articles

Once you have mastered writing press releases the next level up in terms of writing skills is a feature article. Where press releases impart news and are short and to the point, feature articles are about opinion and tend to be 600–2,000 words. However, like press releases there is a basic formula you can quickly learn and adapt.

Different types of publications will require different types of features. You are probably best off starting with a trade publication where the audience will understand your terminology, and you will be writing for a publication and audience you understand well. Regional business magazines can also be a good source looking for articles. The most demanding (and difficult to secure) are national broadsheet press.

Writing a feature can be broken down into: developing the idea, pitching the idea and writing.

Developing the idea

This is a creative process and you need to develop a system for collecting ideas that could include:

● Keep a file of possible ideas, for example, news stories, facts, interesting case histories;
● Jot down ideas as they come into your head and explore them later at your leisure to see if they might grab the readers' attention;
● Make a short list of your organisation's interests you believe you can write about, which will engage the reader;
● Read features, lifestyle sections and op-eds (opposite the editorial page articles) of a range of newspapers, magazines and trade publications to get an idea of the kind of stories they develop as articles;
● Consider whether your idea has a particular angle, is it fresh, is it timely? For example, if you are a wedding planner you might write an article in May/June of unusual weddings or the latest trends;
● Think of a hook, you may have an idea but it needs something in the news or that is current that allows you to make the article topical.

Pitching your idea

This can be daunting, but as you get more proficient in writing this will get easier. The first few times you write an article the features editor will want a detailed written synopsis (effectively a plan). You need to consider:

● Who to pitch your idea to – read around – which publications are more likely to be interested – in other words what is your market;
● Your strength is that you are a specialist in a particular subject area. This is what you should focus on;
● Your key contact is the features editor. Phone them up and briefly explain your idea. If they are interested they will want you to send them a short synopsis;
● The synopsis should include a title, an introduction that sets the scene, your premise, the core facts/arguments, supporting material such as examples, quotes, statistics, and the conclusion.

Writing a feature

If you can write a reasonably good press release you have the level of writing skills for a feature, it is merely a matter of being aware of what is required.

- Check the length and deadlines for the article from the Features Editor;
- The title should grab the readers' attention whether by intrigue, amusement, curiosity, etc.;
- Use a stand first to set the scene – this is usually one short sentence after the title but before the main text which sums up the article or puts it into current context. This could be a fact, interesting quote or anecdote;
- The lead paragraph needs to be punchy and interesting and in essence should sum up the angle you are taking;
- The main body should include key facts, arguments and quotations. The Features Editor expects a professionally written piece so avoid puffery, at most only one or two quotes from your organisation – you get a mention at the end through your contact details/blurb. Therefore, you should include examples and quotes which illuminate your case but are not puff for your organisation;
- The conclusion should sum up your point of view and usually should link very closely with the lead paragraph;
- Features Editors nearly always want photos to go with copy, therefore try and get some pictures taken to accompany your text.

Writing a stand first: For example, an article looking at whether mass communication is declining might have a stand first of 'With 15 million viewers watching Jonny Wilkinson kick England to rugby victory, Nigel Jackson asks whether this is the last hurrah for television?' Sometimes a subeditor from the publication will write this. A good way of thinking about this is, why write this article now, why is it current?

A selection of feature articles

What follows is a selection of different event-based features that have been paraphrased to include the core material each covered.

1 By Mamta Sharma, *Koramangala sees boom in corporate event management* – looks at how in Koramangala, an upmarket area of Bangalore, India, there has been significant growth in corporate events management. The article quotes a number of event managers who talk about how much growth they have experienced, in what type of events and identifies popular venues. However, the article provides balance by pointing out some of the challenges the industry in Kormangala faces. At the end it predicts what might happen to the market in the next few years.

> Source: *Times of India* 14/5/14 online at: http://articles.economictimes.
> indiatimes.com/2014-05-14/news/49846612_1_event-management-
> koramangala-corporate-event (accessed on 15 June 2015)

2 By iBID, 'What do you look for in an event management company?' – this blog started by establishing the author/company's credibility in answering this question. It then introduced five numbered and measurable elements of what to look for when hiring an event management company. The basis of these was to ask a series of questions. The article ends by suggesting that if the reader needs help they can get in touch.

> Source: iBID 23/3/15 online at: www.ibid-events.com/what-do-you-look-
> for-in-an-event-management-company/ (accessed on 15 June 2015)

3   Monik Makadiya, *Four core event management software features you need for your next event* – identifies as a problem the ability to choose the right software for your event. Suggests that the answer is to be found by addressing how four features meet your needs. The obvious benefit for Monik is that he works for a ticketing agency and his details are provided at the bottom.

Source: Event Industry News 4/12/13 online at: www.eventindustrynews.co.uk/2013/12/04/four-core-event-management-software-features-need-next-event (accessed on 15 June 2015)

The first of the above articles follows the more traditional article in that it is 'neutral' in tone and could be written by a journalist. It sets out the problem and then offers a solution. It provides a range of facts and figures and opinion from more than one source. It presents a slightly different viewpoint as well. Finally, it concludes with a view of the future. The next two articles are more typical of those we have found within events management; namely, that they are written in a less 'neutral' way. The author is not observing and commenting on trends *per se*, rather they wish to establish their credibility by commenting on them in the hope that others will contact them and use their services. Both approaches are legitimate, but be careful if your main purpose is essentially to get your contact details given out at the bottom that you do not come across as too 'salesy' about you or your company.

Being picky, the one criticism we would have of all of these three articles is that the hook could have been stronger. Why does this article need to be written now? Your article could have been written for some time but you need to explain why the subject is important *now*.

Stunts

Where press releases and feature articles are primarily based on writing skills, stunts are a creative process designed to present an idea visually. It is worth noting, however, that the media will probably hear about it because you will send them a press release. The whole purpose of a stunt is to receive media attention – if photographers do not turn up it is a failure. As a consequence, you need to give a lot of attention to devising stunts that will interest a picture editor: the picture must tell of and link to the message.

6.2 Definition box

What is a stunt?

A stunt is an event organised solely for publicity purposes, to gain attention to a product, cause or event. As a result, it does not automatically require an audience other than from someone recording it and reporting it to others. While primarily the media is the main target, an event may record the stunt itself and then use the internet to promote it.

There are two main types of stunts:

- Photocalls and press conferences;
- A newsworthy event.

Photocalls are commonly used to launch a campaign such as a charity fundraiser. Award/s ceremonies, red carpet events and celebrity photo opportunities are all considered a type of media event, where the event is orchestrated for the sole purpose of introducing certain narratives into the media. Press conferences are either held because you have a crisis and the media is clamouring for information, or your event or story is so significant, such as a mega-event, that the media may be prepared to be briefed together. However, press conferences are notoriously difficult to arrange – why should the journalist attend? – so, for most, a press conference will be rare; rather, photocalls will be more common. However, during elections and high-level sports events, press conferences are more frequent.

Stunts are sometimes known as pseudo-events, which Boorstein (1962) suggests are based on hype rather than being real. The formal hammering of the last link of the American transcontinental railway 1869 was believed to be the first pseudo-event because the use of a solid gold link attracted journalists to witness it in Utah.

Other stunts are designed to support a cause. For example, a trade union received widespread coverage when a number of apparently naked pensioners standing behind a huge banner on Bournemouth beach complained about the loss of company pension rights. Here, a dramatic picture supported the story; the naked pensioners who were being apparently stripped of their work pensions.

Examples of stunts that have been done include flash-mobs and skydiving. When devising a stunt, Jackson (2013) suggests the key is spending time to come up with ideas, while Williams (2010) suggests three things to consider when creating a successful stunt. These include 'going for shock value, giving your customers a way to share your video, and staying true to your brand'. This means that when thinking of a stunt or street promotion to promote an entertainment-based event or festival, appreciate that it requires careful consideration and must still be noteworthy and interesting. Remember, to make the promotion successful you have to keep it legal (Preston 2012). You also need to consider avoiding activities that would be contrary to the overall message of, or embarrassing to, your event, organisation or sponsor. In other words, will your stunt give out the wrong message?

Most stunts are contrived to promote a product or organisation. For example, the *Guinness Book of Records* recognises that Harrah's Cherokee Casino Resort (USA) in Cherokee, North Carolina, holds the record for the largest gathering of Elvis impersonators in one place (895) (www.guinnessworldrecords.com/world-records/largest-gathering-of-elvis-impersonators). This stunt helped to promote the casino. To promote the ASB Classic 2015 tennis tournament in Auckland, New Zealand, sponsor ASB created a stunt, Best Ball Boys in the World. Leading tennis players Venus Williams and Svetlana Kuznetsova played an exhibition match where the ball boys were three dogs (https://blog.asb.co.nz/2015/01/meet-the-best-ball-boys-in-the-world.html). This stunt gained significant media and viral coverage.

Practical media relations checklist

- Practise writing releases – practice makes perfect;
- Construct a mechanism for capturing news stories, this might be a dedicated meeting, walking around talking to people or a regular meeting agenda item;
- Keep a log book that records which media you spoke to and the result – consult it regularly and learn from it;
- Have a press page on your website with your latest press releases;
- Produce 'action' photographs, not just heads and shoulders;
- Target key journalists, seek to build a relationship with them and do not rely just on press releases;
- Monitor what happened to your release, learn by noting how journalists wrote it up;
- Arrange to meet journalists or invite them to your event;
- Jot down a range of possible topics you could write a feature on, and wait until the right 'hook' comes along;
- Start by offering to write a short feature for a trade or free business magazine or a blog;
- Always write a feature article as if you were a neutral journalist;
- With feature articles, always think pictures – what pictures can you have to help illustrate the point?
- Stunts are a creative process, only try them if you or your team are creative.

Discussion questions

1 You are organising a sporting event, how can you develop different stories for a series of releases? Think about what is unique or different about this event, how and when people can sign up for it, well-known competitors and why it is happening.
2 Your event decides that it needs to devote resources to media relations. Your boss has limited experience and the expectations of what can be achieved and how journalists work are unrealistic. This is a common scenario, how do you handle this and meet the needs of journalists at the same time?
3 Feature articles require more work and writing skills than a press release, what therefore are the reasons why you should consider features? Does this suit particular types of events or organisations?
4 Devising a stunt is not an easy process. If you feel it will be worthwhile, how will you come up with one creatively and develop ideas? What mechanisms will you use to devise stunts?

Further information

Books

Bland, M., Wragg, D. and Theaker, A. (2005) *Effective Media Relations: how to get results*, London: Kogan Page.

Lloyd, J. and Toogood, L. (2014) *Journalism and PR: news media and public relations in the digital age*, London: I.B. Tauris.

Websites

Feature articles on events management in India: http://articles.economictimes.indiatimes.com/keyword/event-management

Examples of current stunts: http://prexamples.com/

www.youtube.com/watch?v=wOptT637vSY – event manager being interviewed for an in-house video.

www.youtube.com/watch?v=JVMpDb5716Q – event manager being interviewed at World Sports Destination Expo.

http://scouts.org.uk/supportresources/593/public-relations-activity-badge/?cat=7,64,172&moduleID=10 – the Scouts Association public relations activity badge.

www.theguardian.com/global-development-professionals-network/2013/mar/27/tips-for-writing-a-features-article – *The Guardian* runs a feature writing competition and offers some advice.

Chapter 7

Merchandising

Introduction

Our last chapter in this section on printed material is slightly different to those preceding it. While clearly the message is important, what is key here is what it is printed on. Instead of using paper the message is likely to be on a desirable item such as a bag, mug or T-shirt. To the receiver of the merchandise the product has value; to the event organiser it provides a means of getting out a message. This chapter will first look at the meaning of merchandising; it will then assess what the benefits are for event managers. We shall then look at how to select and use the correct merchandise for your event. The fourth section will identify how to source merchandise for your event. The bulk of this chapter will focus on how event managers can use merchandising to reinforce their messages, but our last section will assess how events can be used to offer giveaways. By the end of this chapter students will be able to:

- Identify the meaning and benefits of merchandising;
- Select the correct merchandising for their event;
- Construct a promotional campaign for an event using merchandising;
- Assess how events can be used as a merchandising tool.

What is merchandising?

Merchandising, which is sometimes referred to as offering giveaways, corporate gifts, goody bags or swag marketing, is primarily a promotional tool. However, there is also a stream of merchandising that is designed to generate income as there are products associated with an event that can be bought. Merchandising as a primarily promotional tool can be associated with any industry and so events are just one of many industries applying it, whereas merchandising as a form of revenue generation is closely associated with events (but not exclusively since other industries, such as retailing, use it as well). We naturally think that if we attend a music festival or a sporting event we may buy something that shows our allegiance to that band or baseball team. Indeed, such allegiance applies equally to other events, such as a political rally where attendees may buy or be given a baseball cap or foam finger with their desired candidate's name or party on it.

Merchandising can also be a way of saying thank you to staff, paying them in kind or differentiating them from attendees. Staff wearing the same branded clothing act as a means of reinforcing the corporate image of that event. This is especially common with volunteers who will see a free T-shirt as a reasonable perk. Moreover, with staff wearing items for sale they are effectively acting as walking billboards.

Merchandising at events should not be confused with visual merchandising, which is the presentation of a shop and/or its products in an attractive way to enhance sales. This is not to say, however, that events will not use visual merchandising to present their merchandising products to increase sales. Merchandising is not inherently about the display; rather, what is important is the meaning the buyer or beneficiary ascribes to the merchandise.

7.1 Definition box

What is merchandising?

Simply put, merchandising is the use of any tangible item by an event to raise awareness of it prior to the event, enhance the experience of attendees during the event or provide a means of remembering the event afterwards. These three roles are not exclusive as merchandising can indeed attempt to achieve all three – before, during and after an event. Such merchandise could be functionally useful, such as a key ring or hat, or merely decorative, such as stickers. Typically, merchandising includes some form of branding. It can be either a 'free' giveaway or a purchased product, but in both instances the intent is to link it with the positive experience enjoyed at that event. For many events merchandising is more than just a promotional tool, it is also a very important income stream.

The list of merchandise that an event manager could use is almost endless but might include pens, mugs, clothing, USB sticks, mouse mats and piggy banks. One of the key features is that normally the merchandise involves some form of personal interaction, which offers the provider of the merchandise opportunities to build relationships. For example, if you are at an event and they offer a free newspaper, typically it will be handed out by someone and not just lying around for you to pick up. So the event or its sponsors has two bites at the promotional cherry: they potentially get to speak to individuals; and these individuals 'promote' their product/s or brand to others by wearing or using it.

While most of us would associate gifts and products with merchandising, the Promotional Products Association International (www.ppai.org), an American trade association, suggests that the scope of merchandising is wider. They also consider awards such as employee recognition and commemoratives as promotional products. Thus, being named salesperson of the year would be considered merchandising, as would a pin badge celebrating an anniversary for an organisation.

Using merchandise is also a method of attracting attention, and can be done using larger-than-life replicas of a product in the form of a mascot or display item. Chas Clarkson is a Christmas decoration company in Australia which specialises in creating very large display pieces to raise the profile and visibility of Christmas activities (www.chasclarkson.com.au/).

Merchandise marketing is the process of creating awareness and customer loyalty using merchandise (www.printperfection.com, 2010), and is an ongoing strategy. Therefore, it is another means of getting your message out there in front of your (or the sponsors') key targets. However, in addition, it is a good way of providing a reminder about your event, long after it has finished. For example, one of the authors got a bright yellow umbrella from the Tour de France over ten years ago. Whenever it rains and that umbrella is used, it does not just remind the author of having attended the event but also promotes the brand to passers-by. If used in this way, and not just simply thrown away, merchandising offers a potentially long-term branding strategy.

Some events will use merchandising as a way of opening up additional revenue streams. For example, a band touring around a country will have music, T-shirts and the like for sale that bring in additional income. For the buyer of the item they provide a keepsake that reminds them of the event, or says something about them as a person. Thus if you go regularly to an event, such as a play or professional sport, and you purchase a programme, when you look at it later it acts as a reminder as to what you were doing at that time. If you wear a certain item of clothing it pronounces your interests, and possibly how 'cool' or 'hip' you are (or otherwise). So after London 2012 a number of people wore merchandise that could only be purchased at the Olympics, as this stated they had been present. In this case, wearing merchandise implied exclusivity, and so potentially offered the wearer kudos. Indeed, this probably explains why the organisers of the London 2012 Olympics raised £85 million in revenue from merchandising and licensing, such as mascot toys, commemorative coins, stamps and badges (www.olympic. org/news/london-2012-publishes-its-final-report-and-accounts/199870).

Merchandising tends to work in three ways. First an event may license the right to sell products and then pays a flat fee or a percentage of revenue. Second, they may license others to sell products at their event, which is very typical with sporting events which may have deals with clothing manufacturers who sell their wares, and give the event a proportion of the revenue. Third, to have the products made for them and then sell them direct, taking all of the profit.

The International Licensing Industry Merchandisers Association (www.licensing.org/ education/intro-to-licensing/) provides a simple definition for a license: 'A license is an agreement through which a licensee leases the rights to a legally protected piece of intellectual property from a licensor – the entity which owns or represents the property — for use in conjunction with a product or service.' Events are a common area where licenses are purchased.

Some merchandising is so attractive that it develops value in its own right as a discrete market. This is especially so with programmes for concerts, sports events, posters and tour programmes. For example, looking at one specialist website, a 1979 souvenir tour programme for Swedish pop group Abba's tour of Europe and North America retailed at £35 (http://991. com/Buy/PresetList.aspx?pageID=9839).

Merchandising is a channel that certain types of events use, perhaps more than in other industries. This form of promotional channel is less likely to be linked to encouraging sales, and more about building relationships and linking to experiences.

Table 7.1 provides a typology for categorising merchandise products. Clothing and equipment are often worn during the event, but their real marketing value is after the event. Clothing in particular is a very common form of merchandising, whereas equipment tends to be linked to more specialist events/audiences such as sports or particular careers. Printed material is typically something which the event attendee will enjoy reading at the event (such as a programme) or afterwards (such as a book related to the event). Functional gifts are designed to have some tangible use to the receiver, be that at home or work, and by comparison knick-knacks are primarily small decorative items for use in the home. Personal statements are similar to knick-knacks in that they are small, but they are typically worn by or are attached

Event merchandising

Event Merchandising Limited (www.eventmerch.com) is a leading London-based merchandising specialist. Their services include designing and manufacturing creative products for corporate requirements to selling at live events, from devising licensing programmes through to running online shops. Event Merchandising seeks to deliver goods and services that elevate a company's brand perception. Clients are in industries such as sport, entertainment, corporate, film and charities. Event Merchandising support events from those that require a one-off consumer order through to large well-known brands at major events, such as London 2012, the BBC, Walt Disney, Diversity, IMG, The Rugby World Cup 2015 and Rio 2016.

Managing Director Jeremy Goldsmith offers advice on how events should utilise merchandising 'As a term event merchandising means promoting desirable products that are sold to generate revenue, promote a brand in its best possible light or as a marketing tool.

If an event is considering using merchandising for the first time, our advice is to speak to an expert who will be able to have a good understanding of your event, and should be able to look at their data of similar events to help guide you. The exact advice will depend on the event, the number of people attending, is the merchandise to be paid for, is it a ticketed event or is it free, is it being used as a marketing tool to support the brand through lanyards and T-shirts worn by staff or is it revenue-generating, and how strong is the brand? We generally sell more at ticketed events than those that are free.

Deciding which products to stock and new trends to buy can be difficult. It is easy to get carried away with the choice. Often less is more, more often. It does depend on the size of the event, but if you were a band playing at a 3,000 capacity venue you might have one T-shirt, a cap and possibly one other product. If you have a wider range of products they will spend the same amount, but some of your products may be unsold. Whereas, at London 2012, a huge event, there were 22,000 product lines for sale. Typically clothing is the primary revenue generator, usually providing 50% of your revenue and sometimes up to 80%. What to sell also depends on the strength of your brand, the stronger the brand the more likely people are to buy products.

Events should aim for selling 90–100% of their stock. To avoid having unsold stock comes with experience and understanding your event and market, but if it is a one-off event this can be difficult to tell, so it is always best to ask for advice from experts who know your type of event. My advice is to be conservative when choosing what to select for sale until you better understand the event.

The nature, type and size of the event affect what are the latest trends, as it differs across different events. For example, over the past few years for sports events, technical, or performance, clothing has grown in importance. We, therefore, try to mix and match the product to each different event.

You also need to be innovative. For example, we recently did a Dr Who Musical and came up with a conductor's stick with a Tardis on it; this was consistent with the theme of the event. This product sold well, so it is important to be creative. People tend to buy what they recognise, so if they see a poster or brand, this is what they want to buy, so do not try to be too clever and offer something they do not recognise.

From a marketing point of view people wanting to buy your brand is very flattering; they may be wearing a T-shirt with your brand on it for some time. Buying your branded product shows that they are part of your club, this is especially so for sports, entertainment and music events. When you are selling a product it is important that they are of a good quality as they are promoting your brand.

Even at the same event there is a big difference between giving goody bags and retail sites, as we did at the Rugby World Cup 2015. We handed out goody bags at the venues on behalf of DHL which was designed as a marketing tool, with the main marketing offer being a Clap Banner. We handed out over 500,000 which gave brand awareness for DHL because it was fun (it was a noise-maker) and it was very visual – it was seen on television and mentioned by the press. Indeed, the Clap Banner has now been adopted by Leicester City Football Club at every home game as a means of helping the atmosphere. At the same event we also looked after onsite vending at various stadium and fan zones. Here, because we are selling the product it tends to be of a higher quality than a giveaway. They also tend not to carry the sponsors' branding. One important thing to bear in mind if you have both giveaways and sales is that they do not lead to conflict. For example, if you are selling T-shirts you should not also be giving away T-shirts.

One of the problems events face is when to order merchandise. Our advice is as long as possible, for example if the items have to be manufactured in the Far East the lead time is normally about three months. A long lead time gives you the luxury of planning, saves money and means getting it right. However, if it needs to be done quickly if it can be, for example a T-shirt can be printed in a day but it may not be as well planned.

If you are managing the sales of merchandise yourself there is some clear advice. You should try and turn your sales team into brand ambassadors, so provide them with a briefing document on the products and brief them on the brand at the event. With some brands that are hot you do not have to do this, but with most you do. Your briefing should cover what to do if there are customer service issues, and explain how they should speak to customers. We also abide by the old adage that the customer is always right.

The better the display the better the perceptions from the customer, so tips are:

1   Put items of high value on display even if you will sell few, it lifts the look of the overall product range. For example, it you have a jacket that costs £100 but only a few will be sold, place it in a prominent place.

2　If you have a hot product that you know will sell, then make sure this is displayed in a prominent place.

3　Make sure that you have clear signage so that customers know what the price is and have them laminated so they look professional.

4　If you are provided with a basic display area, be creative. For example, if you are a band and you are given just a table, do not just fold your tour T-shirts onto it, people won't look at them; rather, think how you can best display them, for example using manikins.

Display is something we pride ourselves on, but each event is different.

When we are looking at the return on merchandising it is important to do a profit and loss based on the costs against sales. We use software that manages this by inputting variables, but a small event could simply use a spreadsheet. For example, if your T-shirt costs £3 each and you will sell them at £15 each, you can work out how many you need to sell to break even.

Another figure we use is the "per head spend" at the event. For example, if 10,000 people are expected and the "per head spend" is £3, then there will be £30,000 spent at the event, and we need to work out what they will spend it on.

There are a number of possible developments in event merchandising which are worth watching such as "print on demand" which we have seen at events, and the quality is getting better. This can take some of the risk away as it is possible to have a stock of blank T-shirts, for example, and then take them to an event where they are printed. It is also possible to use software to provide real-time reporting, so that as soon as a product is sold it can be viewed via your phone. 3-D printing may become a means of printing off souvenirs.'

to a person. Badges can include those worn by delegates at a conference, but we have more in mind those aficionados who collect badges related to their interest. For example, according to Outsourced Events (www.outsourcedevents.com) at the 2015 Mobile World Congress in Barcelona, Google Android was very successful in encouraging mobile industry professionals to find and collect a series of Android pin badges throughout the exhibition centre. Food and drink is a specialist area and by its very nature tends to be small, durable and packaged products that could include sticks of rock, tins of mints and biscuits. If the event is celebrating a seasonal occasion such as Christmas, these sweets lend themselves to be easily branded to the time of year. A niche area is awards and prizes where clearly the intent is that the recipient will display them either in the home or at work.

The merchandise industry is always evolving and responding to new trends, and one of the more recent categories is sustainable products such as shopping bags manufactured from recycled plastic. Organisations that sell such merchandise are probably seeking to suggest that environmentalism is important to their event. Merchandising catalogues offer a dazzling array of different products, most using their own different classifications. We suggest that our typology helps you identify nine types that may be relevant for your event by which you can measure all the myriad brochures you read.

Table 7.1 Types of merchandise

Category	Examples
Clothing and apparel	T-shirts, hats, caps, foam hands and umbrellas.
Equipment	Typically with sports such as bags, golf clubs and footballs.
Printed material	Programmes, magazines and books.
Functional gifts	Mouse mats, electrical items, pens, mugs, bags, USBs and lanyards.
Knick-knacks	Decorative home items such as thimbles, paper weights, small cuddly toys and ornaments.
Personal statements	Badges, stickers and balloons.
Food and drink	Typically tend to be sweets, chocolate and bottled water.
Awards and prizes	Branded awards, prizes and certificates.
Sustainable	Typically recycled products such as bags, paper-based products and clothes.

It is possible to go a stage further in understanding different types of merchandising. Figure 7.1 identifies three core features that help us to understand the nature of merchandising. The first component to identify is the audience, which could be an individual or an organisation (or very occasionally both). For example, at a music concert it is likely the main target is what individual attendees want, but at a conference any merchandise used by an individual is likely to be used or seen within an organisational context. Hence, our first difference is whether we are looking at B2C or B2B merchandising. The second component is the value that the merchandise offers, which could be intrinsic or extrinsic. Intrinsic means that it has some personal probably non-monetary value to the individual such as a keepsake or as knick-knacks as in Table 7.1. For others they may have no value and be considered rubbish or clutter, but to that individual they have meaning. Extrinsic are those that many individuals would consider have value, often monetary, such as a smart bag, camera or diary. This makes extrinsic potentially more desirable, but we should not overlook the value of something like a stress ball to some individuals. The third component concerns who is gaining most from the merchandise. Is the focus on what it says about the event or the individual attendee? For example, events that see themselves as environmentally minded are making a clear statement about their event and its ethos by providing recycled merchandise. Whereas an individual might buy a piece of clothing from an event because it says something about them that they wish to be associated with when they wear it.

While Figure 7.1 provides a stark either/or scenario we note that it is possible that large or complex events could offer both options for each of these three factors.

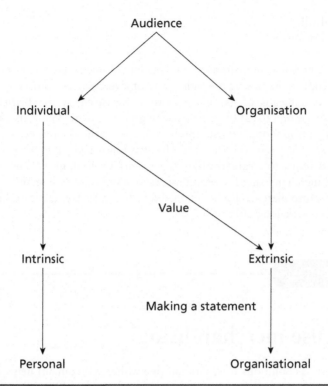

Figure 7.1 Segmenting merchandising

Why use merchandising?

For some events commercial selling is the prime purpose of the event, and so they act as merchandise markets. The most obvious ones are conventions and fairs that focus on one particular interest such as sci-fi, comics and gaming. For example, Star Trek Las Vegas a four-day convention in August 2016 featured collectibles as one part of a wider range of activities including celebrities, autographs and parties (www.creationent.com/cal/st_lasvegas.html). On a smaller scale Bolton Comic Con has a similar format of stars, stalls and people dressing up (http://northwestcomiccons.co.uk/). One venue, The Merchandising Mart in Chicago, tries to bring buyers and sellers together by listing trade shows, conferences and special events (www.mmart.com/find-a-show-or-event/).

However, for most events merchandising is unlikely to be central to its success, and if you do not have any merchandising your event will probably not fail as a result. What merchandising can do is to help enhance the atmosphere at your event and provide branding opportunities for both you and any partners or sponsors.

When we are assessing branding we are looking at how customers and potential customers perceive an event or host organisation. A blog posted by Promotional Products Business (2013) identified five reasons for using promotional merchandise:

1 Promote your company's skills.
2 Improve relationships with customers.
3 Improve sales meetings.

4   Promote goodwill.
5   Attract new customers.

Common to all of these five motivations is how merchandising enhances links with customers. Like an event itself, merchandising is another way of leveraging customers.

Merchandise is a means of gaining attention. Research by the British Promotional Merchandise Association (2012) of sales/marketing professionals found that the most popular reason for why promotional merchandising was used rather than other methods was that it targets customers effectively (69 per cent). This was followed by brand messages last longer (52 per cent), and ability to create loyalty (46 per cent). Overall, they found that 63 per cent use promotional merchandising for brand awareness and re-branding. What these findings suggest is that because merchandise is retained by the recipient it continues to do its job of securing brand exposure long after the event.

CASE STUDY

Why use merchandising?

Shared Services Solutions International (www.sharedss.com.au) helps organisations grow through both membership services and merchandising. Shared Services Solutions can both supply merchandise and manage its sale at events. Managing Director David Friend explains how events can best use merchandising 'Events should consider merchandising because it can make good additional income at events, but you need to have very experienced operators to manage the programme. You can make good income, but can also lose a lot of money if you have too much unsold stock. If well planned, financially it works well at events as you can take advantage of event crowds.

To make best use of merchandise the locations of the outlets are very important. They must be located in high traffic areas and be well publicised and have relatable quality merchandise.

We help develop a detailed merchandise implementation strategy which needs to cover:

- Develop quality product;
- Do not get greedy on retail prices or they won't sell;
- Complete a financial analysis of the viability;
- Use reliable suppliers;
- Be careful not to buy too much stock as it is better to sell out;
- Ensure size specs are accurate;
- Employ reliable staff.

We find that in membership-based organisations members will buy merchandise to support the organisation, if they are encouraged.

In addition to branding, merchandise can have a functional purpose within an event. For example, Indian-based Reliance Communications (www.rcom.co.in/Rcom/personal/home/index.html) is one of the International Cricket Council's (ICC) partners, and at matches between international teams spectators are given cards with a 4 on one side and a 6 on the other. So if a batsman scores a 4 or a 6 they hold up the relevant side. Television coverage frequently shows spectators, especially children, holding these cards up. They are in effect actively participating in the atmosphere of the event, and at the same time Reliance's branding is prominently featured.

Choosing and using merchandising

The British Promotional Merchandise Association 2013 research identified the consumers' perspective to receiving promotional merchandise. Of the 1,000 UK-based respondents the top branded gifts they have received are outlined in Table 7.2. The research highlighted 15 gifts of which the top five are mostly fairly small and fit in with our category of functional gift items. What is most interesting for event managers from this research is that the most popular place where respondents expected to receive such gifts is at an event, with 81 per cent of respondents. The next popular, hotels, was at 49 per cent some way down.

This suggests that possibly one of the first criteria to assess whether to use merchandise is the type of event you are organising. Table 7.3 identifies some of the events that might use merchandise, the type of merchandise and why to use it. We can see that most events are likely to be interested in merchandising because of the branding and income-generating opportunities it offers. The exact type of event probably shapes the motivation for, and nature of, merchandise. For example, some events such as sports, political and music are essentially tribal with attendees supporting this team, politician or band as opposed to another. As a result, by buying merchandise, attendees are saying a lot about themselves and who they support.

We have noted the possible promotional and commercial advantages of merchandising, but there are some important fiscal and logistical factors to take into account before finally deciding whether to use merchandising and which merchandising to stock.

1   Who and how will you decide which items will sell? If you have run this event several times you will have internal data on sales, but for the first time it can be risky. If products are left unsold what do you do with them?
2   Where will they be stored? Some items such as clothing can be quite bulky to store and transport to the venue, so you need to factor in the logistical problem and cost of storage.

Table 7.2 Branded gifts with a company logo received

Branded gift	Percentage of respondents who have received one
Pen	62
Mug	35
Key ring	32
T-shirt/sweatshirt	25
Drinking glass	24

Table 7.3 Use of merchandise by events

Type of event	Why use merchandise	Types of merchandise
Sports	Generate income.	Clothing.
	Encourage spectator participation.	Printed material.
		Personal statements.
	Branding.	Equipment.
Music/entertainment	Generate income.	Clothing.
	Social identity.	Music.
		Printed material.
		Personal statements.
Political	Generate income.	Printed material.
	Mobilise support/branding.	Knick-knacks.
	Social identity.	Personal statements.
Hobby	Generate income.	Functional gifts.
	Social identity.	Knick-knacks.
Exhibitions/conferences	Raise visibility.	Functional gifts.
	Brand awareness.	Food and drink.
		Awards and prizes.

3 You are an event manager not a retailer; you are not necessarily an expert in preventing theft. Moreover, very often the way such merchandise is presented is not as secure as it might be in a shop. Do you insure your stock? Develop security measures and how can the venue help you?

4 Who will be your merchandising staff? Do they have the required skills? What briefings do they require? For example, how will you record and account for sales, and by whom and how will new stock be managed? What safety protocols have to be introduced?

5 Retailers and supermarkets use psychology to work out how best to display their products so they sell those they wish to sell. How will you organise your display to sell key items?

6 Have you taken into account the costs of setting up production and postage?

7 At what point do you order your merchandise? Order too early and it can affect your cash flow, order too late and they may not turn up in time.

8 How will customers pay? If you are going to take credit card transactions at the event you should seek professional advice on how to manage them. A number of companies offer specialist services, such as: www.support.omnovia.com or www.cvent.com.

Wiscombe (2010) advises that if goods can be sent post-event this can avoid some of the problems regarding storage and not to order too many items.

Other questions to consider include:

● What are you using merchandise for? For example, if motivation is to generate an income stream, then you need a clear understanding of what your audience will want. If it is to help enhance the sponsors' branding, then you need to identify those things which the audience will keep, display or use during or after the event. What products will you use as merchandise? Is it clothing, keepsakes or tangible products? In what way does your merchandise support your brand and the key messages you want to get across? Thus, if your message is environmental, your products should reflect this; if encouraging a hedonistic experience at your event, then your products should reflect this by encouraging fun.

● The cost, and then evaluating the return on investment, of merchandising is a key issue. If the purpose is to provide a gift, then the quality is likely to be higher so the cost will be greater. A cheap, poor-quality gift is probably going to have a negative effect on your branding and reputation. If we are looking at giveaways then the nature of the event and audience are key. If you have a mass event with a lower grade of audience then your giveaways are likely to be cheap. However, if the size of audience or its importance is high, then the quality and so the cost will be higher too.

One person the authors know who sources and buys gifts and giveaways for a large organisation said that when they started, 'It felt like I was a child in a sweetshop.' They soon realised that they needed to establish good relationships with their suppliers and understand what their audiences wanted for each different type of event.

When you are looking to source merchandising you may not get it right to start with, as you need to understand the needs of your audience and event. However, once you have this knowledge it will become easier to get the right products. Assuming you source possible merchandising from a company with a brochure or a website, there are a number of factors that shape the final price, and what is cited in the catalogue will not be the full cost. So if you are thinking of getting a branded product made, say a mug, bag or pen you should:

1 Secure three different quotes and make clear to each company that price is the key determinant.
2 Recognise that in many countries the catalogue/website price will not overtly include any tax liable, such as Value Added Tax.
3 Normally if you ask for several hundred branded mugs, for example, be aware that there will probably be a small one-off setup charge before manufacture can begin.
4 Usually the greater the number of units the less the price for each product. So 100 units might cost £10 per unit, whereas 1,000 units might be £9 per unit.

Sourcing merchandising

One of your big issues is working out where is best to source your merchandise, and the issue will probably be too much choice. The British Promotional Merchandise Association (2012) sought to find out where their sample found information about merchandising. By far the most popular source, at 70 per cent, was their current suppliers, so they were most likely to ask those they dealt with for ideas for new merchandising. The next most popular at 53 per cent was catalogues, which presumably was important if they did not know what they wanted, as comprehensive brochures could provide ideas. The third most popular source at 33 per cent was the internet where presumably they would type in merchandising ideas within a search engine such as Google. Internal sources such as their creative department or agency (26 per cent) and co-workers (23 per cent) were less popular for sourcing ideas.

There are a number of trade shows where it is possible to find out the latest products and trends in merchandising. For example, in November 2015 the Sports Merchandising and

Licensing Show (http://sportsmerchandiseandlicensingshow.com/) was held at the Great Hall of Stamford Bridge, the home to professional football club Chelsea FC. A very specialist show is the PGA Merchandise Show (www.pgashow.com/) held in Orlando, Florida, in 2016, which showcases the latest equipment, apparel and other products specifically linked to golf.

Using events

This chapter so far has considered how events use merchandising and so we have assumed that the event exists first and then merchandising is an add-on decision. However, a niche area is the creation of events whose sole purpose is as a mechanism to provide promotional merchandise, typically in the form of free giveaways. Very often these are campaigns where an organisation is seeking to raise awareness, for example when Sensodyne wanted to demonstrate its new products for sensitive teeth it set up its Great Sensitivity Test near London Bridge. They created three different zones which included dental checks, a 4-metre-long molar and a *Guinness Book of Records* attempt (www.hotcow.co.uk/portfolio/sensodyne-case-study.htm).

Such events are closely associated with the idea of experiential marketing. The concept behind this is that customers are no longer solely influenced in their buying behaviour by price, but that they wish to engage more with brands. Therefore, marketing needs to encourage an emotional response, such as pleasure or happiness. It is within the rapid growth of experiential marketing that some merchandising may be viewed.

Anchor Butter ran its Anchor Cheddar Tour in early 2015 to 'Save the cheese sandwich' (http://whynotthinkpeople.com/portfolio/anchor-cheddar-tour/). This involved the Anchor Butter team visiting cities throughout the UK and giving away 564,592 freshly made sandwiches. In addition, 54,179 people signed up to their petition to save the cheese sandwich. This tour allowed Anchor to speak to a large number of people direct, create an experience (eating the sandwich) and generate significant media coverage. The campaign was launched to reflect the fact that many younger people did not eat cheese sandwiches any more.

Discussion questions

1 Consider the reasons why you still use merchandising long after the event you attended. How can you then encourage others to do the same for an event you are organising?
2 Those new to merchandising at events can make easy-to-avoid mistakes. Who will you seek advice from so that you avoid possible pitfalls, such as buying too many or the wrong products?
3 Is merchandising, be it free giveaways or sold products, more appropriate to some events or can it apply to all?
4 How will you assess your 'per head spend' at your first event? What are the implications for you of this measurement?

Further information

Book

Morgan, T. (2016) *Visual Merchandising: window and in-store displays for retail*, 3rd edn, London: Lawrence King.

Websites

www.promota.co.uk/
https://bpma.co.uk/
www.narms.com/
www.licensing.org/
www.inc.com/guides/201107/how-to-make-great-brand-merchandise.html

PART III

ONLINE MEDIA

This section assesses the main digital tools that events use.

Chapter 8

Websites

Introduction

For many events web technologies are the first promotional channel they turn to. For most of us when we are talking about the web we do not refer to a single technology, but join together several within the one term. However, for ease of understanding this chapter will deal with what can be referred to as websites, the next chapter will look at social networking sites separately, and the last chapter of this section will look at email. In practice, all three are interlinked and usually events do not use just one of these technologies. This chapter will start by identifying what is a website, and then will explain why an event should use one. The core of this chapter will assess the design and content aspects of a website by considering how to create a good website. Having then designed our site the chapter will address how to market it so that more people visit. Finally, we shall consider the management of your site, especially how to evaluate and improve it. By the end of the chapter students will be able to:

- Present a case for using a website as an effective promotional tool;
- Identify the key components of a well-designed website;
- Understand how to drive traffic to your site;
- Put in place systems to continually improve your site.

What is a website?

A website is the term for a series of web pages hosted on a server and available via a network. Each individual web page is merely a document that is available to the viewer. The web designer has to use a software package such as HTML (Hypertext Markup Language) to construct each page. Therefore, a website is a collection of related web pages, and so it can be viewed akin to a single document. The web author is the person who writes the text/content on the web page. However, such a simple description of a website does not tell us how it is used. Some websites are little more than an electronic brochure (Jackson 2003); they are essentially a static document used like a flyer, leaflet or newsletter that does not utilise the discrete architecture of the web. Whereas what the web offers is the ability to create interaction in a way not normally possible outside direct face-to-face contact. The argument is that by engaging more with your website, visitors are more likely to attend your event.

8.1 Definition box

What is web communication?

Web communication is essentially a means of promoting a message online, which can either be purely informational, such as this event is happening when and where, or persuasive as to why you should attend. The means by which tickets are purchased, e-commerce, can be included. It is a flexible method of getting across and/or reinforcing messages to both large amorphous and small targeted audiences. It is merely a technology, and while this imparts a cultural perspective, what matters is the content of messages. Web communication is versatile and can be private, public, a monologue or a dialogue.

Why an event should use a website

For many now this question would be re-written as 'why not?' Yet it is a fact that not all countries have high levels of internet access, typically where education levels are low, the technological infrastructure is poor or incomes are low so the application of the internet is less developed. However, we shall assume that your event is taking place in a country with a high level of internet access.

Event websites can be used as a one-way monologue, simply trying to get across their message. Typically, this is evidence of a transactionary marketing approach. So, if you see an event website that essentially just tells you what is happening, when and focuses on the value of the event, and at the same time provides no mechanism for you to engage with the site, then you are reading an electronic brochure. However, the potential of the internet goes much further than this, alternatively a website may be used to encourage dialogue between the event and potential attendees. For example, the forum page of the V-Festival website (www.efestivals. co.uk/forums/forum/15-v-festival/) enables interaction between attendees prior to the event. Research by Jackson (2013) found that most events use websites for both one- and two-way communication. In terms of the didactic approach he found that 94.7 per cent of sites offered

---

8.2 Tip box

Why have a website?

The first decision you have to make with any internet tool is to answer why are we going to use it? In short, for our event what is its purpose? If the answer is merely because everyone else has it, then this is not a good motive. Rather, have positive reasons for your web presence. This seems to be common sense, but many events do not appear to ask or satisfactorily answer this question.

---

the event programme, 52.2 per cent explained the event history and 56.5 per cent offered news about the event. Yet at the same time 63.2 per cent had a social networking site, 55.5 per cent a microblog such as Twitter and 50.7 per cent used videos. We would assume that the number of events using social media platforms will have increased since then. The data suggests that most events do not provide one approach or the other, rather a combination of both.

Although a different field to events (politics), Jackson (2008a) provides a typology (Figure 8.1) for understanding how organisations may use the web. He suggests that only 5–10 per cent of organisations are *pioneers* who have a clear vision as to why they are using web technologies. Another 25–30 per cent are *magpies* who use the internet to gain competitive advantage. The rest are either *technophobes* who make little use of the internet, or *bandwagoners* who adopt web technologies for the negative reason that everyone else has and do not really know why and how to use it effectively. If this typology applies to events, then just over a third have a clear idea as to why they are using web technologies. This reinforces our strong view that if your event does not know why it has a web technology then do not waste resources on it.

This typology may help event managers to decide whether they should adopt web technologies, but they also need to assess what a website can do for them. We suggest that websites can have at least two different purposes, although some websites may try to do both:

1 Brand website – this is designed to build customer goodwill, collect feedback and supplement other sales channels. They are not designed primarily as a sales channel. Rather they offer a lot of information about the organisation, its products and people. This can be very important for service-based organisations such as events. For example, the IT conference and exhibition IT Soft 2016 (www.indiasoft.org) provides a wide range of detail on its website for exhibitors, sponsors and delegates, but it appears each completes an email form, and then presumably payment takes place off the website.

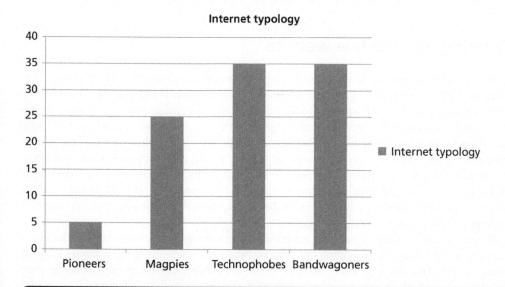

Figure 8.1 Event online typology

Source: Adapted from Jackson 2008a

2   Sales website – seeks to engage the customer in order to try and gain a sale (or at least make that sale more likely), therefore the content attempts to entice the visitor to buy. There will be information, but the design of the website encourages visitors to purchase tickets. Probably more likely for manufactured products, though it can apply to events, especially B2B and entertainment-based such as sports or music. For example, the Newport Flower Show, rated one of the top 100 events in America, has a large 'Purchase Tickets Now!' button in the middle of its web page (www.newportmansions.org/events/newport-flower-show). A sales website would normally have an e-commerce facility so you can buy online.

Having considered its overall purpose, we suggest that a website has the following benefits:

- It can provide a means of reaching new audiences. Because the web is not limited by geography anyone can visit your website, and it is possible that some living beyond your normal catchment area might be interested in attending an event that otherwise they might not have heard of. This makes it very useful for tourism destination events where the target audience is not local.
- It is relatively cheap. There are the costs of setup and management, but because there are no print and distribution costs it should be a cheaper marketing channel.
- It can be quickly updated. New material can be added, existing information such as ticket availability can be updated immediately, unlike with printed material such as flyers and posters.
- Unlike most printed material it can encourage feedback, which can provide market research.
- Using the appropriate tools it is possible to measure and evaluate its use precisely.

The overall benefits of the web, and especially e-commerce, are summed up by Gangeshwer (2013) who looked at how websites are being used in India. What is unique about the web Gangeshwer argues is that it is both a transaction medium and a physical distribution medium at the same time. As such, it is particularly suited to ticket-based events.

Creating an effective website

As noted above, an event is likely to use its website for two main purposes. The first is to raise awareness of your event to encourage people to attend, which is likely to be true of every event website. The second purpose is to lead directly to sales and so requires an e-commerce aspect, although smaller events are unlikely to need this capacity. This feature is most likely for events that need to bring in money early for cash-flow issues or when the sheer number of attendees means handling tickets/entrance on the day would be slow, problematic and affect the attendees' event experience. The types of events that are likely to have an e-commerce facility are sports, music and large agricultural shows. For example, the NFL (National Football League) website for the Super Bowl Fifty (in 2016) gave details on how to buy tickets and VIP packages (www.nfl.com/superbowl/50).

When we are looking at creating an effective website we are assuming that the event manager will probably be managing the process, rather than actually using software skills to create the site. Therefore, the event manager needs to be aware of basic principles rather than the nitty-gritty detail. To achieve either purpose effectively we need to understand four related factors: the nature of the web; how we read online; website design; and content.

The characteristics of the internet

We believe that the web is now central to event promotion, but it needs to be used properly, and to use it best an event manager should understand its characteristics. We suggest that the following factors will shape how you use a website:

1 User-led
   The internet implicitly suggests a slight shift in the power balance between the sender and receiver of a message (Ollier 1998). Typically, when promoting your event offline you decide who receives your message, and what you want to say. With the web the user has more opportunity to decide what information they access, moreover with search engines if they do not find what they want immediately they click off to other websites. As a web author this means that you need to think not just about what you want to say, but also what the visitor wants to know. This is not to overstress the shift in power, but the internet is more user-led than most other communication channels. As we shall see, this characteristic will influence a number of your design decisions.

2 Non-linear arrangement of information
   In a website, unlike a brochure, information is presented in a non-linear way which enhances the user-led characteristic. While the visitor will often arrive at the home page, after that they choose which page they visit and in what order, not the web-host. You, therefore, lose some control in how the visitor accesses your content. However, one way of trying to control and direct how visitors access your information is to use hyperlinks within the site. Enmeshing is the means to use such links to guide the visitor to where you want them to go next (Ollier 1998). Jackson (2013) found that 96.7 per cent of event websites used hyperlinks to direct web visitors around their site. For example, a short 50-word introduction for new visitors to the outdoor opera festival Glyndebourne (www.glyndebourne.com/about-us/new-to-glyndebourne) included three hyperlinks.

3 Writing on the web – a journalistic approach
   Writing on the web is very different from authoring a newsletter, press story, poster or flyer. Where in a brochure you can afford to take your time to get across your point, in a website you have to get straight to the point or your visitor will be off somewhere better. For example, Morris (2000) suggested that where a printed promotional document might have 1,000 words, a website should use 100. Each website has to be short and to the point, utilising multimedia such as graphics and images. For example, the home page of the London edition of the Holi Festival of Colours World Tour (http://holifestival.com/uk/en/index) explains in 105 words how to buy tickets, why to buy them and the details of the event. When we write normally, a paragraph is usually in the 140–170 words range, yet in fewer words than that this event has communicated all the necessary information. Brevity is key to writing on the web.

4 Both synchronous and asynchronous
   The internet creates a changed time frame for communicating, allowing for both asynchronous (not concurrent) and synchronous (live) communication, depending on what the receiver prefers (Grieco and Holmes 1999). The receiver could access a message, and respond to it, at a time to suit them, for example with any website that provides a chat feature. This means that you can have a live chat function but your visitor can also engage with your site when you are asleep.

How we read online

Before we can start thinking about website design and content we need to understand how visitors to our website 'read' it.

As the internet has become a central part of our lives, there have been a number of books and articles that have looked at the possible psychological effects of web technologies. An idea of possible relevance to us can be found in a YouTube clip: www.youtube.com/watch?v=aXV-yaFmQNk. This implies that technology has rewired our brains. In October 2011 Jean-Louis Constantza posted his one-year-old daughter using her fingers to move icons on an iPad's touch screen. When presented with old media in the form of magazines she uses the same method with her fingers, but obviously it did not work, and she appeared confused. The conclusion Constantza comes to is that for those who have used digital technology from an early age it is recoding our minds. You may or may not accept his viewpoint, but what we cannot ignore is that if we seek to communicate via the internet, the Gutenberg diagram and the Z-pattern outlined in Chapter 2 may not work as effectively as they do offline. Indeed, research by Nielsen (2006) suggests that we read a web page very differently, first in terms of the order and second that we scan, not read. This type of 'scanning' has been referred to as the F-pattern which implies that when you are using the internet you need to construct your message and its design very differently.

Neilsen (2006) conducted an eye-tracking study where cameras were placed on computer screens to see where the eye went when people were reading a web page. He used such eye-tracking technology to identify how 232 users looked at thousands of web pages. He found that users' main reading behaviour was fairly consistent across many different sites and tasks, and looked broadly like an F. There are three main components to the F-pattern:

1   Users first read in a horizontal movement, usually across the upper part of the content area. This initial element forms the F's top bar. This line does not go all the way across the page, though sometimes it is broken and continues with a small 'blob' on the far right.
2   Then users move down the page a bit and then they read across in a second, normally shorter, horizontal movement which forms the F's lower bar. There may be more than one such movement, but each horizontal movement gets shorter.
3   Last, users scan the content's left side in a vertical movement which forms the F's stem.

We suggest that the F-pattern provides you with a useful tool, but we also note that practitioners do not always follow it. Jackson (2015) looked at whether political parties applied the F-pattern to their websites during the 2015 UK general election campaign. He found that they did not. The existing literature suggests that parties use their websites for two main purposes: providing information; and resource generation (such as encouraging donations). These were precisely the two features most likely to be outside the F-pattern, and so the least likely to be seen by visitors. Had the F-pattern been applied we argue that these websites would have been more effective.

Using eye-tracking technology a heat map can be produced. The diagram is colour-coded with red being the hottest in terms of where the eye goes most, and then orange/yellow, then blue and lastly grey, being cold areas that the visitors simply did not look at. This suggests that if your most important information about your event is in the grey areas, your web visitors simply will not take it in. The F-pattern clearly encourages you to be brief – to get the key information in the top and down the left of the page. Indeed, Nielsen advises getting the key information such as logos, when the event is, why attend etc., into the first two paragraphs.

The F-pattern suggests that we need to work out the priority of information. The most important content, be it words, images or symbols, should be placed across the top of the design where it will be seen first. The second order messages should then be placed on the left side of the page, where the use of bullet points may help the eye take it all in without having to move much. However, as noted above, one very important finding from this research is that people do not read online in the same way they might offline, rather they scan quickly for information. Therefore, you should focus on making sure that the key information you want to get across is within the F.

There are two health warnings with the F-pattern. First, Nielsen's data was collected using left-to-right languages, and so may not apply in the same way for right-to-left (such as Arabic) or pictorial (such as Japanese) languages. Second, Nielsen's data was from websites set up for PCs or laptops, the reading behaviour of handheld devices such as phones or tablets may be different and the F-pattern might not apply.

To test further his point that we scan, not read, a website, Nielsen (2008) conducted additional research that assessed 45,237 views of web pages. He found that on average web readers read at most 28 per cent of a page, and more typically 20 per cent. This means that the bulk of your message is not being taken in, and so you need to consider what are the best visual cues to get your key points across. Nielsen's research was broadly supported by Manjoo (2013) who found that for the website *Slate* most readers only scroll down to 50 per cent of the article. This suggests that most people will not read all of a web article. Both projects reinforce the importance of highlighting your key messages, and doing so in a way that is noticeable to the visitor.

Website design

Website design encompasses a wide range of activities for creating and managing a website, including the code, graphics, authoring and evaluation. Thus, when you are trying to improve your website you are likely to consider the words, images, colours, composition and typography.

Before we consider how to design a good website, we need to identify what can go wrong:

- Out of date information;
- Pages difficult to use;
- Visitors being unable to find what they want.

Research by Kim et al. (2003) found that if visitors cannot find an item on a website then 50 per cent of them will leave. Indeed, if they have a negative experience, at least 40 per cent will not return to the site. They suggest that the way to avoid such mistakes is to create criteria by which your website could be benchmarked. These criteria are for the event manager to decide, but they could include:

- Currency;
- Information;
- Authority;
- Clarity;
- Accuracy;
- Ease of use;
- Audience;
- Navigation.

They identified over thirty possible criteria, the key point is for an event to decide what is important for their website.

One of the more popular approaches for explaining why technologies are adopted is the Technology Acceptance Model (TAM) (Davis et al. 1989) which states that the ease of use coupled with the usefulness of the technology are key. Tan et al. (2006) used a panel to assess the process of buying a computer online, and found that the best sites focused on the users' needs. In particular, they identified features that influenced users' opinion of a site: how easy it was to get around the site; how comfortable it was to use; and whether they enjoyed the process.

Your website should be easy to use, physically attractive and appropriate for the audience. The purpose, be it primarily promotional or sales-driven, will shape your design.

We suggest that there are five areas you need to consider in constructing your website:

1 Your audience – what are their needs likely to be?
2 Speed – how quickly can information be accessed/downloaded?
3 Navigation – how easy is it to find what visitors want?
4 Content – what information should it contain?
5 Security – yours (can it be hacked?) and your visitors' (will their details be safe, especially financial?).

We suggest that design aspects are to be found in both the navigation and the content. Using a questionnaire of 130 e-commerce users Gehrle and Turban (1999) found that speed of page loading was the most important feature, followed by content and then navigation. This suggests that simplicity in terms of design and access are more importance than abundance (i.e. having too much information is a mistake).

To help you design an effective website we suggest that you concentrate on four areas:

1 Words – key messages and calls to action;
2 Images – the use of pictures, video and music;
3 Architecture – how you structure information;
4 Navigation – how easy it is to get around.

Words

It is often said that content is king online, but too many words can create a site that is impenetrable. We suggest you keep it simple, use easy-to-read language and mix up text with images. Be clear in what you want to achieve: is there branding (yours or your sponsor's) that you want to get across, are there particular products (such as ticket deals) you wish to promote? The words set the tone for how you will be perceived. For example, the Gold Coast Airport Marathon (www.goldcoastmarathon.com.au) 'About' page succinctly explains the event and offers clear reasons why a visitor should sign up for it. In addition to a variety of images that support the text, this page essentially has three separate components. The first paragraph in 45 words provides a compelling case to attend:

> The Gold Coast Airport Marathon is held annually in one of the most popular holiday destinations in the world. It is Australia's premier road race and was the first marathon in the country to hold an International Association of Athletics Federations (IAAF) Road Race Gold Label.

This well-crafted short paragraph makes two clear points. First, this is a popular holiday destination so this is more than a race, and can therefore appeal to both runners and their families. Second, this is a prestigious race.

The next paragraph then provides the details, and the longest section highlights in more depth 12 relevant features to the race.

The authors of this page have clearly sought to entice readers with short evocative messages, and then subsequently provide more detail for those readers who want it.

Images

We all know the old adage that a picture is worth a thousand words, and this is especially true with websites. Images, be they static or moving, attract the eye and keep visitors on the site. In part they achieve this because we want to look at attractive things/people, but it is much more than social attractiveness. A visual can provide a cue for where we want visitors to look. Galfano et al. (2012) found that if the image in a picture is gazing at text in the website we are likely to follow its gaze. Here is a way of getting visitors to focus on what you consider your most important text.

However, images can also cause us unintended problems. A large or visually appealing image may gain the attention of visitors, but it might not be supporting our key messages, such as the call to action. Therefore, make sure that your image and message dovetail.

Architecture

Web architecture is how you structure, organise and present your content. It is driven by your users' needs. In Chapter 3 we dealt with the factors that can affect architecture: colour; design; and typography. The basic principles apply online, but obviously the context and technology affect the details. Cyr et al. (2010) found that the use of colour within websites could elicit emotions (especially trust and satisfaction) and change behaviour. For example, they found that of their sample of 90, yellow sites were viewed as unappealing and blue sites were viewed favourably.

One important website design consideration is the amount of white space; this is the proportion of a page left empty around the margins and between text and images. A good website sees white space as a friend: it helps to keep a site 'clean' in terms of feel. How often have you visited a website and felt it was 'too busy'? This is normally because there is too much text and not enough white space. Remember, if you have lots to say, use hyperlinks to another page where you can expand – do not try to cram everything onto one page.

One key part of setting the tone of your site is the typography, which is essentially the 'body language'. This includes the font and font size. We discussed in Chapter 3 that the two main types of font are serif and sans-serif. Serif fonts are usually easier to read offline because they help the eye maintain attention. However, the resolution of websites is lower, usually at 100 dots per inch, compared to 1,000 dots per inch for printed material, and so sans-serifs are the norm. Sans-serif is better in smaller type, as with websites, because they are less likely to be blurred.

Navigation

We noted earlier with TAM that being easy to use is important to the adoption of a technology. The use of navigation buttons, icons and providing a search facility are key to providing this. In large part, navigation comes back to the purpose of your site, for example, a sales-led site should make sure links to the product/buying pages are easy to find.

An important part of navigation is that it is short and to the point, therefore brevity is important. Too much text and information on the screen turns people off; one way of dealing with this is to have more pages but with less text. A good test will be to see whether you can get all your information onto one screen. You will note that architecture and navigation support each other; a good architecture should enhance the navigability of a site.

How to make your website popular

You need to drive traffic to your website. This can be achieved through offline communications highlighting the website, the obvious ways being to have the website url prominently displayed on posters, flyers and at the venue itself. In addition, many organisations have turned to other online tools, such as email, e-newsletters, Twitter and Facebook as a means of driving traffic to their websites. Websites are more of an integrated communication channel, repeating messages on more than one route to market, but also providing slightly different content via different channels. For example, the website for the 2015 ISA World Surfing Games in Nicaragua (www.isasg.com) has Twitter, Facebook, YouTube and Instagram. Thus, visitors to this website can get more information, engage in discussions and watch videos and images of the action. The website is therefore the means to bring alive this event.

A web surfer might find your site by accident, but why do they come back time and time again? The main answer is that you need to provide them with a reason; typically this is content that regularly changes. A 'sticky' website (Jackson 2003) encourages repeat visits by offering a range of either fun or interactive things to do, or it provides new updated content. For example, the Rugby World Cup 2015 website (www.rugbyworldcup.com) gave frequent updates on ticket sales, transport links and partnered hotels, fixtures/results, chat groups and fan pages. In short, for those interested, there is a wide range of material; some of it is interactive, and it is updated.

The management of your website

The way in which many people hear about an event is by using a search engine such as Google, Yahoo and Bing. Typically, someone might type in to a search engine 'something to do on a wet and windy Wednesday in York', and then see what comes up. When we typed in this phrase to Google, the first page was a real mixture that included horse racing (there is a racecourse in York), restaurants and New York in America. We did not look beyond page two.

One of the easiest ways of measuring the effectiveness of your website is to internally audit it. Here you need to try and see your site as a visitor would. For example, ask:

- Does it get across your key messages?
- Is it easy to find information?
- Do all the features, buttons and links work?
- Does it work on different platforms, such as PC, tablet and phone?
- How long does it take to load?
- Is it easy to read (both the content and the design)?

The other useful evaluating tool is to conduct some form of search engine optimisation (SEO), or web analytics, which help to assess traffic trends and behaviour, referrals, sales etc. Web analytics can be used to see how many people have visited the site, and which links have been clicked through the most. Web analytics can normally also be used to show from where in the world the site was accessed and how long the visitor stayed on the page.

When you seek to find out some new information, the chances are that you will Google it. Moreover, the chances are that you will look no further than the first two pages of Google on the word(s) you search. Google employs a range of algorithms to decide where websites should rank in any particular search. Search engine optimisation is the art of securing a high Google ranking.

Google does not make this easy, it regularly changes what it gives weighting to, and you will find many guides and consultants claiming to offer the solution. Indeed, just Google 'what factors do google say they rank'; we found nearly a million responses. What we can say is that the domain name, keyword tags (the more you pay for the higher you are likely to be in the ranking), content, especially user experience, links to your site and number of mentions are likely to affect your ranking. One of the reasons many organisations use a range of internet modalities such as Twitter, Facebook and Instagram is that they raise your Google ranking through more mentions.

Before you spend a lot of money on hiring a consultant, we suggest that you start by reading the Google Search Engine Optimization Starter Guide (http://static.googleusercontent.com/media/www.google.co.uk/en/uk/webmasters/docs/search-engine-optimization-starter-guide.pdf). This short guide does not give away any secrets but it will help you to understand how you can improve your navigation and content and how you can promote your site to improve your ranking.

8.3 Definition box

The use of apps

Apps, or applications, are software that can be downloaded to mobile devices and tablets, and if your PC has Windows 10 an app is a means to performing a task on a tablet or phone. Some may already be defaulted on your hardware, but many apps need to be downloaded. Such apps could be free to download or may incur a cost. Organisations may create free access to apps in order to make it easier for a customer to find or use what they want. Phone companies run some form of mobile shop from which you can download an app.

Apps have become a bit of a buzzword and many event managers have looked at how they might use them. Indeed, there has been a growth in the number of companies who can design, create and manage an app for an event; though note this is not a cheap business, to develop your own discrete app rather than purchase someone else's with the development often costing many thousands of pounds sterling. Apps can be created for a wide range of event-related functions, such as streamlining registration, encouraging networking between delegates and providing real-time voting and updates. There are a range of off-the-shelf apps that as an event manager you can purchase to help improve the efficiency, communication and experience of your event. For example, *Boomset* focuses on registration, *Evernote* is a means of keeping all the notes and images relevant to your event and *Foursquare* helps conference delegates keep track of where their colleagues are.

CASE STUDY

The Appointment Group Global Events website

The Appointment Group (www.appointmentgroup.com) is a global events and travel management company. With offices in the US, Australia, Singapore and the UK it provides a range of event management services to support events around the world. The Appointment Group explains how it designs, manages and uses its website.

In April 2014 with the Global rebranding of The Appointment Group (TAG) new global brands were announced. In conjunction with the rebranding, TAG launched a new website. The site includes significant layout updates and features clear distinctive navigation, in a strikingly modern and vibrant visual design.

The Appointment Group (Global Events) website is essentially the shop front of our company. Its objectives are to present visitors with the wide range of services we can offer on a global scale, attract new business, and we are currently entering a new phase; we are trying to make a conscious effort to use the website as a Sales and Business development tool. Furthermore, the challenge was to create divisional sites that would be catered to the specific requirements and target market of each division, whilst maintaining a "group" feel, layout and structure the Board of Directors were very keen to maintain.

Now that we feel the website is at a good standard we are taking steps to:

1 Become more visible on the web (SEO);
2 Publish interest-driven/original content;
3 Relay this content via social media.

The primary of these steps is to, slowly but surely, convert visitors into clients, using the website as a commercial and business development tool.

When considering the design of the website it was the wish of the Board of Directors to have a visually striking and image-rich website that would present the different divisions under one collective roof.

The main objectives of the Global rebranding were:

1 To give a global emphasis on each of the divisions;
2 To streamline the Style Guidelines globally for improved branding and perception;
3 To offer each division its own identity whilst maintaining a thin red line between all of the brands of the group;
4 To encourage cross-selling;
5 Easy navigation.

This is why all of the logos of The Appointment Group have common elements. One of the elements we have introduced in the 2nd phase of the website redevelopment late 2015 is the introduction of the meta-header. This was an essential new feature of the website that allows a user, regardless of what website or page they are on, to navigate to any other part of the website in one click. This allows extremely easy access to the information regardless of what you are looking for (see below). In addition, this allows us to feature any news relating to that website division with ease to ensure maximum impact.

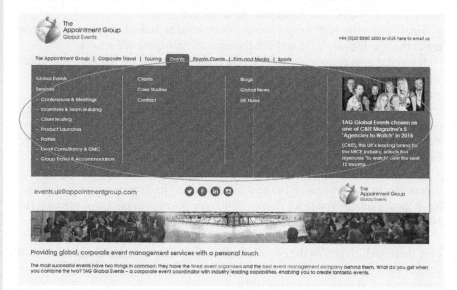

The colour of the logo is one of the identifiable elements of each division. This divisional colour is used throughout our corporate documentation website and any other marketing or business development collateral. Each divisional space was tailored within the pre-established "framework" and style guidelines to cater for the mores specific requirements of their target market. In the case of TAG Global Events, the company has an extensive sitemap presenting the key services this division has on offer. It was our objective to demonstrate that from private parties and product launches, to large corporate incentive trips, the TAG Global Events team manages every detail, giving the host a seamless experience and maximum return on investment.

The imagery was also of great importance. A good picture can display not only the magnitude of events one organises but also the type of clientele we deal with, our degree of innovativeness and the quality of the work. If a "wow factor" is achieved through the image on the page, visitors are far more likely to look at the content in greater detail.

The choice of fonts was motivated by two principal factors: aesthetics and cross-device compatibility. We were conscious that to keep maintaining one image we were obliged to use fonts that were compatible with: websites/different browsers/iPads/tablets/iPhones/regular smartphones, but also other systems such as Microsoft Outlook.

If we were to use standardised fonts for all mediums we needed to ensure they would be supported by all of these systems. If fonts are chosen that are incompatible with certain devices or software, that software will convert the text into whatever font it can support and consequently, as a company, you have no control on how your emails and/or website can come across.

Finally, we wanted to keep a balance between text and white space in order to make the text legible, clear and not too overwhelming for the reader.

It is our aim to choose images that reflect our company, our services and where we operate to the best of our ability. We want to ensure to tick enough boxes for any type of visitor that comes across our website.

The TAG Global Events Services page, www.appointmentgroup.com/tag-global-events/services, is, for example, a page where we display in quite a concise manner the key services we are able to offer all our clients. Each of these services is illustrated by a picture depicting that type of event to keep it as relevant and clear as possible.

The TAG Global Event Blog page, www.appointmentgroup.com/tag-global-events/blogs/, is a little more fun and playful due to its "social nature"; again we have chosen imagery that we think will have a positive impact and enhance the blog it compliments.

The great majority of the events organised by the team will have a photographer on site which allows the client to capture key moments. The Events team will usually then request whether we can use some of this imagery for the purpose of our website and other marketing collateral.

Along with the global rebranding of the company in 2014 we decided to look at changing the content, keeping our potential customers and clients at the forefront of our mind.

What were event planners and bookers looking for? What type of information would make them want to get in touch? What type of events would they be looking for? What content would make them want to contact us? Finally, we needed to bear in mind the global reach of the website and establish how to effectively cater for clients that could be located in various countries around the globe.

For users we have built what we call a geo-location system. The geo-location feature identifies where a user is accessing the website from and will cater certain elements to that user in order to improve their website experience.

According to the location the user is based at, UK/US/Australia/Singapore, certain elements in the header and footer will be changed (see illustration below):

- Contact telephone number;
- Address in the footer;
- News feed will be their local UK/US/Australia/Singapore feed.

The Appointment Group | Corporate Travel | Touring | Events | Private Clients | Film and Media | Sports

The Appointment Group Global Events

Providing global, corporate event management services with a personal touch.

The most successful events have two things in common: they have the finest event organisers and the best event management company behind them. What do you get when you combine the two? TAG Global Events – a corporate event coordinator with industry leading capabilities, enabling you to create fantastic events.

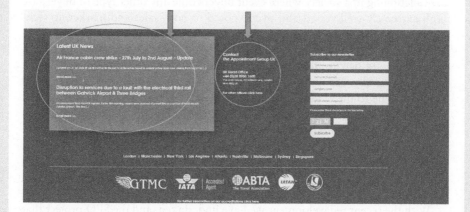

On the Events website, in particular, we have catered the text to a global audience. As we in fact arrange events globally for many of our UK, US and Australian clients we found it important that those elements transpired in the copy.

Furthermore, we ensured both blogs and case studies we publish are varied in nature and location. Whatever we publish we try to ensure, to the best of our ability, the content is relevant to one or several of the locations we are established in.

The copy we produce and publish needs to be a fine balance between information and yet not enough detail to make yourself indispensable. It is the objective to answer the standard type of question any potential client would ask themselves in the copy of the website:

- What key services does TAG Events offer? → "We have the expertise and skill to organise a great range of events to perfection, see the list of services we offer."
- How can using TAG Events be of benefit to our company? → "We take the hassle and stress and time investment off your shoulders. We have specialists that work alongside you to make your event the best it can be."
- How can TAG Events offer value? → "We have relationships and buying power that allow us to offer cost-effective solutions."
- What type of events have TAG Events completed in the past? → "Our case studies demonstrate some of the fantastic events we have organised for our clients."

The next aim is to entice people to contact us and enquire about our services.

Popular elements to the website are usually the recruitment and about us pages as they are always looked at by people researching the company and/or looking for positions. It is actually far more challenging to drive people to pages you want them to go to, the services and contact us pages for example.

In our case this is partially due to the fact the market is extremely competitive and that people, as they do for any other type of purchase, love "browsing". We are functioning in a society where event buyers (like any other type of buyer) are both extremely well-versed and overexposed to both sales and marketing techniques. Capturing their attention and pulling them in is extremely difficult when no pre-existing relationship exists.

A very good way to drive people to where *we* would like them to go, which are coincidentally also well-visited pages, are blogs and content that are original and add value to the reader. That is why we are investing in the creation of that type of content that is then used in newsletters, published on our social media channels etc. When you create interesting content that can both sell your expertise as an Event Management company and educate the reader at the same time you generate interest, which is a valuable tool to obtaining new business!

In terms of evaluation we have always kept an eye on website performance via Google analytics which offers a good overview of performance.

With the recent redevelopment we have undertaken, and the SEO project that is in its infancy, we shall be receiving detailed reporting on the visitors who will land on our website, such as which pages they navigate, most effective keywords, and how long they stay on the pages. This will then allow us to determine what pages are most popular, establish why and keep on tweaking content, structure and imagery to improve the impact of the website and gain a greater amount of business via this medium.

For those events looking to use a website we would advise:

- Think about your audience – who are you communicating to?
- What would you like your website to achieve?

- Bear in mind navigability – people want easy access to information.
- The more your website is on trend, the quicker it will be perceived as outdated. Redeveloping costs a lot of time and money.
- Never consider a website totally done: a website needs maintenance, tweaking, updating and care.
- Create interesting content that can be advertised through social media. Think "thought leadership".'

Discussion questions

1 If we assume that you want to use your website as a one-way communication tool to promote your events, how do you 'square the circle' that many of your attendees will want a conversation with you via social networking sites but that you may not?
2 When thinking about the look and feel of your website, how will you utilise the F-pattern, font, typography and colour? That is, what are the key principles you will apply for designing your website?
3 Content is king with the web. How will you decide how to develop new material and what design and authoring tricks will you use so that your text meets the needs of your visitors?
4 What data do you require to effectively assess whether your website is doing what you want it to do?

Further information

Books

Blumler, J. and Katz, E. (1974) (eds) *The Uses of Mass Communications: current perspectives on gratifications research,* Beverly Hills, CA: Sage.
Major, I. (2013) *Website Marketing: how to use Google webmaster tools,* E-book: Ian D. Major.

Articles

Courtois, C., Mechant, P., De Marez, L. and Verleye, G. (2009) 'Gratifications and seeding behaviour of online adolescents', *Journal of Computer-Mediated Communication,* 15 (1): 109–137.
Weinreich, H., Obedorf, H., Herder, E. and Mayer, M. (2008) 'Not quite the average: an empirical study of web use', *ACM Transactions on the Web,* 2 (1): 5–31.

Websites

For more detail on producing a website, have a look at:

www.webdesignerdepot.com/2012/12/20-creative-and-inspiring-event-websites/

www.amiando.com/eventwebsite.html

www.websitemagazine.com/content/blogs/posts/archive/2014/03/21/5-reasons-visitors-leave-your-website.aspx

http://wpeventsites.com/creating-an-event-website/

http://planning-an-event.com/2012/event-website/

www.socialnomics.net – site with lots of videos with statistics of online usage.

www.workcast.co.uk – agency that provide online events.

www.xtmotion.co.uk/ – web designers who specialise in producing event websites.

www.searchengineoptimising.com/seo-guide – advice on search engine optimisation.

http://design.tutsplus.com/tutorials/9-essential-principles-for-good-web-design--psd-56 – how to design a website.

Chapter 9

Social networking sites

Introduction

This chapter will focus on tools that have often been codified under the umbrella term Web 2.0 applications: these include Facebook, Twitter, LinkedIn, Instagram, YouTube and Pinterest. Although technically not part of a definition of social networking sites (SNS) we will also include weblogs, or blogs, because they can be used to encourage interaction. This is a fast-moving area with new tools developed each year. Thus part of the trick with using social networking is the ability to assess the application, or not, of each new tool to your event. In short, if a new internet tool helps you complete an existing function better, more quickly or more cheaply or it creates a new function that adds to the experience of your event, then you may well adopt it. If not, why waste the energy and resources? This chapter will assess the benefits, but also potential issues of encouraging interaction in the form of co-production of content. We shall start by looking at the wider conceptual issues that set our understanding of how these tools differ from websites *per se*, then we shall look at each of the social networking tools. Throughout we shall assess how events use interactivity and co-production of content. By the end of the chapter students will be able to:

- Assess the benefits and costs of using Web 2.0 applications;
- Create an interactive approach to a social networking site;
- Understand how to offer co-production of content;
- Utilise each social networking application.

Web 2.0 and interactivity

Very simply, it can be suggested that websites are very text-based, informational and one-way, whereas social networking sites are more interactive, conversational and two-way. This is a simplification; as we saw in the previous chapter, websites have the capability also to be interactive and encourage dialogue. However, we do see slight differences in how different web tools are used. Websites tend to be used primarily as a means by which events can get out their key messages. Social networks enable events to build on this information by developing and enhancing relationships with potential customers through encouraging dialogue (both between the event and its audiences and between audiences). For example, an SNS enables you to ask attendees to vote for the best entertainer, speaker or part of the programme. This might be technically possible on a website, but it is easier to manage on an SNS. The result is that attendees are offered an added-layer of participation in your event.

It has been suggested that the difference between how websites and SNS are used can be explained by the terms Web 1.0 and Web 2.0. The former refers to the provision of information that is top-down (by the event), whereas with the concept of Web 2.0 (O'Reilly 2005) conversations are encouraged through an architecture of participation. In short, the means to develop conversations exist and are given prominence in the site. We suggest that trying to view websites as Web 1.0 and SNS as Web 2.0 is probably not helpful. We do not deny that there may be a difference between Web 1.0 and Web 2.0 applications; however, we focus on what the event is trying to achieve. Therefore, all events need to promote their basic details through information, and for some (though not all) it is appropriate to encourage conversations. Therefore, we see websites and SNS as complementary not opposing tools.

CASE STUDY

Applying SNS in different ways to similar events

Holi – festival of colour – is an annual Hindu festival with local festivals taking place all over India (and in other countries). The website of the Jaipur Elephant Festival (http://elephantfestivaljaipur.com/), which is part of Holi, is primarily an information-based website designed to attract tourists. Its home page has seven paragraphs of information about the event, with a booking hyperlink repeated three times. The picture gallery designed to showcase the event offers professionally produced brochure-style pictures. The Holi Cow Dehli Festival, a private paid-for ticketed event, is also part of the Hindu festival of Holi, it also wants people to attend but promotionally it takes a very different approach. Their Facebook (www.facebook.com/holicowfestival) is full of the experience of attendees. There is a short bit about the event, such as when and where, but the focus is on a gallery of the experience of attendees. While posts are clearly led by the organisers, attendees offer their own comments and discussions take place. Most are along the lines of who is attending and what fun they had, but some are slightly critical; for example, there was a discussion about the inability of booking online from abroad for technical reasons. The other obvious difference is the pictures; there are far more in number but they are also very different in source, the site is full of 'action' pictures obviously taken by attendees themselves. We do not suggest that one approach is better than the other; rather, we observe that they are different in content and style even if the purpose (to inform and/or sell) is the same. As a result, we can see a case for an event having both a didactic and an interactive approach.

A third interpretation is provided by Jackson and Lilleker (2009) who suggest that what may actually happen in practice is not a pure Web 1.0 or Web 2.0 model; rather, Web 1.5 which is in effect a compromise. Here events recognise that interactive tools are popular, but they still want to use their websites primarily to get across their message. Thus they may struggle to find a balance between wanting to control their message, and encouraging user input. Events probably want to use their online presence to control their message, but individual web users now expect to interact with sites. Web 1.5 implies that some events feel that they have to have interactivity because their competitors do, but they still want to focus on their key messages. The genie of dialogue is out of the bottle, and this can lead to some friction between what hosts and visitors want.

Imagine that you are going to attend a festival, you might visit the official Facebook page. You may want some basic information about the event, but you will probably also want to be able to contact other attendees, speculate what the event will be like and possibly even air a gripe or complaint. In short, visiting this site is part of the atmosphere of the event, even before you have attended. Now let us assume that you are the marketing manager of another festival. Here you may well view your Facebook page in a very different light. For you it involves allocating scarce resources to manage, update and moderate. Consequently, to get a return on investment (ROI) what you will probably want to focus on is getting your key message out. If you are clever you might use it as a marketing intelligence research tool. It is understandable that you view your Facebook page very differently from an attendee.

Before we can look at the tools we need to understand some key terms. A very simple and useable definition of social networking sites is that they 'allow information sharing and interactivity amongst users' (Loss et al. 2014: 161), and so encourage users to upload their own details and then to communicate with others (or others commentate on what they place on the SNS). As a result, SNS lead to networks between people who choose to meet virtually. Given that people want to attend an event, it is not difficult to see why they might want to communicate prior to the event (and indeed during and after) to enhance their experience.

9.1 Defining event social networking sites

Social networking sites are technologies that inherently encourage interaction, sharing of material, comments and dialogue between two or more website users. Event-based SNS can be organised by the event itself and so are designed to get across key messages, or they can be provided by an independent third party, who is interested in that event, type of events or the sort of people who might attend that event. SNS encourage interaction by providing an architecture that enables users to post their own content, be it comments, images or video. SNS enable virtual relationships to be created, or existing physical ones to be enhanced. They provide a means of adding to the event experience before, during or after it. Content is therefore co-produced between the event and its SNS visitors. Such content can be administered and moderated by the event, so they maintain quality control. Or few controls may exist on how and what content is posted by visitors. SNS can encourage virtual communication between an event and its users, and/or horizontal communication between event attendees. An SNS is merely a technology; what matters is how it is used, and the approach to using it by both the event and its web visitors. An SNS is not a fixed concept, it has many different possible layers.

We offer a health warning for events considering using SNS. From the outset the social aspect of such sites implied that they were linked to individuals and not organisations. This does not mean that events cannot use them, but it does mean you need to think how you will manage them, and why others would access and engage with essentially a corporate body and not an individual.

The term social media is often used interchangeably with SNS, but do not conflate the two concepts. The idea of social media predates the internet, as it encourages the exchange of content, but this could apply as much to the telephone as Facebook. Therefore, if you use the term social media, be aware that your SNS, such as Twitter, is merely one of many social media, not the only social media. This is why this chapter is specially focusing on the use of internet tools of social media (i.e. SNS), not the wider concept.

Facebook is the dominant social media site in the world and in September 2012 had more than one billion users worldwide. At the time of writing (2016), Facebook now claims over 1.5 billion active users. Those who use Facebook can select which brands or companies to comment on, or 'like', as well as what information they would like to subscribe to. There are a number of ways that marketers can use Facebook, from creating a business profile page and interacting with their target audience through 'status' updates; creating events and groups for specific purposes which can be joined, followed or 'liked', as well as developing adverts that can be viewed while other users are online.

As an event manager you want to use your web tools to get across key messages and develop relationships, and your web visitors may want to have their input. Therefore, you need to understand how to develop co-production of content, whereby the technology encourages visitors to participate with their ideas and comments. Thus your visitors are not merely passive

9.2 Co-production of content

Co-production of content is where an event creates a website and then encourages others to post their own ideas, material and words on that website. The overall framework of the website is set by the event, but it creates parts of the site where others have the opportunity to add content. Such content can take many forms but it could be an image, video or typed text. Such content can be one-offs or enable a conversation as others respond and add to it. Co-production of content means that the content of the site is no longer the total preserve of the web host. It enables event or event website visitors to have their say, be it positive, negative or neutral in tone.

recipients of your messages, but also contributors. Conceptually, this means that you need to stop viewing yourself as the sole producer of content, and web visitors as only consumers. Rather, as James (1991) suggests, we can conflate these concepts now to consider produsers where your visitors also have something to offer.

Co-production of content can take many forms. Table 9.1 outlines some of the possible tools for developing content interactivity, and what their event applications could be.

For events we can see some possible benefits:

● Providing an SNS can encourage visitors to return more frequently to your website;
● Making an event feel more 'human' can have reputational benefits;
● They can add value to event attendees by enhancing their experience;
● They can help build relationships between the event and its attendees;
● They can help build relationships between event attendees;
● It is easier for your event attendees to stay in touch with the event and other event attendees;
● If analysed, discussions can provide useful market intelligence.

Of course there are also some possible issues that events should consider before creating an SNS:

● The resources required to moderate and administer a site;
● The possible negative reputational impact of 'trolls' if they regularly abuse your visitors;
● Libellous comments on an event's website can lead to litigation;
● Security needs to be addressed to prevent hacking.

Table 9.1 Types of co-production of content

Type of content	Event application
Forums	Typical to sporting and music festival events. Can help create excitement prior to the event, help visitors plan to meet and can add insight/perspective afterwards of how others viewed the event.
Opinion polls/surveys	Any event. Essentially benefits the event, but may give visitors the opportunity to have their say.
Upload visitor pictures/ videos	Any event, more typical with B2C events. Provides an insight into the experience of others at an event, and so possibly enhancing your experience as well. Likely to be moderated by the web host.
Competitions	All types of events, but especially for those that wish to capture data from their visitors.
Reviews	More likely with sites independent to an event. Appeals to a desire to have one's opinion heard and possibly acted upon, for example, a theatre performance.

Table 9.2 SNS strategy

Questions	Event response
Why have an SNS?	Agree and write down a clear measurable purpose(s).
Which SNS will you use?	Identify and assess which ones other similar events use.
	Assess who in your team has, or can learn, the necessary skills.
	Evaluate the resources required.
What is the content to be included?	Identify the processes by which you will develop content.
	Allocate an author(s) responsible for updating material.
	What will your audiences want to know?
	What are the key messages you want to convey?
When will messages be sent out?	Are you going for a single hit where all information goes out, or drip-feed over a period of time?
	When do you need your audiences to make decisions?
How will you use SNS to support your brand?	Beyond the immediate information you are conveying, what message about your event/organisation do you want to get across?
	Where will your logos, brand images and straplines go on your SNS?
Will SNS be part of your website or have its own url?	Is your website the dominant online tool, or are SNS of equal importance?
What can you learn from your competitors?	Do a structured analysis of their SNS using clear criteria, such as design feel, content, likely effect and interaction.

If you feel that SNS will help you promote an event, then it can be useful for an event to develop a social networking marketing strategy. Here an event seeks to use SNS to achieve its communication, promotional and branding aims. As Wordstream (www.wordstream.com/) suggests, this is a deliberate approach that aims to share content, videos and images for marketing purposes. Social networks allow businesses to engage with their audiences and network with other professionals, creating the impression that the organisation has a 'caring side'. Companies can frequently provide relevant updates to audience members.

Thus you need a strategy or plan of how you will use SNS to communicate your desired messages to your target audience, and the tools you will use to do this. Table 9.2 outlines how you might evaluate and develop your SNS strategy.

Weblogs

Weblogs are different from websites, being essentially a published real-time online diary. There are two main types of weblog, those that emphasise the diary and comment aspect, and those that emphasise hyperlinks (Blood 2000). The former allows a blogger to promote their ideas, whereas the latter act as a filter, looking at what exists on the World Wide Web that might be of interest to visitors. It is the former that is more likely to encourage feedback from visitors. Weblogs are very diverse in that there is no one dominant style or activity, but common to all is that they share information.

We can identify two types of event bloggers; those who are using their blog to promote their own event, and those who act like an independent commentator offering opinion on a range of events. An example of the former is the National Wedding Fair held each September at London Olympia. This show has a website that includes a blog (www.nationalweddingshow.co.uk/blog), which although it does promote aspects of the event is much more than this, and feels like a magazine, offering articles on subjects that do not at first feel like a plug for the event. The approach then is to add value to the event by acting more like an independent wedding magazine, with lots of interesting wedding-related content as opposed to more overt event content. The blog supports the event as a soft sell.

One of the best known event management blogs (www.eventmanagerblog.com) is provided by events consultant Julius Solaris. This comprehensive blog contains posts that cover a range of planning, marketing and technology issues, which affect the delivery of a good event. It provides expert analysis on a range of topical issues relevant to events management. A similar approach is taken by http://eventjuice.co.uk/blog which proffers advice on topical issues. However, it is different from Solaris's blog in that it is provided by a collective of eight bloggers, each of which has their own specialism.

While eventmanagerblog is associated with an individual, others such as http://blog.planningpod.com are used to establish the credentials of a company. The rationale appears to be that if you like our content you will like our company providing you with an event-based service/product. Similarly, http://velvetchainsaw.com is a popular blog that comments on event issues provided by Jeff Hurt at Velvet Chainsaw Consulting, specialists in the MICE industry (Meetings, Incentives, Conferences and Exhibitions). The extensive content on developments in conferences helps establish their credibility as experts in this field. In both instances these agencies are using blogs as a soft sell.

Some event-based weblogs do not have an association with a specific event or event management consultancy, rather, they are nearer to journalism by generating income through advertising. Thus Live Music Blog (http://livemusicblog.com/) provides reviews, photographs and videos of American music festivals, gigs and venues. It is, in effect, a free online magazine that specialises in live music.

Most blogs are linked to either commentators or those seeking to promote commercially their event manager credentials. It is very difficult to find one supporting an event, which suggests that the individual event would probably be best off not using weblogs. However, an interesting approach has been taken by the singer Moby, whose blog (www.moby.com/journal) provides a series of personal posts, but also helps to promote his music and touring.

Although blogs are not necessarily one of the key event online promotional tools, with over 250 million Tumblr blogs in 2015 (www.tumblr.com/about), they can be an effective way of influencing the wider agenda. However, as most weblogs are ignored it is important to develop a reputation for providing good content. Someone like Julius Solaris has now reached critical mass with his blog, and is clearly a market leader in offering a wide range of event-based opinion.

The advantages a blog offers an event include:

- They establish the event or consultant as an expert in the field;
- They add value by providing new information for visitors;

- They provide a means of covering a relevant issue in depth;
- They can assist the evaluation of an event website or drive traffic to it;
- They can help to differentiate an event from its competitors.

However, blogs can be time-consuming in terms of coming up with ideas, writing posts and responding to comments. If you allow posts from visitors then you need to manage this, first to prevent slanderous or commercially harmful comments being aired. Second, if you offer a comments feature and do not respond this might suggest that you do not really care for the opinions of others.

We suggest that blogs are more appropriate for those who offer a service to events by using them as a means of establishing their credibility, rather than events themselves.

As noted above, there are different types of blog, but we would suggest that the key issues to address before creating one are:

- What will be the purpose of the blog?
- Are your target audiences likely to read it?
- What resources do you need to manage your blog?
- How will you measure its impact?

There are blogging platforms such as Wordpress, Tumblr and Blogger that are available free to download and access. Clearly it makes sense to look at each of these, speak to other bloggers to get their advice and choose the one that best suits you.

One of the first points to recognise when writing content is that you are primarily seeking to set yourself as an expert. Blogs are not a hard sell. Rather, your content is more likely to be of interest to people within your event industry.

Having written a blog our advice is:

- Before you create it jot down a plan of the first half-dozen or more likely posts you will write;
- Decide how often you want to post, and be aware that it is so easy to start with loads of posts and then run out of steam;
- One very successful blogger we know blogs virtually every day, he posts items he has read, discussions with others and material published;
- If you allow feedback, check posts and respond regularly;
- Identify which publications, websites and other bloggers might publicise your site.

However, as a cautionary tale: after a couple of years the blog became too much work and was given up.

Microblogging

Microblogging sites such as Twitter, Tumblr and Plurk appear to be a response to the limitations of blogs. McFedries (2007) suggests that the requirement of writing lengthy and considered posts on weblogs is a 'hard slog'. In contrast, microblogging is a 'quick-ping' media, which allows people to post brief updates of up to 140 characters. Therefore, microblogging has lowered the barriers, in terms of thought investment by users (Java et al. 2007). Twitter has become popular because users, who are referred to as tweeters, can send and receive messages via a wide range of delivery mechanisms. Users of Twitter can be classified as followers and followed. Some tweeters have more people follow them than they follow, so they are largely broadcasting messages. While others have more reciprocal relationships with users and may both follow and be followed by a distinct community, or may simply follow a wide array of tweeters in order to gain news and updates without personally communicating a great deal.

The dominant microblogging site is Twitter, which started in 2006 and at the time of writing had over 320 million active users (https://about.twitter.com/company). Twitter can be used by organisations in a variety of ways:

● To build their company brand;
● To make new contacts or enhance existing relationships;
● To share ideas and to see what other people are writing about;
● To follow news stories.

One example of the use of Twitter is provided by Silverstream TV (http://silverstream.tv/twitterwalls), which provides a service for events where they can create TwitterWalls. This enables event attendees to tweet about the event which can be seen on screens displayed throughout the event. These are very popular at awards ceremonies, but have also been used at conferences and trade shows.

When considering whether to use Twitter an event manager needs to consider:

● What information will you include on your profile?
● How often will you tweet, and what information will you include in your tweets?
● Will you include any photos, videos or links to your website?
● Who from your company is responsible for writing/responding to tweets?
● How will you monitor/evaluate the success of using Twitter?

In the months running up to the 2016 Olympics the organisers' Twitter account (https://twitter.com/rio2016en) focused on qualifying events and previews of events, and offered a lot of images and video coverage. It was primarily informative and top-down with limited interaction with other tweeters. While also providing information, the racing championship Formula E (https://twitter.com/FIAformulaE) took a slightly different approach, seeking to bring fans closer to the teams and racing drivers. There were features on the drivers, a lot of video and pictorial images showing the action and they responded to some of the tweets from others. While generalising, and how close the event is timewise has an impact, Rio 2016 was more informational and Formula E appeared to have more of a relationship-building aspect.

If you are going to have a Twitter account for your event there are some terms you need to be aware of. A hashtag is a key phrase which begins with a # that allows like-minded people to search for tweets of interest. For example, at many events the organisers, commentators, attendees and sometimes those watching on television may use hashtags. Thus the Amsterdam Dance Event each year makes use of hashtags (https://twitter.com/hashtag/ade?lang=en-gb) and acts as a community for those interested in this event and alternative music in general.

What many events want to do is hit a critical mass where their event is trending (being 'spoken' about by tweeters). This is measured by the number of tweets using a specific hashtag. Events that are trending are likely to gain more followers, as tweeters are able to follow what is happening by viewing trending conversations.

If someone else posts or copies your tweet, then this is a retweet. This allows you to reach new audiences as the people following them will get to see your account, in effect, word of mouth (mouse).

We believe that Twitter, if used well, is a good promotional tool. It allows you to provide regular updates. It is also a way of establishing your credibility in a field. There can be inter-action and conversation, but it is unlikely to require too much management. Twitter fits well within our definition of Web 1.5 – it encourages interaction but is primarily a means by which events can control their message.

Facebook

Facebook is probably the dominant social media site in the world, as we noted earlier claiming over 1.5 billion users. According to Holzner (2008) Facebook users are smart, affluent and internet-savvy whom marketers seek to reach, suggesting that traditional marketing methods will no longer work with these online users. The users can select which brands/companies to comment on, or 'like', as well as which information they would like to subscribe to.

There are a number of ways that event marketers can use Facebook. These include creating a business profile page and interacting with their target audience through 'status' updates; creating events and groups for specific purposes that can be joined, followed or 'liked', as well as developing adverts that can be viewed while other users are online. The adverts use information from people's profiles to identify which adverts would be most suited to them. Well-known television survivalist Bear Grylls uses Facebook to promote some of his adventure-based events. For example, the Facebook page of The Bear Grylls Survival Race promotes a series of challenges he has organised, with videos, comments from participants and details of the events. As well as providing information, the organisers engage in conversation with many of the posts. The Facebook events section of a Facebook page shows which events others in your networks are going to or following and so suggests them to you too. It is possible to create a Facebook Event page where you invite people to your event and hope that they promote it to their friends. However, things can get out of hand with Facebook, for example in 2010 Paris police banned a 'Facebook aperitif' party where revellers intended to enjoy cocktails under the Eiffel tower as this broke a ban on drinking alcohol in the area (Reuters 2010).

There is a community on Facebook dedicated to events management (www.facebook.com/eventm/), which can provide access to information and ideas on subjects of relevance to you. It can therefore be a useful resource for you.

When considering whether to use Facebook think about:

- Does your Facebook profile match the company's branding and ethos?
- What information will you include on your profile?
- How often will you post, and what information will you include for, 'status' updates?
- Will you include any photos, videos or links to your website?
- Are others able to write on your profile, and how will you monitor this?
- Who from your company is responsible for updating your profile?
- How will you monitor/evaluate the success of using Facebook as a marketing tool?

Comic-Con International is a well-known comic convention held annually in San Diego (www. comic-con.org/). It is a non-profit educational corporation dedicated to creating awareness of, and appreciation for, comics and related popular art forms, primarily through the presentation of conventions and events that celebrate the historic and ongoing contribution of comics to art and culture. Comic-Con has used Facebook since 2009 and currently has over 1.7 million likes of its page. Comic-Con shares updates and information about itself and its conventions and events.

CASE STUDY

Facebook shares updates and information about Comic-Con and our affiliated conventions and events

David Glanzer, the Chief Communications and Strategy Officer for Comic-Com, explains why they decided to use Facebook, how they use it and with what effect 'Social media has grown in popularity and many of our attendees take part. It made sense to us to have a presence. We use it to mirror announcements we have on our own website and blog. Facebook is a method by which we disseminate information. Social media in general has been effective in distributing information and driving people to our website/blog, which often features more or additional information. Along with our other promotional tools social media is an effective mechanism to reach core elements of our attendees. For this reason it has proven valuable. For those events thinking of using Facebook for the first time I would suggest that they take time to review the policies and procedures, and see if and/ or how best it could be utilized to benefit the organization.'

If Comic-Con tends to use Facebook to disseminate information, Oktoberfest in Munich (www.facebook.com/OktoberfestMunich/info/?tab=overview), one of the world's most famous beer festivals, takes a slightly different approach. An early adopter of Facebook in 2007, information is being disseminated but they also encourage attendees to send in pictures and talk about their experience. In addition, there are numerous videos sent in by attendees made available on their YouTube page.

Comic-Con and Oktoberfest have different approaches to how they use Facebook; we are not suggesting that one is right or wrong, just noting that your event could view its Facebook page either as a means of providing information alone or also of encouraging dialogue.

As with Twitter, there are Facebook pages provided by industry publications that provide up-to-date industry news. Such general sites include: www.facebook.com/pages/Conference-News/110867218948494?sk=info and www.facebook.com/pages/Conference-and-Meetings-World/110579492314051?sk=wall—so what is the value?

Facebook is often the most popular SNS in many countries, and it appears to encourage more dialogue than Twitter. It probably, therefore, requires allocating more resources to manage it. It is also worth noting that virtually every commercial organisation we have spoken to views both Twitter and Facebook as a means of driving traffic to their website.

LinkedIn

LinkedIn serves a niche market, but as it is aimed at professionals it is very influential. Launched in 2003, by 2015 it claimed to have 400 million global users (https://press.linkedin.

com/about-linkedin), but its value is not so much in numbers as who its users are. It is simply a global network that allows professionals to communicate with each other, though each link has to be either an existing relationship or recommended by a third party. Von Rosen (2012, p. 4) defines LinkedIn as 'A social networking platform that allows you to connect, engage, and do business with other professionals by making the relationships of your business network visible and by giving you the tools you need to connect with them.' There are other online business networking sites; however, LinkedIn offers the most options and interactivity.

Von Rosen (2012) suggests that the reasons for using LinkedIn are:

- Increasing your ability to be known;
- Finding others;
- Learning new knowledge and sharing your own;
- Connecting with other LinkedIn members;
- Demonstrating your social marketing 'savvy'.

We suggest for your event the value of LinkedIn is not as a promotional tool, but as a network whereby you can make useful contacts, either to sell your event services or to help you put on an event.

Like Facebook and Twitter, LinkedIn can be used either in the form of a person or a company profile page – it is more likely to be one of these rather than a page set up just for an event.

Before creating a business profile you will need to create a personal profile (known as a professional account on LinkedIn, a bit like a virtual CV). Your LinkedIn profile is discoverable through internet searches, which means anyone in the world can view your profile. However, you have control over which parts of your profile are visible by editing which sections can be viewed by the public (Von Rosen 2012). LinkedIn is therefore a means of finding out more about your industry, promoting yourself and getting content to B2B audiences. Perhaps more importantly, LinkedIn has over 2 million groups where like-minded professionals can come together to discuss ideas, problems and news. The largest event manager-based group is The Event Planning & Event Management Group, which at the time of writing has over 305,000 members (www.linkedin.com/groups/60415/profile). These groups can be good sources of technical help or ideas for suppliers to use. Moreover, like Twitter and Facebook, people can and do respond/comment on others' posts.

LinkedIn can also be used for endorsements – so people within your network who you are connected with can endorse you for various skills, and write you recommendations that will appear on your profile. These endorsements can help to increase your credibility within certain areas.

We suggest that the value of LinkedIn is that it has blogs from event professionals discussing latest trends in the industry, and could be a useful way for potential event managers to 'problem solve' as there are many question-and-answer groups.

Pinterest

Pinterest, the visual bookmarking service launched in March 2010, had over 100 million active users by 2016 (http://expandedramblings.com/index.php/pinterest-stats/). It is a social media network that is growing rapidly, and which primarily focuses on the sharing of images including recipes, crafts, jewellery, fashion, inspirational quotes, photography and more. Pinterest has a very clear demographic with 85 per cent of users being female, and the most popular age group on Pinterest being 25 to 34 (http://expandedramblings.com/index.php/pinterest-stats).

One of the key reasons why organisations use Pinterest is that people who are referred products on Pinterest spend 70 per cent more money than visitors referred from other channels (Boris 2013). As such, this could be a useful marketing tool for your event products and services.

Pinterest allows you to create your own 'boards' to help you group images or Pins. However, Pinterest no longer accepts new boards; rather you have to choose one of the existing 1,927 boards. The most popular boards include food, fashion, religion and crafts. If your event is in these, or other fields, this may be a tool by which you can find out useful things. It is not so much used by events, but rather for event services, for example, related to weddings, planning, design ideas and marketing. The images often link to external websites providing more information. There is also an event management Pinterest page (https://uk.pinterest.com/explore/event-management/), which provides access to a range of services.

Users can also pin things from anywhere/any website, you are not limited to things that are already on Pinterest. For example, if you see something on a webpage that you like, if you have Pinterest added to your search bar, you can pin things from the page that you were on to a board in your Pinterest account. This would then be visible to anyone who searched for it or who follows you.

Serrano (2015) recommends that Pinterest can be used to create an official guide of your event, especially if it is corporate, so that it may include speakers, key features and activities. Another way that you can use Pinterest is to collect and post images from your attendees.

Discussion questions

1 You may come under pressure to automatically have a social media presence. If you are creating a new event, which SNS should you have and why? Consider what you would do for each of these different events: (a) a local community event; (b) a trade show; (c) a regional sports competition.
2 You have let the genie out of the bottle and you offer a Forum, Facebook page and accept images from attendees. Why? What are you hoping to achieve and what could go wrong?
3 You decide that you only have resources to manage one SNS. Which channel do you choose and why?
4 Just having the appropriate SNS is not enough, you need to offer good copy. What is it that makes potential attendees find, read and return to an SNS? Consider how the size and type of event might affect the answer.

Further information

Books

Fuchs, C. (2014) *Social Media: a critical introduction*, London: Sage.
Standage, T. (2014) *Writing on the Wall: social media the first 2,000 years*, London: Bloomsbury.

Websites

Social media marketing: www.wordstream.com/social-media-marketing
Event planner blog rankings: http://www.blogmetrics.org/Event_Planning
Twitter tips: www.forbes.com/sites/kenkrogue/2013/08/30/31-twitter-tips-how-to-use-twitter-tools-and-twitter-best-practices-for-business/

Online media

Tips for successful marketing through Facebook: www.business.qld.gov.au/business/running/marketing/online-marketing/using-facebook-to-market-your-business/tips-for-successful-marketing-through-facebook

Tips on LinkedIn marketing can be found at: http://blog.event.com/2014/03/top-7-tips-use-linkedin-groups-promote-event/

www.eventmanagerblog.com/eventprofs-linkedin – useful tips on Pinterest marketing: http://blog.tailwindapp.com/using-pinterest-for-events/

Chapter 10

Email

Introduction

Much of the commercial and academic focus over the past 15 to 20 years has been on the eye-catching parts of the internet, first the World Wide Web and then increasingly social networking sites (SNS). As each of the tools we discussed in the previous chapter was developed they generated significant social and media attention, and benefited from a bandwagon effect, based on the fact that they were considered by many to be the next must-have technology for businesses. At present, there is growing interest in wearable IT, 3D printing and mobile payments (such as Apple Pay), and many events may consider in the next few years whether and how to adopt them. However, we suggest that one tool has become the 'Cinderella' of internet technologies, namely email. Yet in the long run email may actually be the most powerful online tool an event has in communicating and building meaningful relationships. We argue that while email has a lower profile than other internet modalities it can be the most persuasive. We suggest that many people are more likely to respond to an email than something posted on Facebook or Twitter, and this also probably applies to direct mail sent via LinkedIn, which is arguably the same as receiving an email. This chapter will consider why and how to construct an e-direct mail campaign. It will also explain how to produce an e-newsletter that covers the development of stories, the content, format and evaluation. By the end of this chapter students will be able to:

- Identify the legislation affecting the use of email;
- Construct a coherent and effective email/message;
- Assess when to use an email campaign;
- Justify why and how to construct an e-newsletter.

Using email

The invention of email is accredited to Ray Tomlinson who was working on the American military precursor of the internet, the ARPANET. Tomlinson created email in 1971 when he used the @ symbol to denote which person and computer a message was being sent to. The technology quickly developed and expanded in use from a narrow academic circle. A detailed report by The Radicati Group (2015) found that the number of email users (both commercial and consumer) will increase from 2.6 billion in 2015 to 2.9 billion in 2019. In 2015 some 205 billion emails were sent and received each day. These figures dwarf those highlighted in the previous chapter, supporting our view that email can be a more powerful tool. To put this into perspective, The Radicati Group's research found that the average office worker now sends or receives 121 emails a day. While many people may use text messaging and SNS for personal interaction, the above figures suggest that email is still the dominant channel, especially for commercial or official communication.

Email is simply a means of sending a message electronically in digital format from one computer to another. It is a way by which event communicators can inform, persuade and seek to mobilise colleagues, participants, attendees, suppliers and interested third parties. Email is essentially a private message, the electronic form of a posted letter, but it is flexible; your event can send an email to one person (say a supplier), or to many thousands (such as past attendees) at the same time. Downes and Mui (2000) suggested that email would be a 'killer app' fundamentally changing communication, society, business and politics forever. While the jury is still out on this prediction, one of the reasons why email is ubiquitous is that it can be delivered by several technologies be it PC, tablet, mobile device or even a watch.

The basic rules outlined in Chapter 5 on direct marketing apply when using e-direct mail, though the nature of email, and the law relating to it (see below), are different.

The advantages of e-direct marketing over postal direct marketing are:

- It is significantly cheaper;
- It is quicker to set up and get responses;
- It encourages dialogue;
- Software can enable some evaluation, such as how many open the email.

For example, in the same way that we can use web analytics to measure the effect of websites, we can use email analytics to assess the impact of our emails. An event can get add-ons to its email account, such as https://bananatag.com/email-tracking/outlook/, which will track how many people open it and which links were clicked on in the email. This particular software is free to sign up for, but there are also paid-for services such as the America-based Litmus which provides a number of e-direct mail services including email analytics (https://litmus.com/). Most e-newsletter software will have some sort of analytical feature in it too.

In the same way that you can sign up to the free service, Google Analytics, the same service is available for email, for example (https://developers.google.com/analytics/devguides/collection/protocol/v1/email). This allows you to track who opens an email and which links/pictures they open. You can then assess which content and images are attracting interest and which is largely ignored, so you can make changes based on hard data not guesswork.

The main limitation with e-direct marketing is setting up and managing your own list of contacts. While each country has different laws regarding direct mail, in the UK you can buy a database for postal direct mail based, for example, on the electoral register. However, you cannot buy an email list, rather you need to create your own.

Although in danger of 'teaching grandma how to suck eggs', we feel that it is important to understand how to construct an effective email, especially to someone you do not know well, or are contacting for the first time or whose attention you have to grab quickly. We are mindful that email has developed its own style of writing and norms. It is often the first impression your event creates with someone, and getting it wrong from the outset will affect your reputation. Email can be an instant reactive communication, and we have all probably later regretted an email sent where emotion rather than rational thought has been the dominant feature. By going back to basics and making sure each email we send meets set principles we are likely to minimise any negative effects, and maximise its impact. Given that email is such a common tool this may seem unnecessary, but just look at the emails you send and receive: how many appear unattractive, are not well written and do not really require you to do anything in response?

An email has four main components: the audience; the subject title; formatting; and the message. There can also be a fifth, namely attachments.

To

The first key issue is to whom to send your email. If it is a colleague or someone involved in your event whom you know well, then this is not an issue. Where selecting the audience becomes more problematic is when you are emailing a person for the first time, or there is a large number of recipients and/or they are external to your organisation, such as with potential attendees. As a basic principle, the sort of issues we discussed in Chapter 5 on direct marketing are likely to apply here, but there may also be specific conventions or legal issues you need to be aware of with email. If you are sending out what might be referred to as a marketing email campaign, say trying to get people to attend your event, you must be fully aware of the law in the countries you are operating in and sending emails to. The approach recommended by the Direct Marketing Association (www.dma.org.uk), the UK trade body representing direct marketers, is that there are different accepted practices for postal and e-direct mail. They suggest e-marketers get permission to send an e-newsletter, so people opt-in to receive it regularly.

There is likely to be some form of anti-spam legislation that seeks to regulate against unsolicited marketing emails. For example, in the UK the main relevant piece of legislation is an EC directive from 2003 which is law, The Privacy and Electronic Communications Regulations (PECR), though the Data Protection Act 1998 can also be relevant. The PECR covers telephone, text messaging, faxes and email. The Information Commission's Office (ICO), which has the power to enforce the legislation in the courts and can impose fines of up to £500,000, provides useful advice (https://ico.org.uk/for-organisations/guide-to-pecr/introduction/what-are-pecr/). While the regulations are primarily aimed at those companies which provide a public electronic communications network/service, so-called spammers, it also applies if your event markets by email. And while most events probably already do, rather than take the risk, we suggest that you automatically comply.

PECR has two main rules, with the first applying to all emails and the second only to unsolicited marketing emails.

Rule 1:
- Your email address must not be concealed;
- Receivers must be able to contact an email address to opt out.

Rule 2:
- Marketing email messages cannot be sent unless the receiver has previously given their permission.

There is, however, a limited exception to an event's own customers, sometimes referred to as the 'soft opt-in'. As the ICO states, this means that, 'The idea is that if an individual bought something from you recently, gave you their details, and did not opt out of marketing messages, they are probably happy to receive marketing from you about similar products or services even if they haven't specifically consented. However, you must have given them a clear chance to opt out – both when you first collected their details, and in every message you send.' The soft opt-in does not apply to prospective customers.

Such legislation applies to how you might contact by email possible attendees of your event, but the same strictures do not apply to businesses you might wish to contact. Here you need to be aware of the nature of the business. The ICO advice is that sole traders and some partnerships count as individuals and so the regulation above applies to them, however it does not to apply a corporate body (though the Data Protection Act might). The ICO concludes that you can send marketing emails to companies, but it is good practice to keep a 'do not email' list of any companies that object. Remember this applies only to the UK, in other countries different rules probably apply.

We could find evidence of anti-spam legislation in about 40 countries, but an excellent summary of the relevant global legislation is provided by Lionbridge, a global marketing and language provider (http://content.lionbridge.com/know-global-email-regulations). What is important is to know the legislation that applies in the country you are sending from, and if applicable the country you are sending to.

You might sometimes decide to cc (carbon copy) people, only do so if you feel that it is important for them to know about the email. You do not want to be known for overloading people with unnecessary information, as they may then ignore the email you really want them to read. You are unlikely to use cc when emailing potential attendees, but you might copy in staff or suppliers so that they are informed of what is going on.

Blind carbon copy (bcc) is a more controversial tool, which prevents the recipient from knowing to whom else an email is sent. This is perfectly reasonable if sent to customers so they do not get others' email addresses, but if the recipients know each other it is possible it might be considered discourteous. It also raises issues of what your salutation will be as you cannot use a name, and so this is no longer a personalised communication. Therefore, we generally advise using a mail merge so that each communication to attendees is personalised.

Before you actually send your email, double-check that all you want to send it to are included.

If you fear that your event is, or may become, a victim of spam, then Spamhaus (www.spamhaus.org/organization) is a non-profit international organisation that can provide advice.

Subject

An email without a subject is more likely to fall foul of anti-spam software, so always have a subject. Your subject should be viewed like a headline.

The prime purpose of the subject is to encourage the recipient to open it, and so you need to think carefully about what would be attractive. Research by MailChimp identified which types of subjects are more likely to be opened (http://kb.mailchimp.com/campaigns/previews-and-tests/best-practices-for-email-subject-lines). They advise that those which are short (50 characters or less), tailored and descriptive are more likely to be opened, and that those which are cheesy, use jargon or overused words are less likely to be opened.

For most people the subject is the first impression they have of you, and can be key to whether they open the email or not. MacArthur (2016) assessed 17 successful email lines, suggesting the five most successful subject styles are:

1 Reason why lines – such as five reasons why you should attend.
2 Benefit lines – have fun while you save money.
3 Question lines – do you want a new job?
4 Testimonial lines – why the Prime Minister supports this charity fundraiser.
5 How-to lines – how to make money from your event.

We would add that key to any marketing campaign is to test, and we recommend trying out different subject headings to see which is most likely to be opened. For example, you could use the email analytics software we suggest above and send out two or more mailings using different headings so you can test which is more likely to be opened.

Formatting

Keep the format simple so that it is readable; use one of the more common fonts that PCs and Macs offer such as Arial, Calibri or Tahoma. While it is possible to use a much wider range of fonts, especially if your event has a particular tone, most receivers will want it to be simple. So use black or dark blue colour type (and stick to one colour only), size 11 or 12, and avoid fancy background schemes. We would also suggest avoiding the use of capital letters (this is considered to be shouting), but use bold for some terms. When including hyperlinks within an email these should appear as a different colour, usually blue, and then pink once they have been clicked. They should also include text to explain what they link to (images should also be included as best practice for those who use screen readers or are partially sighted).

The message

Emails have developed their own conventions and style in that they are short and fairly relaxed. You are not trying to replicate a letter, rather an email briefly gets across your message or it sets up an attachment or somewhere else to go for more detailed information. The advice that follows is based on a recipient whom you either do not know or who is not a personal friend and the relationship is essentially professional:

- The salutation. One of the authors recently received a fundraising appeal which began with 'Dear list subscriber', not unsurprisingly no donation was forthcoming. Some people keep emails very informal and start with 'Hi', but if you are trying to win business/gain attendees a more formal start may be appropriate, for example 'Dear' and then insert their name. However, if you are using a gender term such as Ms, Mrs or Mr, make sure you get it right, and if you are not sure of the gender use the full name. One alternative we use is to say 'Good morning John'. It is just a slightly more personal way of starting and usually elicits a similar response. The purpose of the opening is to be polite and respectful.
- Although emails are more relaxed than letters, double-check all the details. Never send an email until you have carefully proofed it. Is everything factually correct? There must be no typographical errors or misspelling of names/places. Any mistakes will immediately undermine the effect of your email. Take your email seriously, like any other piece of writing, and we would recommend as with other documents that you read it aloud to check that it is getting your message across in the way you want.
- Avoid jargon and text speak, rather write your sentences as you would for a letter, brochure or flyer, though note that your paragraphs may be shorter than a letter.
- Keep it short, the attachment or web hyperlink is the place for the detail, an email is in effect an executive summary. For most emails we would recommend keeping them to three or four short paragraphs, and avoid, unless necessary, writing so much text that the recipient has to scroll down.
- Provide a polite and appropriate closing such as 'Regards', 'Yours sincerely' or 'Best'. If the authors start with 'Good morning', we tend to end with 'All the best'.
- Provide a signature. The signature at the end of the email acts almost like a letterhead, and should help with a professional tone. We suggest keeping it fairly simple: your name, job title and contact details. If you have a latest product, achievement or event you might

hyperlink this, but avoid overly long or 'humorous or wacky' signatures that you think reflect your personal style.

Attachments

Very often the email acts as the hors d'oeuvres to whet the appetite, with any attachments as the main meal. An attachment is simply a file in whatever format you choose that is attached to the email. However, be aware that not all email systems work the same way, so unless you know differently, it is probably best to put the file in one of the basic formats such as Plain Text, RTF or PDF. We would always recommend PDF as you then know that the recipient will see what you see and that the formatting will not change in between. We also suggest that before you send the email do check the size of the attachment to ensure that it will not clog up the recipient's inbox.

Email policies

In the same way that most businesses have a telephone policy, such that calls must be answered within four rings, we suggest that you devise an email policy for how you handle inbound emails. Some organisations offer an auto message reply that says something along the lines of 'We have received your email and will be responding in due time'. We are not convinced by such messages, rather we would prefer that you have a time frame by which you reply to emails, say two working days. This is especially important if you are dealing with attendees. Remember that compared to letters, email has changed our perceptions on how long it is before we expect to receive a reply.

E-newsletters

E-newsletters are an application of email, in the form of a newsletter offering information and sometimes special offers. They act as a 'reminder facility' (Ollier 1998), whereby stakeholders regularly 'hear' from an event. They can be in a variety of formats, such as an email with the

---

10.1 Tip box

Managing email

The old time management system of one-touch paper works well for email. The idea is that rather than shuffle work around several times before you act on it, you should handle the paper once. Thus when email comes in, it makes sense to keep on top of it by trying to deal with it as soon as you can. You can use Outlook to create folders where you store emails that have been successfully dealt with, and any that are left in your inbox are pending/live. The authors have thousands of emails of completed work in Outlook folders, but typically only 50–100 'live' emails in the inbox of outstanding work. This is a manageable number and easy to check whether you need to chase up on something.

newsletter as an attachment or hyperlinks to websites, or a very common approach is to have a short taster paragraph and then the reader needs to click to the full story. Software is available (usually built in to the e-newsletter software) that allows the sender to know exactly what the receiver has done with the e-newsletter, has it been opened or not, which pages/stories have gained most traffic and has it been deleted? One of the more popular products for producing e-newsletters to a set design style is MailChimp (www.mailchimp.com), which, for example, allows you to look at the open and click-through rates of your e-newsletter. Jackson (2008b) found that the use of an e-newsletter before and during an election campaign could make the difference between being elected or not, so over a sustained period this is potentially a persuasive channel. E-newsletters need not be used just as a one-way route from sender to receiver; with the touch of the reply button the receiver can send back their solicited or unsolicited views. Indeed, if you send out an e-newsletter you are tacitly inviting subscribers to respond. Though we note that some companies send out e-newsletters from email addresses you cannot reply to, rather inviting you to respond to a specific contact address.

We argue that e-newsletters can provide a number of tangible benefits for events:

- It is cheaper and quicker to produce and send a newsletter by email than post;
- It can build up relationships with your key audiences;
- It can encourage feedback or market intelligence;
- It can be an effective means of promoting offers.

Some organisations use e-newsletters as a means of promoting their event expertise to events. For example, Cvent who provide software solutions to event planners send out a monthly e-newsletter to some 130,000 event planners in America (www.cvent.com/en/supplier-network/email-newsletter.shtml). Interestingly, and rather unusually, although they provide their own copy they also use this as an income stream by making it a means by which 'sponsors' can access their subscribers by offering their content in set slots.

It is worth noting, however, that there are possible downsides to having an e-newsletter. There are two essential issues. First, to use an e-newsletter effectively does require committing resources (essentially building and maintaining the database, and identifying the content). These need not be onerous, but cannot be ignored. Second, sending an e-newsletter is no guarantee of success. Nowadays many people subscribe to a range of e-newsletters and then end up deleting them when they arrive. In large part this is either because really they did not want the e-newsletter in the first place, its content adds nothing of value or the time lag between editions is too great (or in some cases too frequent). An article in 2013 by Boost Blog Traffic (http://boostblogtraffic.com/create-a-newsletter/) argues that e-newsletters have been replaced by SNS. We understand the point this site is making and it is valid; e-newsletters are not a panacea, but we note that Boost Blog Traffic collects email addresses, so even though they do not have an e-newsletter as such, they do recognise the importance of an email database. We would certainly agree that e-newsletters are not appropriate for every event, but we would disagree that SNS has automatically replaced them, as online audiences are heterogeneous with a range of different likes and requirements.

How to produce an effective e-newsletter

We suggest that there are five components to creating an effective e-newsletter: its purpose; the database; management; content; and analysis.

Why have an e-newsletter?

As with any form of the internet the absolute first decision to make is to agree what the purpose is for having it? Do not decide to have one just because your competitors do, you need to know what tangible benefits it should provide you with. It is not a one-off tool; rather, you will need to offer an e-newsletter on a regular basis. An e-newsletter is a slow burn, it will not lead to overnight success, but it can be a key factor in changing the relationship between a contact or customer and an organisation. This implies that an organisation using an e-newsletter places a high priority on building relationships with key audiences (usually but not only customers). The intention is to build, over time, trust and loyalty, so that a customer will spend more money over a lifetime. There is, then, a clear link with relationship marketing.

You need to set clear goals, which might include:

- Raise awareness of your event;
- Change the reputation of your event;
- Increase sales/attendance;
- Secure market intelligence for new events.

The Dorset Chamber of Commerce and Industry seems to view its e-newsletter as a benefit of membership, stating that events can be promoted to its members (small and medium-sized companies) via its e-newsletter (www.dcci.co.uk/events/events-management).

The database

The basics of this we have dealt with in Chapter 5 on direct marketing, but the key question is to decide who should be your audience. Should it be all of your customers or only those at some events? Having decided this will shape the content of the e-newsletter.

The initial source of the database will come from your existing customer base (but take into account relevant legislation concerning permission marketing). However, you will need to expand beyond this. Ways this could be achieved might include:

- Display a subscribe button prominently on the home page of your website;
- You could put a 'share with a friend' button on the e-newsletter so it can be forwarded on;
- Promote it via other communication tools, for example include a link in your email signature;
- If you provide special offers via any of your communication tools, these could require an email address;
- Collect email addresses at events; be they your own or others', such as exhibitions that you attend.

To a degree the nature of the database depends on how sophisticated you wish to be. One simple option is to provide just one e-newsletter that goes to all subscribers whoever they are. Another is to provide a tick box when they subscribe to which e-newsletter they wish to receive. This could be done by topic, such as food, music, events-based on geography etc. More likely it would be by type of person such as corporate, individual or whatever is appropriate.

Management

Having decided why you need an e-newsletter, the first detailed issue to address is to decide how frequent it will be. We recommend that you plan at least a year ahead when it will be published (and roughly what each issue will focus on). It would make sense, where possible, for each issue to be spaced out broadly equally, say three months apart, but the type of factors you might take into account include:

- The size, frequency and nature of your event. If your event is annual you may only need to send an email out twice a year, but more frequently if it is monthly. If you have a lot of events or the audience is large then you might send it out more frequently.
- Timeliness – will you set dates and find content to fill it, or will it be content-led based on particular time periods in the cycle of your event when you have something to say?
- Your resources – it takes time to produce; if you are a small event with a small team responsible for all tasks it could be a burden. Whereas if you have a dedicated marketing team this could easily fit in with their other tasks.
- Integrating your communication – what other communication have you planned and how does it fit with this? It could be that you want to send your e-newsletter out at a quiet time when you have no other activity, or you may decide you want to send it out at busy times to reinforce other messages. Indeed, some organisations send out an e-newsletter at the end of the year as a thank you for being involved with the company/have a good festive period.
- You certainly might think of using an e-newsletter before, during and after your event.

Obviously, a key management issue is who is going to do what and by when? As noted above, you will require someone who can collate, input and update the database, but who will be responsible for the content? And, more importantly, how will they collect ideas for what the e-newsletter will contain? We recommend that you select one person responsible for getting ideas, and that they need to talk to those people organising key aspects of the event to identify what will be happening and when. Key to this will be persuading people of the value of the stories you capture. You will then need someone to write up the stories (this need not be the same person who collects the stories but often will be).

Probably the last setup management decision is to decide what type of format you will use. It is rare that e-newsletters are in brochure format where you access all the material in one go; more common is the use of links for the reader to click to access the material. We normally use a short taster sentence, often with a thumbnail picture and then the reader has to open the link to read the whole article.

Content

On the internet, content is king and the currency of an e-newsletter is that it adds value or provides something usually not available elsewhere. This could be additional information or a special offer. For example, D&S Events, based at Donington Park Grand Prix race course, specialise in motor-based events. They produce a newsletter every two to three months which might offer driving tips, special vouchers for courses and promote their upcoming programme of events (www.nfegroup.co.uk/newsletters-library). So do not just promote your events, have something interesting to say that adds value. The reader of an e-newsletter is looking to get material such as offers that they cannot get elsewhere (Chaffey 2003). For example, the Oake Manor Golf Course in Somerset in England encourages people to sign up to their e-newsletter on the basis of 'You'd be amazed at the activities and offers available' (http://oakemanorevents. co.uk/signup-to-our-free-email-newsletter).

General principles to apply with your content include:

- Needs to be regular;
- Provide the subscriber with value: essentially it provides something that they cannot easily get elsewhere;

- Be easy to read;
- Cover a range of topics;
- Consider encouraging feedback;
- Use it if a quick response is required.

Only send out e-newsletters when you have something to say, rather than rigorously stick to a date, say every third Thursday of the month. Furthermore, consider how they provide added value for the subscriber (not all of the content will, such as the news, but ask yourself the question).

You should also consider:

1 When a new subscriber signs up, automatically send them the most recent version.
2 Have a privacy statement.
3 At the end of each e-newsletter make it possible for recipients to unsubscribe. For example, at the bottom of the e-newsletter the authors produce we have the following three links which allow us to keep our data up to date:

>   Add us to your address book
>   Unsubscribe from this list
>   Update subscription preferences.

E-newsletter task

The V&A Museum of Childhood (www.vam.ac.uk/moc/) uses e-newsletters as a means of letting people know when it has events and exhibitions. Those who sign up receive six emails a year that provide details of forthcoming activities. In addition, the V&A Museum of Childhood cross-sells by encouraging people to sign up to e-newsletters from the main V&A Museum and Shop as well.

Your task

If you were the marketing manager of an organisation which holds a series of events at regular points of the year, such as a training company, art gallery or charity that was considering an e-newsletter, how would you address the following:

1 What would be the purpose of such a newsletter?
2 Would your focus be on general information of what is on, or would it be to promote special offers?
3 Would you want this to be a one-way communication tool, or could you develop it to encourage feedback, such as using attendees' pictures and stories?
4 How would you evaluate how effective the e-newsletter has been?

Evaluation

You need to note how subscribers respond to the e-newsletter, and what impact it might have on their relationship with your event, for example, do they buy tickets or take up an offer? This brings us back to the point made earlier about what analytics you might have, but we can clearly see that there are certain factors you might consider in assessing how successful your e-newsletter is:

1 What its purpose is – if it is more promotional and reputational the effect of this is harder to measure, but if more sales-led it is easier for you to assess how many purchased the offer contained.
2 Bouncebacks – how many of the emails sent out were not delivered? If this is a high percentage this suggests problems with either how up to date your list is, or that you are falling foul of spam filters and may need to address factors such as your subject.
3 Open rate – simply the number who opened the e-newsletter. This gives a very basic figure.
4 Click-through rate – this is usually more useful as it tells you which links recipients open and so which is the more interesting content. Analyse this and change your content appropriately.
5 Sales – how many bought the offers?

Discusion questions

1 Many, especially younger, people prefer to communicate with their friends and social groups by SNS. When and why should you rely more on email?
2 We tend to take email for granted, using it as a random, reactive and tactical tool when we 'fire off an email'. However, how can email be used as a planned, strategic and powerful tool for your event?
3 If your e-direct mail campaign includes overseas email addresses, what are the implications for you?
4 E-newsletters require resources to manage and produce regularly. What sort of events are likely to benefit from using an e-newsletter and why?

Further information

Book

Jenkins, S. (2009) *The Truth About Email Marketing*, Upper Saddle River, NJ: Pearson.

Article

Schlesinger, M. (2015) '4 creative email marketing ideas', *Employee Benefit Adviser*, 13 (2): 22.

Websites

Producing e-newsletters:

www.campaigner.com/resource-center/getting-started/top-5-tips-on-writing-great-email-news-letters.aspx
www.dmnews.com/email-marketing/section/223/
www.dmnews.com/making-direct-mail-and-e-mail-work-together/article/166004/

PART IV

MULTIMEDIA

This section considers the range of technologies that events use to promote themselves.

Chapter 11

Video and audio

Introduction

A lot of what we have discussed thus far has primarily been word based, in this chapter we shall turn to sound and moving images: audio and video. This is often referred to as AV: audio visual. This covers the technical aspects of putting on an event, and even sometimes the actual delivery of the event itself. It can include sound, music, presentations and the environment, such as lighting and moving images. It was within the lifetime of the authors that video was essentially its own technology, requiring separate hardware such as cameras and projectors. Thus, video was the preserve of a few professionals and hobbyists. Now a wide range of communication technologies, including your smartphone (cell phone), can be used to film and download video materials, which makes video an accessible and popular tool. In the context of events, the use of sound and moving images showcasing previous activities can create very powerful messages. This chapter will start by explaining why an event should use AV, moving on to how an event manager should work with venues and suppliers in using AV. We will then look at how events can best apply first audio and then video, and the impact they can have on event attendees. We shall finish by linking with some of the lessons from social media that apply, by focusing on the possible use of vlogging by event managers. By the end of the chapter students should be able to:

- Understand why you should use AV;
- Brief an AV supplier for your needs;
- Assess the impact of AV on the event experience;
- Identify how to create a vlog.

What is AV?

Many of us may consider AV more in terms of the electrical goods that provide us with our home entertainment, such as an MP3 player, a wide-screen television and tablets. However, as an event manager AV is a broader term that addresses the technical equipment you need to help the logistical aspects of your event, which shape the experience attendees receive. If your attendees need to see or hear your event there is a very good likelihood that some form of AV will be needed. Typically, the term AV implies that you will provide both sound and vision, though it is possible that you might only be offering one or the other. AV covers, for example, creating presentations, setting the ambience and allowing for interaction between participants/attendees through film, music and microphones. For example, the short powerful TED talks (www.ted.com) designed to spread ideas make heavy use of AV. You have probably seen many examples where a charismatic TED speaker is wandering around a stage using a hi-tech microphone to speak to their audience, and in the background projected on to massive screens are fantastic visuals to which the speaker is referring. Without AV these talks would not have the same effect.

AV is now central to the delivery of almost all events. Think of an event you have attended where there has not been AV. There will be very few, possibly none at all. At its simplest level this might be the use of a sound system to play music or give out announcements at a local fête, through to events that are delivered by technology such as video conferencing. Such AV is fairly basic and central to the event, but we have also seen an explosion in the visual aspects at major events, especially musical and sports. For example, each year some 175,000 spectators attend the five-day Glastonbury festival, which has 27 different areas (www.glastonburyfestivals. co.uk). We take for granted that a music festival needs a good sound system, but video now plays a key part. At some of the most popular sites such as the Pyramid stage at Glastonbury it would be impossible with the naked eye to see the detail of what is going on from the back. Thus, the use of huge video screens allows everyone, irrespective of how far they are from

11.1 What is AV?

John Hibdige, Production Manager of JHAV (www.jh-av.co.uk), suggests that 'AV is an all-encompassing term for Audio Visual which can include: sound, lighting, video, staging and possibly even theming. It is difficult to define because it means different things to different people. For example, if you are in corporate events it might simply mean a microphone in a conference suite with a projector. However, if you were putting on a live music event in the middle of a field it would involve lighting, security, screens and sound systems.

AV is a headline for a lot of sub-headings.

For some of our clients AV can mean "magic". It depends on what sector a client is from as to what AV means to them:

- For corporate events it is what they think a client needs for the presentation or conference to happen, for example, the means by which a video can be shown.
- For the live sector, such as music gigs, AV means everything that is required to put on a show.
- For an exhibitor it is everything they require to show off their product, so typically a PA (public address) system, lighting to show off their stand and probably power to run demonstrations and screens to play product videos.'

the stage, to be able to see. Even for larger indoor music gigs it is common now to have such screens. They might just be a camera pointing at the stage so all can follow what is happening, or the band may have their own visual show playing along with their music. Whichever is the case, videos can enhance the viewing experience at music-based events.

We also see that video has had a major impact on elite sport and major sporting events. Venues that offer professional sport in, for example, baseball, basketball, American football, cricket, rugby, athletics and football (soccer) all frequently have screens where fans can see the action and sometimes replays. It is also used in some of the major swimming and diving meets so that spectators can see what is happening underwater. While, like with music, this can enhance the viewing, the use of visuals in sport can go beyond this. For example, we have all seen someone watching a match and suddenly noticing themselves on the big screen, and how they react. They suddenly have their ten seconds of fame, enhancing their experience of and engagement with the event. Many basketball games employ a kiss cam that focuses on couples kissing, and famously witnessed US President Barack Obama and his wife Michelle sharing a 'smooch' during the USA versus Brazil basketball game in July 2012. In a more infamous example at a basketball game in Chicago in January 2015, as the kiss cam centred on one couple the boyfriend refused to get off his phone, leading to an argument between the couple. The day was saved by the team mascot, Benny the Bull, who picked the lady up and swept her away to loud applause. In both examples kiss cam kept the crowd interested at a time when no action was occurring on court.

There are other ways in which technology can help enhance the attendee experience. At the 2015 Rugby World Cup attendees could pay £10 for match day radio, which included listening to the referee when he spoke to colleagues via his microphone. This gave subscribers access to a facet of the game that other spectators did not have. However, AV also caused some problems for the Rugby World Cup. The referee has access to a video referee that he can call on for some close calls. In one early match Fiji were awarded a try and just as the kicker was going to kick the extra conversion points, the big video showed the try again, and clearly the player dropped the ball. The crowd reacted and only then did the referee consult the video referee, and the try was overturned. Here a feature provided for the benefit of paying spectators actually ended up having a material effect on the final score of the game.

Very occasionally AV can play a vital symbolic role way beyond the confines of the event. On Friday 13 November 2015 terrorists struck in Paris, including at the Parc de Princes a major sporting venue, and killed 130 people at several locations. On Tuesday 17 November the French football team played England at Wembley Stadium. A component part of this match, in a sign of solidarity against terrorists, was that the English fans were encouraged to sing the French national anthem, La Marseillaise, before the match started. The organisers put the unfamiliar words on to stadium screens, and in addition, to keep the beat, a recorded version was also piped out on the public address system. Without AV the symbolism of this moment would not have been as impactful.

Another way in which video has played a key role in expanding the sporting experience has been the creation of fan festivals. These are usually events put on at a major competition for fans who do not have tickets for a match, but who can watch it with others via a big screen. Like television viewers the experience is second-hand, but like those at the event the experience is also highly social within a crowd of enthusiasts. At the 2002 football world cup in South Korea a number of unofficial fan fests proved very popular, and FIFA introduced their first official fans fests at the 2006 World Cup in Germany. At these fests thousands of fans can watch games live via the big screen. The concept of spectators gathering together to watch was also applied to the royal pageants such as the Queen's Diamond Jubilee in 2012.

The examples above are primarily examples from major events, but we suggest that the principles behind them can be relevant for smaller events too.

CASE STUDY

Using AV

JHAV (www.jh-av.co.uk) provides tailored technical solutions for your event, from hiring a single item of equipment through to full event production. Production Manager John Hibdige explains what they do, and how to get the best out of an AV supplier.

'More and more clients are seeing us, and other AV companies, as a one-stop shop. They are expecting us to be able to provide all of the services they require. Rarely will a client come and ask for just one service from us, and then go to other suppliers for the rest of their AV needs. Now they look for us to manage the whole process, in other words provide a complete solution to all of their technical needs. Thus we will typically provide all technical services, which can include subcontracting in other suppliers for elements that we may not be able to directly support.

Clients want a supplier to help them achieve what they want to do. For example, they might have a crazy idea and want to know if it is possible. Normally the answer is dependent upon what they can afford, what is feasible and technically possible. Clients want help in achieving their dreams and aspirations. Sometime people don't know what they want and that's where we have to work with them to help unpick their vision.

The fundamental thing about how AV can be used is determined by the nature of the event, the venue and what the event manager and client want to achieve. The client comes to us because they need our support to help them achieve their vision. We therefore need to know what the client wants, so we ask questions and try to understand the end outcome they want to achieve as well as using our experience to guide them through the process. This is why we always try to have site visits; it allows us to test the feasibility of the project. It is a partnership between the AV supplier and the client, and sometimes the venue, to create something that is possible within budget. Quite often we will produce drawings and visuals to share with the client, based on these discussions, prior to deciding on the final proposal, sometimes two people can interpret the same idea in totally different ways, visuals can really help to avoid this. Also they help to design the event, manage layouts and overcome problems in advance of getting to site.

The relationship between event manager/client and the AV supplier can be one that grows over many years of events. One thing to ensure is that new ideas and innovations are made. It is far too easy for this relationship to produce very similar events year on year. We like to try new ideas, suggest innovations and help to keep events looking and feeling current.'

Table 11.1 Why should your event use AV?

Core reasons	Application
Logistics	Communication with staff.
Attendee experience	Add to the visual, aural and sensory perceptions.
Theme/atmosphere	Support a theme.
Income generation	Offer new or differentiated products.
Product requirement	Sound for a music event, lighting for a play or pictures for a lecture.
Secure feedback	Use tablets with questionnaires.

Having provided an insight as to how AV might be used, we shall now identify the core reasons why an event might use AV. Table 11.1 identifies why you would need AV and how it might be used.

As Table 11.1 shows, AV can help with the logistics, planning and running of an event more efficiently. We also recognise that for some events, such as music festivals, public marches and trade shows sound, lighting and images are central to the event provision: without them there is no event. However, perhaps more importantly AV can shape the very 'product' of an event. We have also noted a new development, that of encouraging feedback. Therefore, it is fairly easy to ask attendees to complete a questionnaire on a tablet while at the event. For some events AV is core, whereas for others it is supportive, enhancing the experience.

In the future we are likely to see more of the immersive events, utilising video and augmented reality to create 4D experiences, just as we are seeing in cinemas and theme parks. Event managers are looking for the latest developments to enhance the experiences they are giving their end clients.

What can AV do for an event?

We suggest that AV can help you in a number of ways:

- Complement an event and tie in with marketing and branding concepts, which may include colours and styles;
- Improve the impact and clarity of message. For example, with a bigger screen more attendees can see what is happening, with a better sound system the audience can hear the speaker;
- Improve functionality;
- AV can also enhance an event.

However, AV has limitations, you cannot make a bad presenter look good. You may be surprised to know how widespread presentation coaching is in business management where the presentations are critical to the success of a company. To work out how AV can help your event it is important to ask a series of questions. For example, if you are organising an all-day conference, in a seminar conference room, with 50 delegates, you need to think 'What do I need?' This is likely to include asking about: the power available in the room; size of stage;

access routes in and out of the venue; how many speakers will be presenting; will there be videos/presentations; will speakers be using a Mac or a PC laptop? All of these are linked to the AV package that you will ask your AV company to supply to fulfil your needs.

Another example would be if you are putting on a one-day music event in a farmer's field, then the first questions to ask are not necessarily about the sound and lighting. Rather, you need first to turn the field into a venue. The initial focus is on licensing, security, site logistics such as welfare, fencing, power and access issues, and only once all of that is in place would you look to the sound, lighting, stages, etc.

AV, venues and suppliers

It is possible that you might buy some of the AV you need such as laptops, microphones, lighting and projectors, but you are much more likely to hire in any equipment you need. You might also need to hire the personnel required to set it up and operate it, which is especially probable as an event gets bigger or more complicated. You are most likely to have three main sources of AV: the venue; an equipment supplier; and a specialist AV agency.

For many events, especially smaller ones such as weddings, conferences and auctions, the venue will normally have, and set up, AV such as sound and presentations for a fee (or it may be included as part of the overall price). Even for many larger events, a specialist venue is more likely to have the appropriate equipment, for example a play visiting a theatre will bring with them some equipment, but probably not the lighting, sound or dry ice.

CASE STUDY

How to choose your AV supplier

John Hibdige of JHAV suggests that, 'The first thing is to know what you want to achieve. As a supplier we will first try to establish what a client wants to achieve, what type of event it is and what are their expectations? This will then shape what we are likely to suggest in terms of packages and prices.

Asking for three quotes is normal in the industry. This gives you something to compare, as there are often variations. The cheapest is not always best option, there is a lot of variety in terms of AV equipment used and therefore you need to establish what your event needs to achieve, the results you desire within your budget. What we suggest is that you should work with a supplier whom you feel you can trust, and that you feel will best offer you the service you require. To identify such a supplier we suggest that you look for one who appreciates what you are trying to achieve, and comes up with solutions to help you with this. A good AV supplier wants your event to do well, be successful and build a relationship for the next event.

We tend to offer three different tiers to our quotes. The first is the premium package with high-end equipment, as an example. The second meets all of the

---

requirements and specifications, without extras. The third is the more cost-effective solution.

For example, if we were looking at an awards ceremony the premium option might have additional features, such as the use of social media and screens that attendees can interact with, additional theming and HD screens. The second option would meet all of the requirements and functionality required but may, for example, have standard definition projectors rather than HD projectors specified in the premium package. The lower cost approach would probably have a smaller stage, smaller or fewer screens, less lighting equipment and other technology to create the atmosphere; in essence it would be a pop-up awards ceremony. For a first-time event we may look to offer additional discount on our packages to help the event grow. Sometimes this can mean starting with a lower-cost package, we help them establish the event and look to enhance the offer each year. More and more AV companies try to build events with their clients, so it is more of a partnership.

One of the biggest problems is how to compare the prices in AV quotations. You will never see an exact comparison. The different prices are likely to reflect the type and quality of equipment used, the nature, experience or size of their teams and logistics. It is also important to be aware that some suppliers may have hidden costs. It is important, therefore, to find out exactly what is included in the price, and what extras there may be such as call-outs, extra microphones, screens etc. Sometimes the price of the equipment in the quote is attractively priced to get the business and build the relationship. Often the discount initially offered is not extended to any additional equipment added to the event, and is charged at full rate. This is practice that we avoid, and links back to making sure that the AV company is aware of all of your requirements, we totally understand that events have last-minute changes, and requirements do change, therefore you need to be flexible.

One of the things that can be a surprise to new event managers is the consideration that needs to be given to costs such as hotels and food for crew working on the event, especially if the timings of the event dictate that they need to do very long days which may include a long travel before arriving on site and after the event has finished. In most circumstances the event would cover the costs of refreshments, food and hotels but it is always good to establish whether this is the case early on as it will be built into other costs if not.

Setup and de-rig time can often affect a quotation and the feasibility of event AV. It is important to establish when all suppliers are setting up. For example, if you are organising a single evening gala event then the food and beverage team may want to start setting up the tables earlier in the day but this may affect AV setup and the basic logistics of getting AV equipment into a room. This is where good communication between suppliers, the venue and client is key to establish a schedule that works for everyone. For example, sometimes we would set up the day before if the venue is available or we work overnight or start very early, but all of these options would have an impact on the price for the labour element of the quote and possibly the costs from the venue. The answer to such questions will determine the exact price quoted. Even access requirements can affect a quotation. For example, if you are holding an event on the second floor with only a small lift then additional crew may be required to set up and de-rig.

When creating our quotations we often provide a full breakdown of each area or element so a client can see the full breakdown, this is particularly effective when there are elements the client isn't sure they want or can fit into their budget. Some quotations require detailed equipment specification listed, whereas others require a package-only approach. Again, this highlights the need for AV companies to be flexible and work with the client's needs and specifications.

Sometimes there are unexpected changes that might incur additional costs, such as additional microphones, a lot of these costs can be managed. For example, when working on the initial quote you might ask if the PA system (public address system) could cover up to 300 people, even if you are initially budgeting for 250 – this builds in scope for change. Or say an extra microphone has been built into the quote, an extra speaker is added, does the client want to use the spare and hope nothing goes wrong or order another microphone? If all of the other microphones are not being used, then an answer could be 'use the spare', but such questions affect the final cost and are related to the impact that it has to the continuity, and redundancy is always built into the event costs.

When you are looking to choose an AV supplier, ask for examples of similar events they have worked on. If they have no experience in your field and this will be their first type of this event, then you need to consider whether you will be happy with taking this risk. Always ask questions and gauge their responses. The fly-by-night operatives will probably try to steer you to the solutions that work for them, rather than address what is best for you. It is also worthwhile finding out if there is a dedicated production manager who will be dealing with your event, and get to know them, if this is your first event with a company or it's a new venue there is no harm in meeting up to discuss the requirements face to face.'

An important part of both getting a quote and the actual logistics of your event is the site visit. John observes:

If the supplier knows the event and the venue well, or the requirements are simply for a 'standard' package of AV equipment, such as microphones and projector, then a site visit might not be needed. However, for the vast majority of events a site visit prior to the quote is essential. It allows the event manager to meet and get to know the supplier and for both to ask very precise questions to work out what is wanted and the possible options. With a big new event, say an awards ceremony, it is quite common to have another site visit after the contract is signed, especially as some details such as the room layout might change. Site visits can also be essential to establish the site logistics, access and setup times that ultimately affect the price and overall event feasibility and schedule.

The site visit is key. We always view this as if we are doing an event abroad and it's not possible to return before the event. Therefore, we need to ask all the questions we can, and take all possible measurements we might conceivably need and walk through the venue as if the event was happening. For example, is the lift big enough to get the equipment in or will it have to be carried up the stairs and through a narrow corridor? Or can you hang lighting on the ceiling and what is the height of the ceiling?

Using audio

When we use the term audio we mean a number of things. Most commonly we refer to how an event uses sound. This could be the technical aspects of how the organisers communicate with one another, such as radios or more likely how the event itself uses sound as part of its 'product'. At a rock concert this is fairly obvious, you want to be able to hear the singer and all the different musicians, and at a political rally you want to be able to hear what the speakers have to say. One of the authors recently walked past a mass rally in Cardiff city centre. The banners carried by protestors were clear, but when we stopped to hear what the speakers were saying it was impossible to make out, despite standing only ten metres away. Poor use of a sound system totally undermined the message the marchers were trying to get across. Whereas, conversely, the street DJs at the Notting Hill Carnival use solely the loudness, clarity and quality of their sound systems to attract people to listen to their music.

Music can be used to help set the ambience and themes of an event. So theatre performances might use their soundtrack playing softly in the background as people are coming in. Shocktober Fest (www.halloweenattractions.co.uk/locations/crawley/shocktoberfest) is an event based on Halloween that uses 'spooky' noises around their site to help add to the attendees' 'fear'. At awards ceremonies winners walk up to music – sometimes their own if it is a music awards event – or maybe a song that has some link to what they have won an award for.

Charities in the UK have been able to use the radio to make appeals for funds. Each week there is a short appeal for money for a charity broadcast on Radio 4. Typically, these use a well-known celebrity who makes an emotional appeal for financial support. During 2015 these raised £138 million for charities (www.bbc.co.uk/charityappeals). Another use of audio is within marketing of events to use radio as an advertising medium. Radio 'remains the world's most ubiquitous medium, and is certainly the one with the widest reach and penetration' (Pease and Dennis 1995: xvi). There are more than 40,000 radio stations in the world, far more than television, with radio being the most accessible. There are more people in Africa and Asia that listen to and own a radio than a television set, as it can be used without a source of electricity – making them cheaper to buy and operate (Hendy 2013).

When you are thinking about how you use audio, be it at the event or if radio is broadcasting it, we suggest a checklist to work out how you will use it:

- Who is your audience? What sort of music and sounds are they likely to prefer?
- What is the message you are trying to convey? Then choose music or sounds that support this. Can you present your message using sound?
- How will the audience receive and understand your message that the sound is conveying? How does sound contribute to the event experience?

Local radio stations often work with large local and regional events to broadcast parts of the event live. For example, in 2012 Professor Splash dived from a 30-foot-high platform into 12 inches of milk at the Royal Cornwall Show, an outdoor agricultural show. His show lasted about 30 minutes and the local radio station had two presenters on site explaining what was happening.

It is fairly rare for national radio stations to work in partnership with events. One obvious exception is the BBC and Glastonbury, but the link is with all of the BBC, its television, radio and online coverage, not just radio. Here presenters and programmes are on site and all or sections of their show broadcast live from some part of the Glastonbury Festival. More common are associations between local radio stations and significant local events. For example, Radio Kent, a local BBC station, each year broadcasts some of it shows live from the Kent County Show. This is a three-day agricultural show and given the rural nature of the population of Kent the station presumably believes that its listeners are interested in this event.

Video

Video can be used in multiple ways in order to create awareness about your organisation, a product or a service that you are providing. Video can help capture the personality of your business, due to the world being a visual place (Langton and Campbell, 2011); this can help your business connect with its target audience by creating an emotional relationship. This can be done using theming, music, images, or telling a story. Videos can be planned, in the case of TV advertisements or planned stunts, or unplanned – an audience member could video something from your event (record stunts, something from an event, using a product) and post this online for the rest of the world to see. At their 2013 concert at Wembley Stadium The Killers sang a song, the 'Wembley Song', written specifically for the event. Many spectators filmed it on their mobiles as it was a song they could not get anywhere else. Afterwards an official video was released (www.youtube.com/watch?v=yM3L7VRQALM). This was special for the crowd at Wembley Stadium, as they became part of The Killers' 'history' as it was their first time playing at this venue.

Another form is planned videos which include the filming of advertisements that can be shown on television, the internet, at events, or in public places such as in the cinema. These videos are generally produced using experienced film crews and involve a large amount of planning. Prior to filming, a brief has to be created to determine the aims and objectives of the video, as well as what information needs to be included. This is typically the case with major awards ceremonies where some of the winners cannot attend. It also happens with the live televised annual BBC Sports Personality of the Year award (www.bbc.co.uk/sport/sports-personality). For this to be viable for you, the event needs to be attractive, and you have to have the budget and expertise.

CASE STUDY

Case study video

Silverstream TV (https://silverstream.tv/) provides streaming and live video production for events, for example a live TV channel at the event. Creative director Simon Walton explains how technology is being used by events: 'Video offers a lot to events. If you look at any of the popular social media platforms video is a strong driver. This trend is happening very fast on Facebook, Twitter and Instagram. Traditionally internet search engines are attracted to video, so the visibility of an event can be increased by having video on its platforms. This has been growing and growing.

When we started we did quick turnaround video for marketing an event while it was still on. It has been long recognised that a video link in an email increases click-throughs by some 300 per cent. That trend has continued on social media platforms too. Then the fashion for content marketing led to another wave of demand for video, as exhibitions and exhibitors wanted to market themselves and video is a very powerful way to do that. You do not just reach the people who attend the event, but also those who are touched by the event online. Events can grow their online visitors in addition to their physical visitors, and event managers are recognising these as an important community. We recently supported an exhibition at London ExCeL where there were 35,000 physical visitors and 80,000 visitors on their website during the show. Therefore, the exhibition wanted to serve this bigger audience online with the content available at ExCeL.

When an event is considering video they should go back to the basic objectives of the event. So rather than running off with a fad, they should focus on what they're trying to achieve and what the relevance of the video to the target audience will be. Therefore, you need to start from the right position of creating something that is relevant to your objectives and the audience interests. If you get that right, then the production and creativity will follow.

To produce an impactful online video, start by thinking carefully about what the potential visitor is interested in. How will video add to their understanding more than text and images? People subconsciously weigh up the time versus reward before they press the play button. So short videos can be more attractive. What has changed is that event organisers used to ask for elaborate 3–4 minute set-piece videos about their event. More and more they're looking for shorter granular 30-second videos about particular elements of the event, targeting particular audiences.

Online visitors are usually on a mission to find something. When they come online they know what they are looking for because they have taken a route to get there. So avoid repeating what they already know. That will only annoy them. We see that websites tend not to put all their videos onto a separate page as they used to in the early days of online video; rather, they are peppered throughout the website.

When you make videos which are granular in short segments they can be pinged around in social media and email campaigns. The video has become part of the marketer's toolkit to be rolled out responsively at relevant times.

People like to be entertained or surprised, so if you have a video which has a twist or humour they are more likely to share it, which in turn helps develop a sense of community.'

Vlogging

A vlog is essentially a blog that is primarily presented in video form. In the early part of the noughties some commentators predicted they would take over from blogs because of the power of video. However, they have remained a niche area; rather, the use of YouTube has dominated the video field.

Typically, with a vlog you are creating podcasts that can be accessed. You are, in effect, creating your own television station. The basic principles of blogs and vlogs are the same, but clearly the technology involved with vlogging raises some issues regarding the quality of your material. If the quality is not good, it is unlikely that you will get repeat visitors. As a result, a single vlog entry will probably take more of your time than a written entry, though, obviously, get the images right and the impact could be greater. That said, the technology is becoming more affordable and easier for the vlogger to use.

Producing a short video is now a common way of showing how good your event was. Thus, www.sointofashion.com produced a vlog of the Lifestyle Business Network Event at Strandzuid, Amsterdam, in September 2015. The video showed that the network meeting was enhanced by a fashion show. Indeed, sointofashion posts a series of blogs on events they attend. Vloggers, like bloggers, can influence opinion about your event, indeed some events now consider inviting vloggers in the same way they would the media.

While we observe that vlogging is becoming a medium in its own right, and some people make money out of it, we suggest that vlogging is of secondary relevance to events. Of greater application is YouTube.

YouTube

YouTube (www.youtube.com) is the number one place for sharing video content (and indeed the second most popular search engine). Many businesses create video content for the purpose of TV or online promotion (see video section), with the aim of reaching large numbers of their target audience. YouTube enables businesses to create and share their videos with their audiences, as well as for their audiences to share their videos. Users are able to create profiles and subscribe to various YouTube channels. By reviewing the channels you subscribe to, as well as monitoring the videos that you watch, YouTube can suggest other videos which the user might enjoy. Organisations can also create 'how-to' videos for demonstrating ways of using their products and finding out more information about the company, and these are ranked on the video search results of Google.

What to do if things go wrong

John Hibdige of JHAV suggests that 'If something goes wrong, say the power fails, it is important to establish what the scale of the problem is, can the event still go ahead or is the issue event critical. Either way the next step is to decide whether there is a budget to find a solution as this affects what the options are. There is always a solution, but they can cost. So if money is no object we would get in a generator, solve the issue and to some degree worry about the money later as the continuity and success of the event outweigh the costs that could be incurred. However, if there is no budget, the event may have to wait until power is restored by normal means, or possibly be postponed or cancelled.

As an event manager you need to remember that sometimes you have to have such uncomfortable conversations. Ideally they should happen in advance of the event, of "what if . . .". The most important thing from a supplier is that the event manager makes a decision and has thought about every eventuality.

Unfortunately no one really wants to talk about the "what ifs" and contingencies, but it is definitely something that's worth giving five minutes' thought to rather than wish you had.

The way to get the best out of your supplier is to have clear communication with them about your ideas and what you want to achieve. If we do not know about it, we cannot help solve it.'

Looking after your equipment

Some events will invest in AV equipment, such as microphones and some basic lighting, and it needs to be maintained. Equipment breaks – the trick to avoiding this is to treat it properly, so put it back in its box, check it after use, carry out repairs if they are needed, clean it regularly and get it serviced. Do simple maintenance such as change the filters in projectors, get equipment PAT-tested for electrical safety and remember that its working properly is part of the success of your event. If you do not look after it, your equipment will inevitably break precisely when you need it most.

How to plan to use AV

A good idea is to create your own form for assessing your needs at a site. Table 11.2 presents a sample of the questions that you may need to answer when conducting a corporate event site visit. Obviously, each event is different and your questions should be tailored to the event that is taking place, and the location. For other types of events, such as festivals, there may be a different set of questions but linked to the same information relating to the event, the site, logistics, infrastructure, timings, restrictions and the client.

> **Table 11.2** Site visit notes template

Corporate Site Visit Notes

The Event – Overview

Client name:	
Event name:	
Event dates:	
Venue name:	
Venue address:	
Venue contact name:	
Venue contact email:	
Venue contact telephone:	

The Venue – Specifics

Name of event room:	
Has the venue supplied a detailed floor plan?	

Are the exits marked on the plan?	
Are all power supplies marked on the plan, including single-phase and three-phase?	
Do you have all dimensions for the room including height (all heights if the head height varies)?	
Is the venue on the ground floor?	
If not on ground floor is there a lift, what size is the lift?	
Have you taken photos of the venue?	
Is there any rigging capability in the roof?	
If yes, do you have information regarding load capacities and rigging locations?	
Have you thought about the ambient light levels in the room i.e. are there lots of windows?	
Is there any AV equipment already in the venue that you can use?	

Table 11.2 continued	
Is there an in-house technical contact and do you have their details?	
Are there any noise restrictions?	
Are there any access restrictions i.e. loading times, curfews etc?	
What is the capacity of the room? Does the venue have seating layouts?	
Is there parking on site for vans? If not, where is the nearest and what are the costs?	
If crew are staying in a separate hotel, how far away is it and what travel options are there?	
Have you discussed crew catering with the venue as part of your wider catering order?	
Have you established the event timings with the venue?	

Describe the route from the position that any vans or trucks park to unload to the venue room, including if there are doorways, steps, lifts, sharp turns in corridors or any other possible obstructions. If access is via corridors and lifts, please note the dimensions of those areas (if possible video or take photos):

Discussion questions

1 AV can be a quick way of 'leaking' money, how do you decide what you want from it?
2 Probably the most important factor is the site visit with your supplier. Conceptualise that it is occurring 3,000 miles away and you cannot return to double-check details. How then will you ensure that you cover all that you need to in the visit?
3 If yours is a regular event, at what point should you decide to buy your own AV equipment, and what management issues does this create?
4 Many marketers believe that YouTube or other visual sharing mediums are the way forward. In what is becoming a crowded market, how will your video stand out and achieve your objectives?

Further information

Book

Miller, M. (2011) *YouTube: online video marketing for any business*, Indianapolis, IN: Que Publishing.

Articles

Smith, A., Fischer, E. and Yongjian, C. (2011) 'How does brand-related user generated content differ across YouTube, Facebook and Twitter?', *Journal of Intensive Marketing*, 26 (2): 102–113.
Waters, R. and Jones, P. (2011) 'Using video to build an organisation's identity and brand: a content analysis of non-profit organisations' YouTube videos', *Journal of Nonprofit & Public Sector Marketing*, 23 (3): 248–268.

Websites

Using video and YouTube:

www.theguardian.com/small-business-network/2014/jan/14/video-content-marketing-media-online
www.dreamgrow.com/8-reasons-why-your-business-should-use-video-marketing/
www.forbes.com/sites/steveolenski/2015/09/10/using-video-in-marketing-why-wouldnt-you/#67122ee66a9f
www.pixability.com/industry-studies/
www.business.qld.gov.au/business/running/marketing/online-marketing/using-youtube-to-market-your-business
www.reelseo.com/video/youtube-marketing/

Using sound in your marketing:

http://contentmarketinginstitute.com/2013/11/audio-enhances-brand-content-signature-sound/
www.campaignlive.co.uk/article/1333725/sound-huge-opportunity-marketers-its-falling-deaf-ears
www.learnmarketing.net/soundmarketinginfluencers.htm

Chapter 12

Images

Introduction

For many people the easiest way to get across a message to them is visually. If we are 'decision misers' (Chaiken 1980) who want to exert as little effort as possible in understanding something and deciding what to do with it, then visual images are probably the easiest way of achieving this. The first section of this chapter will access the general importance in getting across our messages through visual images. We shall go on to assess four ways in which event marketers can use images, starting with photography. We will then move on to illustrations such as diagrams, figures and graphs which have long been used by marketers. Next we will assess the more recent phenomenon of infographics, which combines images with words and data. The last section will consider how to construct impactful presentations, and here we will look at slides and props you might utilise to support you. Images have long had a key role in getting messages across, but technology has significantly enhanced the use of visuals in memes, screenshots and attachments. Social media has revolutionised how we share visual images. A recurrent theme to this chapter is the need to combine your images with what you want to say at the same time. Indeed, typically the image reinforces the words. By the end of this chapter students' should be able to:

- Understand why visuals are so important to event promotion;
- Use a photograph to promote an event;
- Assess which illustrations are best applicable for promoting your event;
- Design infographics that will appeal to your audience;
- Create an effective presentation.

The importance of visuals

Humans are visual beings, and an image can be the best way to tell a story. This point has long been an axiom, but the introduction of social media has potentially added potency to images. Marketing without words enables you to tap into the underlying power of images – emotions. Images can cause people to react, and those reactions can humanise your brand and event, and turn attending an event into an emotional relationship.

If you look at the literature about the importance of visual images you will often see authoritative figures on how we take in messages. Probably the most famous is Meharbien's (1972) formula that 55 per cent of communication is body language, 38 per cent is tone of voice and only 7 per cent is the words spoken. This research was conducted in a specific context and we are not convinced by the precise formulae, as in reality most communication is contextually driven. However, we are convinced that this research and other research provide common findings which should influence the principles of how you communicate. Essentially words alone are not enough, most people only take in so much through the words they read/hear. Visual images alone are for most people probably more effective at getting across a message. The most important lesson is that combining words and images is even more successful than using one alone, and this may explain why infographics have become so popular. We, therefore, advise you not to rely on just words or images, but to combine them so they support and reinforce each other.

There is evidence that in recent years marketers concerned with maximising their return on investment (ROI) have identified two growth areas: events and the internet. Both of these are inherently visual channels, moreover, the rapid growth of social media has further stimulated the use of images. Research by the Chief Marketing Officer (CMO) Council (2015) found that of 177 senior marketers surveyed:

- 65 per cent believe that visual assets are core to how their brand is communicated;
- 60 per cent believe that infographics will grow in usage;
- 27 per cent have a process to manage their visual assets.

This suggests that while marketers believe that images are growing in importance, their ability to use such images needs improving.

The argument is parallel to that made by Pine and Gilmore (2011) that the customer wants an experience. Inherently such experiences are likely to be both visual and tactile. The growth in the use of visual images implies that there is a shift in customer behaviour, that customers want to engage with brands that present themselves visually. More specifically Gupta (2013) argues that consumers are becoming less interested in text and moving more and more towards images, precisely because they offer emotional responses. Events using a range of senses can find themselves in a strong position.

The CMO (2015) research asked respondents which visuals were critical, important or unimportant to their marketing. There were four visual options: photography; video; infographics; and illustrations. Only 5 per cent said images were unimportant. Of the images that were considered critical it was clear that video and photography were the most important, with 46 per cent for photography and 36 per cent for video. Infographics and illustrations were critical for 19 per cent and 15 per cent of respondents respectively. We dealt with video in Chapter 11, but these findings suggest that despite the hype about infographics, it is photography that you should be focusing on first. Get this right and then you can move onto illustrations, infographics and presentations.

Using photography

Why use photography?

Put simplistically, a photograph is an image that is produced by exposing a light sensitive area, typically using a camera. It is therefore the process by which we create pictures. It is essentially a snapshot of a moment in time, which can be spontaneous or set up and staged. At an event you will probably use both.

An old axiom states that a picture is worth a thousand words, and what this means is that images such as photographs can quickly get across a message, which might in written terms take quite a lot of effort. Therefore, pictures provide a very easy heuristic, or shortcut, for our target audience. A photograph can help to reduce obstacles to making a decision, so that a good attractive photograph may make us more likely to do something, and a poor image less likely. In short, a photograph may make the viewer/reader less or more likely to attend our event.

Moreover, some products are more photogenic than others and as an event manager you are in the right business for effective marketing pictures. If you are trying to sell a mobile phone (cell phone), it takes a bit more creativity to get across your message, and more importantly demonstrate its benefits and impact. Typically, you would be advised to use pictures of individuals using the phone in a positive way to make good things happen. This is indeed possible, but for you as an event manager it should be even easier. If you have already run the event, or a similar one, you should have had high-quality pictures taken, in which case it should be very easy for you to have pictures of attendees demonstrating the behaviour or results you wish to stress. And if this is the first time you have run the event, it may, depending on its nature, be possible to set up some pictures to illustrate the event.

The Respect Festival (http://plymouthrespectfestival.blogspot.co.uk/) is a festival and city parade that celebrates diversity in all areas of the community. Every year hundreds of

attendees take part dressed in vibrant colours, which help to create excellent photo opportunities. These photos are used by the festival organisers to promote not only future events but also the ethos that surrounds the festival all year round.

Many photographers and graphic designers suggest a strong geometric shape is key to good composition of images. Figure 12.1 achieves this by having a clear foreground, main focal point and background of the image. This is useful when using photographs for promotion purposes, as it can easily be converted into a poster/flyer where text can be placed on the foreground and/or background without compromising the image.

Figure 12.1 Respect Festival

Big Festival Weekend 2015, Plymouth

Credit: Image courtesy of Plymouth University

However, do not assume that a photograph is a substitute for text. Consider for example that you see a poster with what is to you a very attractive image, and you think 'That looks interesting I would like to go to that', and there are no details such as when and where it is and the cost of admission. In this instance the image does not lead to attendance. Therefore, you should view text and images as complementary, with the text and picture supporting your overall message/point.

We can adapt an approach from tourism destination marketing to why and how we should use photographs to promote events. Tourists seek to escape from their everyday lives and so the prime motivation is new experiences, which is very similar for event attendees. Urry (1990) developed the idea of the tourist gaze, which is the way tourists see a destination. It is essentially a visual snapshot.

So what exactly then is it that tourists focus on? Hollinshead (2002) found that the tourist gaze's centre of attention is on fun/pleasure, the consumption of things, people and places. It is possible for us to take this concept and create an event visual gaze, which would typically be fun/pleasure, people, and experiences.

If we understand what the event gaze may focus on, then our promotional materials will seek to address this. Thus, Jenkins (2003) suggests that young backpackers seek adventure, enjoyment and new friends from such travel. As a result photography used in promotional material for this audience stresses action, adventure and group 'fun'. With a different audience or audience motivations the photographs should reflect this. For example, if our event was aimed at the over 65s, the photographs are more likely to focus on comfort, being relaxed and couples.

Tourism provides us with another insight that may help us to promote events. Jenkins (2003) explained the 'spiral of representation'. Here she suggests that we are attracted to a destination by iconic photographs, then when we visit we take our own perception of these images with our cameras, and when we get home show our friends and this further reinforces the perception of a place. While most events are not 'iconic', this spiral suggests that our marketing should aim to create attractive images of our attendees, who in turn will want to recreate them when they attend, and so enhance their experience.

As a marketer, using photography (or images in general) is an integral part of your marketing campaign. Photos help achieve your marketing objectives and extend readers' engagement with your content.

Using pictures

Pictures tell us, or reinforce, a story and we may use them in general marketing material such as flyers or as part of public relations campaigns. While the pictures you take at your event may be suitable for social media, when we are looking at producing websites, flyers, posters and the like your event needs professionally taken pictures. Therefore, this section is not about taking photographs yourself, but how you manage the process of getting them taken, and then using them effectively.

The good press officer thinks about combining words and pictures to make a more effective message. Journalists are always looking for pictures to help illuminate news stories and feature articles. If your event has occurred before, you are in a powerful position to use previous action photographs to accompany your press releases. For example, the annual Street Machine Summernats Car Festival (www.summernats.com.au) uses pictures both of the cars in their different competitions, but also of the crowd experience. This gives a sense of the action, but also what the impact is on those attending. With a more B2B audience, The International Film Festival on Tourism Films (www.tourfilm.cz) takes a slightly different approach, which stresses the high quality of what attendees receive. Those events aiming primarily at a B2C audience are more likely to emotionally stress excitement and being part of a crowd, whereas B2B events are more likely to stress the rational message of quality of the experience.

Photographs are a good way for you to interact with your audience, by sharing them on social media. The fashion magazine *Glamour* (www.glamourmagazine.co.uk/) does this well – in every issue they have a winning photograph, sent in by of one of their readers somewhere in the world holding a copy of the magazine. This is a good way for your target audience to get involved, and helps to make them feel valued. TripAdvisor is another common example of an organisation that relies on its audience's contributions and involvement. These photos often have a greater impact on viewers of the website than the pictures that are taken by the organisation itself, as they are perceived to be more genuine.

Some events ask attendees to send in their pictures and share them on social media as a way of raising awareness. The organisers of Brain Tumour Day (www.braintumourresearch.org/wearahatday) ask people to wear a hat and send in a picture of them in their hat. Thus supporters may create mini-events as part of a bigger campaign. National Flip Flop Day (www.tropicalsmoothiecafe.com/funraising) offers good images showing how much it has raised using an image of a flip-flop.

You should try to build up a stock of background pictures. For example, of your senior personnel, organisation's activities and what happens at your events. Unless you have a very good amateur, always pay professional photographers to take these background pictures. You also need to introduce an organised library system so you can quickly access pictures. When you are emailing out a press release, as a basic principle attach a picture (usually in JPEG format) and caption of what/who it shows.

In the pre-internet days building a picture library was more complicated as we typically had 35-millimetre negatives that had to be put into individual cases, then within a plastic folder and each labelled labouriously in a logical order. With technology, managing the picture library is far easier and there are a range of programmes such as Windows 7, SharePoint and a variety of apps. However, you still need to remember some basics for managing them, and one of the most obvious is to think of a logical way of naming and filing them. You do not want hundreds of unsorted pictures that might relate to one event. So why not think about what they are of, say participants, organisers, spectators, or where in the event such as behind the scenes, from the stage and in the entrance? What these cateogries are should be relevant to your event, but the main point is that before you start naming them you need to think how you will use them.

You should also remember that pictures will either be used in portrait or landscape format. In the former, the height of the picture is greater than the width and in the latter it is vice versa. So when you are building up your library make sure that you have pictures in both forms, as they tend to fit different purposes, messages and types of publication. Put simply, landscape tends to work well with pictures that require breadth to get everyone or everything in, whereas portrait can work well when you want to focus on individual detail of say one or two people.

Always when you send a picture out with a press release write a caption (often called cut-lines by journalists and picture editors), so that the publication knows what or who is being shown in the image. A caption is vitally important; after the headlines it is often the next likely bit of text read from an article.

A caption provides context or background information which helps to explain the image. Typically, a reader looks at the picture first, if their interest is piqued they will then look at the caption and then look back to the picture, and possibly read more of the article. When you are writing a short caption you must tell the reader what relevant information they cannot get from the picture alone. If you have an awards ceremony with pictures of people giving and receiving awards you need to say in order of left to right who is who. Do not forget to mention any sponsors in the picture; they are effectively paying for the event. If you have a picture of the main speaker at a conference you need to make clear who they are, what they are doing and why the topic is important. A picture of guests having fun at a music festival probably tells the story clearly, but it helps if you can give a name to the people being shown and why they are happy.

Examples of captions

The picture shows from the left John Smith of Acme Events receiving the prestigious Event of the Year Award, presented by Bill Bloggs, Chief Executive of Anytown Rugby Club.

Andy Andyson, Minister for Widgets, giving the keynote speech on 'Growth in the Widget Industry' to a packed audience at the Annual Widget Conference organised by Widgets R Us.

Getting on down from the left Tom, Cobley and All enjoy the first ever public performance from The Preserve opening the show at The Old Timers' Festival, Isle of Wight.

Tips for writing captions:

- Keep them fairly short;
- Offer relevant information that is not obvious from the picture alone;
- Answer questions the reader may have: who is in the picture, why, when and what the story is;
- You want to give the sense of live action at your event so use the present tense;
- Avoid using one style, start and order captions in a range of ways;
- Avoid obvious descriptions of what the reader can deduce anyway;
- Check you have the correct names (including spelling and titles) in the correct order.

Creating an effective marketing photograph

If you are taking photographs as part of a marketing campaign you need to consider a range of elements that you may have to address:

- Are they simply generic images that can be used anywhere within your marketing?
- Are they for a specific purpose?
- Are the photographs aligned with your message?
- What is your message?
- By what means will the message be delivered?
- Where will they be shown?
- What size will they need to be blown up to?
- In what format will they be used?
- Can you crop them?
- If you are focusing on a specific section of the photo and blurring out others, what does this look like?
- How can you use other people's photographs to your advantage?

We would suggest that you first identify the purpose of the image, for example, to inform, educate or sell tickets. Then we would construct the message, such as exclusivity or having fun, and then create or choose a picture that supports this. Finally, we would consider the technical requirements of your chosen channel of delivery, such as JPEG, resolution and number of pixels.

12.1 Tip box

Using photography at events

An experienced photographer who photographs dozens of events a year outlined his biggest bugbear: 'Please do not ask us to photograph the food at your event. It is very difficult to get this right during the event, it is much easier if we arrange with the Executive Chef to photograph the food later. Then the chefs will not be under pressure to deliver, and we do not have people getting in the way. This way we can show off the food much better.'

However, it is not enough to provide photographs, the images must be relevant and help the reader to understand the message. Nielsen (2010) conducted eye-tracking research whereby he was able to identify the factor which determined whether a picture was looked at or not. He found that pictures that tried to 'jazz up' a website were ignored because they were decorative. Pictures that contained relevant information were the ones people looked at. For example, this might include pictures of a product or real people who were viewed because they were considered important. Therefore, Nielsen found that stock photographs, perhaps bought from an agency or downloaded from a free website, showing generic business people in suits, would be ignored. However, pictures of actual delegates at a conference would be looked at. The lesson is clear for events, that you should provide pictures of actual people, at your event, as they will be looked at and will reinforce your message.

CASE STUDY

Photography

Alan Stewart currently works as an in-house photographer for an organisation that hosts over 400 events a year, ranging from the very small and parochial through to events that are quite large and significant in their field. At some of the major annual events that run across several days he has taken up to 1,000 photographs, though for smaller events it may only be 12–20. He has previously worked for a local newspaper and as a freelancer. Alan explains how you can best make use of your photographer and the photographs they take for you:

'Photographs can help events in lots of ways. First, they publicise what has happened to promote the organisation through social media, print media and specialised communications. An event can be very specific in deciding where their pictures are used, so it can increase their reach. Second, we find that we are used a lot as a record that the event actually happened. Say we are photographing a Memorandum of Understanding between two organisations, this is unlikely to be used by the media as a thank you to those that are involved. Pictures can also be a way of thanking sponsors. Most of our pictures are used in websites, social media and promotional publications.

When an event manager is considering using photography to promote their event they should do as much preparation before the event as possible. The photographer needs to know, for example, what the pictures will be used for, how much time there is, what time they have to be there and where? I am always thinking of how much time is required for each part of the event that I will photograph – so how much of the organisers' and my time will each picture take? And is there a way that we can save time?

As a photographer, I always want to know whose picture to take, and what for. So the event manager needs to be clear what you want to achieve, and what the photographer needs from you. For example, I want to know what are the timings of the key parts of the event, what is the style of photography to be taken and its purpose. Essentially I need a wish-list of the photographs to be taken. It is always a good idea to meet up at the venue beforehand to look at what the stage will be like, the lighting and what the Wi-Fi is like. If the Wi-Fi is good we can put pictures out on social media within five minutes of taking them. In the last few years I have noticed that the speed of putting pictures out has got much faster, especially on social media where people are interested in something which is instant. When I started it was said that today's news is tomorrow's fish-and-chip paper, now with social media it can be junk mail very quickly.

The use of the pictures can affect which ones are taken. So if you are going to put out the pictures on social media immediately, then we can use low resolution, but if it is going to be for press release or promotional materials, then it needs to be higher resolution and it takes longer to turn around, say 3–4 days. It is possible for a photographer to switch from one to the other, but this takes time and may increase the cost.

It is important to place the boundaries straight away. If you want pictures of, say, a keynote speaker, and then these to be put onto social media straight away, be aware that this takes time and while I am doing this I cannot photograph the second speaker.

For different audiences we will take different types of pictures. When we are focusing on younger people the pictures are likely to stress fun, be dynamic and possibly colourful. However, for other audiences we may focus on the credibility or importance of them and be more sombre and serious.

When we get the call internally that an event needs a photographer we will talk through the key moments, asking details of the key parts such as details of keynote speakers, when they will be on and the like. This all helps us set up pre-event photographs that we can control and save time. If the event manager needs group pictures we ask what time people arrive, and if anyone is time-restricted and if they are important. If someone is important and is only at the event for a short time we will set up group photographs around them.

What makes a good picture varies: as a press photographer it was to create a visually stunning picture that stopped people turning over to the next page. Now it is to describe that event simply and easily in a visual, and to do so by linking it to the event's key messages. Therefore, before I attend an event I need to do my research so that I understand the organisation and the event. I try to photograph people how I would like to be photographed. I would not want to be pictured eating a chip butty, and so I would not take such a picture. We look to take pictures which are a true reflection of the event, i.e. with people with happy facial expressions and the event surroundings.

We try to treat people, especially speakers and main participants, as if they are important and on the cusp of delivering something important. The pictures we take could in a few years be used if this person becomes well-known.

Some events by their nature are fairly sterile visually and there are ways of making them better. I always look for background screens, pop-up banners and projections that tell us what the event is about. Another thing to look for is people interacting, especially if it is with high-ranking attendees who are important to the organisation. So we are looking for anything that places a person within the context of what they are doing at the event. For example, I recently was taking pictures where a world-renowned podiatrist was giving a talk. I had been pre-briefed that he would have a person on stage for demonstration purposes. Therefore, I was able to get a picture of him, the patient and the audience because I knew what he was going to do.

For something like an awards ceremony I will look for backdrops with corporate logos and try and create a controlled space. So when they get the award I take a picture, hopefully with something in the background, and then take them to my controlled space and take their picture there. It is worth being aware that unless I am told I do not know which is the most prestigious award, or most important person(s) there.

On the day of the event it helps if I have one person to go to if there are issues. If it is a large event, then that person needs to be easy to contact without necessarily being exclusively focused on me.

It is important to try and build up a relationship, you may host several events and if you use the same photographer you will want to know they do what you want. Communications is key to achieving this. I need to understand what the organisation does and what they want from me. It can help to know which and where pictures are used. Send electronic copies of brochures, flyers and the like so I can know what pictures you like, this helps me to understand your approach to marketing materials.

I need to know what the client thinks of the pictures, and sometimes I might say that I was not happy and ask them to discuss with me how we can get them better next time. It is therefore important to have some sort of sweep-up meeting that discusses what worked, what did not and what we could do better next time. This might be one-to-one with the event manager, or it might be at a team meeting. For example, I attended an event for a number of years where we tried to take all the pictures live during the event, and this did not quite work. At the sweep-up meeting we spoke about this, and now we are able to do a number of pre-event shoots.

There are two different styles of photography evolving. For social media the style is one of happy people, very relaxed almost boarding across both work and pleasure. The other style is a more campaigning approach which provides a clear-cut message, it is a more advertising-based approach. Event managers need to decide which style they want as it can get a bit messy if you try both at the same time. Some photographers specialise in one approach more than the other, so you might choose different photographers depending on your chosen style.'

Model release forms

Alan notes that it has become more prevalent for events to use model release forms. 'When we attend an event we ask whether everyone attending has been told there will be pictures taken and that they are happy to be photographed. We put the emphasis on the event commissioner to sort this. Although we are photographing in a public sphere normally we still have to be careful. Technically an event should use Model Release Forms for everyone who is photographed, but with many events this is not practical. One approach is that some events put text on to their promotional material along the lines of "Photographs will be taken and if you do not wish to be photographed, please tell the photographer." Many events will have a board up that says the same thing.'

Using illustrations

An illustration is simply a graphical representation of an idea, activity, factual information or person. It could include a diagram, painting, photograph, map or video link. When trying to present complex data, diagrams such as pie charts, graphs, bar charts, Venn diagrams and cycle charts are a well-used route. Many of these diagrams have a long history, for example William Playfair used bar charts, histograms and pie charts in the late seventeenth and early eighteenth centuries to display information such as the economy of England.

Diagrams are very good ways to display data so that the audience can understand what the data says. For example, Replay Events used a colourful pie chart to explain the results of

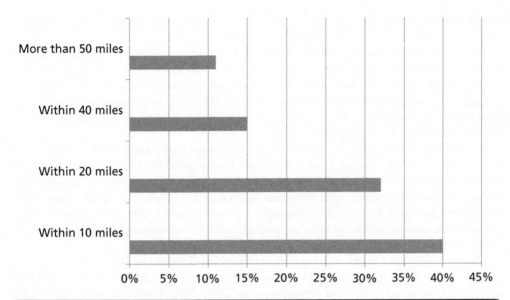

Figure 12.2 Bar chart of geographic attendance

its readers' survey into the 2014 console of the year (www.replaygamer.co.uk/readers-survey-best-console/). They identified nine major machines and the pie chart showed that three were the most popular. Figure 12.2 is an example of how one diagram, a bar chart, can be used to explain data visually. In this instance it quickly shows the geographic spread of attendees. This would be very useful to venues such as conference centres and entertainment hubs to know where to target their marketing.

We have used one specific type of illustration in the form of heat maps. Using eye-tracking technology on event websites or flyers we can test which parts of that promotional material visitors actually focus on. The heat map allows us to tell very quickly if the audience is actually looking at what we want them to look at. If not, we need to change the structure and content of the material.

We suggest that diagrams are more likely to be used for business documents to make marketing decisions rather than in promotional materials. They allow managers to analyse information quickly and make decisions.

Infographics – the new must have?

While we can trace the history of infographics back to the use of pictures on cave walls several millennia ago, and graphs, maps and diagrams have been used since the seventeenth century, it is really in the last ten–twenty years that the term infographics has come into vogue. Indeed, Mazereeuw (2015) found that from 2010 until 2012 the use of infographics increased by 800 per cent. This implies that there is a clear upward trend in the use of this visual tool, suggesting that you are more likely to use it in the next few years.

There is some disagreement over the exact meaning of the term infographics, but we suggest it is a means of telling a story visually by combining images and explanatory words. Infographics seek to combine aspects of design such as colour and font with shapes such as diagrams that are used to demonstrate a key message. One approach to presenting a message is to use an infographic as a way of presenting data.

Essentially with an infographic you are taking data/information and presenting it in shorthand so the reader does not have to read, process and understand a lot of text. You are seeking to cut through the background noise and grab the readers' attention, and get across a key message very quickly. Research by Miller and Barnett (2010) of how people understand health messages found that graphs alone have a limited effect on comprehension, but that graphs combined with text have much more effect.

While clearly infographics are used in brochures, posters, reports and flyers, their growth is being driven by the fact that they can easily be used in social media. We now have a proliferation of image-based sites such as Instagram, Snapchat and Pinterest where infographics can be passed on rapidly. For example, www.tribalcafe.co.uk has produced a detailed infographic of why and how events should use infographics via social media. The latest development in infographics, encouraged by computer technology, provides moving graphics. The clear benefit of these is that they provide interaction.

However, we offer a caution concerning infographics; there are lots of commentators and bloggers using infographics to explain what event managers should do, but we found little evidence of events using them in their promotion. Therefore, at present infographics are a useful learning tool for event managers, but not an effective promotional tool.

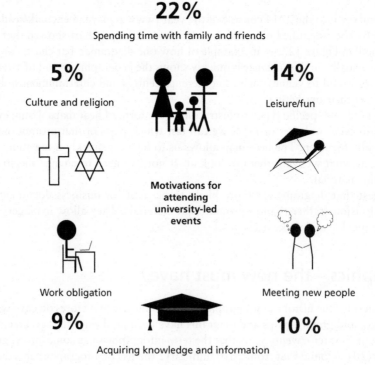

Figure 12.3 Motivations for attending university events

Figure 12.3 is based on a survey conducted by one of the authors with 594 respondents of why people attend university events. Academic statistics are normally presented in tables, but this use of an infographic presents the data in a more accessible way. In particular, the visuals clearly reinforce what each category of motivation is. Incidently, in this particular context you will see that gaining information is the single most important motive.

Powerful presentations

Lights, camera and action: you're on! What you have to remember with any presentation you are giving to an audience is that you are providing a performance. It is not just about what you say, but also how you say it. As an event manager you may have to make a bid proposal to win a contract, brief a few colleagues in a meeting or inform a wide audience. We shall assume that you are presenting to a large audience, and you wish to use visual support such as PowerPoint.

Before we address how to construct and use your PowerPoint slides, we suggest that there are some generic pointers that are key to any successful presentation:

1   Prepare – know what you want to achieve, clearly plan what you are going to say and what you want the outcome to be.
2   Know your audience – who are they, what would they be interested in?
3   Produce content that is tailored to the needs to your audience – get interesting stories, vignettes, case studies and statistics – and learn your material so you can present it effectively.
4   Control what you can control – think about body language, tone, speed of delivery and how you look.
5   Use your visuals to support your message – do not rely solely on them.

PowerPoint is simply a graphics software package designed to enable an individual to produce what in previous years could only be offered by professional designers. A PowerPoint presentation is based on a series of individual slides where you can put text, pictures, diagrams and hyperlinks to websites and video. If you just talk, some of your audience may not focus on your message. We saw in Chapter 2 when we considered VARK that we take in messages in different ways. As well as reinforcing a message, PowerPoint helps us reach more learning styles.

There is a concern that there can be 'death by PowerPoint', that it can be overused, and this is a very good health warning when using this presentation tool. If a presenter comes to rely too much on their PowerPoint slides, akin to an emotional crutch, then its impact is diluted, or even becomes a negative. We must be aware, therefore, that PowerPoint is merely a tool and should not take over – the star of the show is us, the presenter, and what we have to say.

One tip for using PowerPoint is provided by Keshaven and Tandon (2012) who suggest using the mnemonic FIRST:

Flow (one)
Idea (per slide)
Relating to the customer
keeping it Simple
and use appropriate Transitions.

What this suggests is that you need to set up each slide at the end of the previous one, and that whatever you put in a slide must be relevant to the audience and be easy for them to understand. PowerPoint is not a place for too much complexity.

Our advice is that with a PowerPoint presentation you are telling a story, so you need to be clear what your narrative is and what you want to get across. While each presenter and presentation is unique, we suggest that you consider:

- Keep graphics simple – do not overcomplicate the message, for example if you have a diagram do not make it too complex, the audience will switch off if it is too difficult to understand;
- Your slides need to support your presentation, not distract from it, for example if you have a slide with loud or very bright colours your audience may look at this, and not listen to you;
- Think in terms of headlines not minute detail. If you are going to use bullet points limit yourself to three or four each slide;
- Do not have too many slides – this is when we tend to have 'death by PowerPoint';
- Do not talk to the slides and just repeat what the audience can read;
- Do not be too text heavy, relying primarily on bullet point-based slides – think about images, statistics, quotes and diagrams that break up the content – infographics may be very useful;
- Make sure your slides can be seen from the back of the room – so the size of images and text needs to be quite large;
- Choose appropriate simple fonts such as Arial and Helvetica, and avoid narrow or funky fonts because they can be more difficult to read;
- Have a contrast between the background and the text, for example black text on a white background, or vice versa;
- Remember, some colours, such as red, can be problematic for people with eye or other conditions, so do not over-rely on them;
- Avoid using too many fancy transitions and animations; if all your slides are spinning in and 'whooshing' out you might make your audience feel a bit ill.

PowerPoint is a good tool for briefing and informing others, it tends to fit best with educational or information-based events, such as conferences. One of the authors saw a novel use recently in a church where PowerPoint was used to get the attention of a packed audience primarily made up of children. It was a way of keeping their attention.

Another form of presentation used by some is Prezi (www.prezi.com), which is an alternative to PowerPoint. It is a cloud-based presentation software that creates slides but navigation is by a pathway; you do not click from slide to slide but from point to point, and each slide zooms in to the content. By its very nature it encourages slides to be visual rather than bullet point. If an audience has not seen it before it will be refreshing, but ultimately it is merely a means of presentation and some people find the zooming in and out a problem. However, we recommend you try both PowerPoint and Prezi and see which you or your audience prefers.

Those with Macs might use Apple Keynote (www.apple.com/uk/mac/keynote/), which is very image-based and helps you use drop in and use images, videos and the like. It is a more touch-based presentation which might be very powerful if presenting an idea to a small audience, perhaps using your tablet.

An alternative or supplementary to PowerPoint is the use of props to help illustrate your point, and keep the audience's attention. The term 'prop' has been borrowed from the theatre or film world where actors use a prop in their performance to help tell the narrative. A prop is something which can be kept hidden, brought out to illustrate a point and then put away again – you want the audience to focus on it when you want them to. If you have a bigger audience your props probably need to be physically larger so they can be seen, though a live projector screen can address this.

The Royal Gunpowder Mills (www.royalgunpowdermills.com/) is an ex-rocket research station which is now a visitor attraction that demonstrates what it did, and seeks to enthuse children about science. A series of speakers present a range of concepts using props, for example Professor Nitrate uses explosions to help explain science. Museums commonly use a range of large props, for example the Natural History Museum (www.nhm.ac.uk/discover/diplodocus-this-is-your-life.html) in London has a full-sized cast of a diplodocus dinosaur near the entrance, and the Smithsonian Air and Space Musuem uses displays of the original Wright 1903 Flyer and the Apollo 11 Command Module. Charity fundraising events often use a big cheque to show how much has been raised, often for a photo opportunity.

The authors have witnessed a Chinese New Year event where an actor was dressed in a panda suit to hand out flyers to help promote the event. This is clearly an example of a prop, the panda bear suit, being used to get across the point. It could easily have been achieved by the use of a dragon or Chinese dancers. While possibly the bear suit is a bit cheesy and uses stereotypes that perhaps we should be challenging, it was easily recognised by others and they swiftly understood the link to the event.

Props also link carefully with the design themes of an event. For example, if you are organising a tropical beach-themed event indoors in a hotel you might want a lot of green plants that look like palms or banana trees, exotic animals such as blow-up plastic flamingos and possibly even some sand and shells. If your event is celebrating a historical event you might want appropriate costumes.

In addition to helping to get a point across, props can help break up the monotony of a presentation, adding a different tone and speed and sometimes even humour. This can help keep the audience's attention.

Discussion questions

1 Photographs appear to be the most important of your visuals, what are the simple steps you have to take to make best use of them?
2 Do particular visual images such as diagrams, presententations and pictures work better for particular events and audiences? Or do these visual tools work equally well for all events/audiences?
3 How will you measure the impact of your visuals?
4 At some point you will need to use a professional photographer, how will you choose the right one for your event?
5 How can you make best use of the amateur pictures taken by your staff and attendees?

Further information

Book

Smiciklas, M. (2012) *The Power of Infographics: using pictures to communicate and connect with your audiences,* Indianapolis, IN: Que Publishing.

Articles

DeVan, M. and Baum, N. (2013) 'Public speaking: creating presentations that are awe inspiring now yawn producing', *The Journal of Medical Practice Management,* 29 (3): 204–205.

Henley, C. and Burgess, L. (2014) 'What a picture! Mind the copyright', *NZ Business*, 28 (1): 49.

Websites

Some useful tips on using photographs can be found at the links below:

www.cmo.com/articles/2013/1/28/why_images_will_lead.html

Using photographs to support content marketing: http://contentmarketinginstitute.com/2012/04/using-photographs-to-support-content-marketing/

The shift from words to pictures: www.forbes.com/sites/onmarketing/2013/07/02/the-shift-from-words-to-pictures-and-implications-for-digital-marketers/

Ten dos and don'ts for using stock photos: www.slideshare.net/HubSpot/10-dos-and-donts-for-using-stock-photos-in-your-marketing

Seven ways to spice up your online marketing using photography: http://www.toprankblog.com/2013/01/nmx-2013-photography-marketing/

Exellent detailed guide for using PowerPoint http://blog.hubspot.com/marketing/easy-powerpoint-design-tricks-ht

Chapter 13

Exhibition stands

Introduction

When we consider exhibitions, we need to be aware of two related, but different components. For most of us exhibitions mean an event where people or organisations come to show off their wares at a venue, such as a trade or consumer show. However, exhibitions also relate to organisations, such as museums, which exhibit at their own premises as part of their core business. Exhibitions are a major global subset of the events industry, for example in China in 2013 the sector was worth 387 billion yuan ($62 billion), which represented a 10.6 per cent annual increase. This growth reflected not just more income, but also that the number of exhibitions was up 1.8 per cent to 7,319. In America there is an Exhibitions Day in June on Capitol Hill designed to explain to American legislators the value of the $71 billion plus that the exhibition industry brings to the US. The explanation for this growth is that exhibitions deliver a marketing message. As a consequence, exhibitions can represent a major marketing tool, and this chapter will start by considering what an exhibition is, and explain the different types and the impact of their nature on the exhibitor. It will then outline why an organisation might want to have a stand at an exhibition. We shall go on to consider how to maximise the marketing effect of attending an exhibition. Having decided to attend we will consider how to drive traffic to an exhibitor's booth, and how it can stand out. We shall finish by evaluating whether it was worth attending. By the end of the chapter students will be able to:

- Decide whether you should attend exhibitions in general or a specific exhibition;
- Identify how to exhibit successfully;
- Understand how to construct a stand;
- Assess the return on exhibition attendance.

What is an exhibition?

Exhibition, trade show, food festival, ExPo and convention, you have probably heard most of these and many more terms, but what do they actually mean? While their exact nature, purpose and audiences may differ, we argue that they are essentially the same thing, and the term exhibition is a useful catch-all. Morrow (2001) identified three key characteristics:

1   Not permanent;
2   Happens at a specific time;
3   Seller and buyers meet and interact.

The first two parts of Morrow's definition could apply to any event, but it is the third characteristic that clearly identifies exhibitions. Black (1986) makes essentially the same three points, but also adds that the products and services are likely to be within a specific industry or discipline. So an exhibition is not a market where anyone comes to sell their wares, rather it is a bringing together of a group of producers and potential consumers within a specialist interest, such as food, IT or Star Wars memorabilia. Moreover, while money may indeed exchange hands, at for instance craft fairs and food festivals, how does a training company 'sell' there and then go on to sell its courses to an HR manager at the Human Resources Summit in Berlin (www.europeanemploymentforum.eu)? In short, an exhibition occurs because it benefits both buyers and potential sellers to come together in one place.

13.1 Definition box

What is an exhibition?

We suggest that the key to understanding the term is the phrase 'exhibit'. An exhibition is any event where an individual or group of people seek to 'exhibit' their work or services to others. It could be art, a product, a service or a concept. It is therefore very broad in scope, allowing a group to self-define that they are exhibiting. However, just the act of exhibiting alone is not enough, it also needs to attract an audience that is interested in what is being displayed. An exhibition implies some sort of physical or virtual coming together between those who have something to exhibit, and those who are interested in seeing, learning about or buying it.

The main differentiation between exhibitions is between trade and consumer shows. The former are targeted at 'trade', those in the industry such as manufacturers and retailers, whereas the latter are aimed at individuals who want to buy for themselves. Typically, an order placed at a trade show will be much larger than someone buying at a consumer show. For example, one of the authors had a client who made funky wedding shoes who used exhibitions as a significant sales tool. When they attended trade shows a retailer might want 100 pairs of shoes sent to them, whereas at a consumer show each buyer is likely to buy only a single pair.

An example of a trade show where the main audience is suppliers, retailers and professionals within an industry is CLEANMET Asia 2016, held in the Marina Bay Sands Expo and Convention centre in Singapore in July (www.cleanmetasia.com). It focuses on cleaning and management technology aimed at those in the industrial and cleaning industries. This exhibition is not a stand-alone; there is also a conference where each event helps the other, though the conference is probably the more dominant of the two. Many delegates to the conference will also visit the exhibition, and a possible smaller number who want to come to the exhibition primarily then sign up for the conference. Here an exhibition is part of a symbiotic relationship. Many other organisations provide an exhibition as a means of adding value to a conference, for example in the UK the political parties view this as a very good income generator (Jackson 2009). Therefore, when you are looking to be an exhibitor or attendee do not look just at the major exhibition lists, but also consider other events that may have a suitable audience in one place.

Some trade shows are huge. The Consumer Electronics Show (CES) January 2015 in Las Vegas attracted 170,000 who registered (109,507 were attendees) and 3,631 exhibitors (www. cesweb.org). However, this show is a bit of a misnomer as it is not open to the general public, rather to industry professionals such as buyers, analysts, store managers and engineers. Indeed, the event is so popular that the CES created an inaugural event in Shanghai China in May 2015 specifically to target the growing Asian market. The indications are that for some shows the limitation is not the size of the audience but the venue, hence why CES have expanded overseas.

Consumer shows tend to be a little different from trade shows where manufacturers, suppliers and retailers seek to reach individual consumers. They can be very specialist with a fairly small but highly interested audience, such as the Fall Cottage Life Show in October held at The International Centre in Mississauga, Ontario, Canada (www.shows.cottagelife.com). The exhibitors include those who provide boats, docks, builders, green solutions and arts and crafts. It is clearly of interest if you live in or have a second home or a cottage in a remote area of Canada. Thus, this exhibition brings together a small, but highly motivated audience with a specific industry to provide solutions to practical problems.

Many consumer shows appeal to hedonistic motivations; they aim to give pleasure to attendees. Thus the BBC runs a series of Good Food shows at the Birmingham National Exhibition Centre (NEC), and elsewhere in the UK, that are simply about enjoying food. Therefore, the range and numbers of those interested is very wide. While clearly attendees have to have some disposable income to spend, the prime motive is an interest in food, so in terms of demographics and geography there is no one dominant audience. Thus at the BBC Good Food Winter Show for the price of their entrance fee attendees will be able to see celebrity chefs cook, learn to decorate a Christmas cake or sample and buy food and drink products from hundreds of exhibitors. According to its ABC certificate in 2012 there were 80,009 attendees at this show. Attendees simply get access in one venue to a huge range of food experiences.

Smaller exhibitions can play an important role in the supply chain of very small or start-up companies. For example, every weekend throughout the UK, sports halls, hotels and schools play host to very small locally focused exhibitions such as arts and crafts shows. Here people trying to earn extra money, establish their business or break into new markets might sell, for example, homemade pickles, jewellery or woodwork. They regularly attend such exhibitions in order to make sales and enhance their reputation: they are actually a core sales tool without which the business would probably not exist.

Virtual exhibitions

One niche area that has not really taken off as much as originally expected is that of virtual exhibitions (VEs). Here an exhibition effectively takes place online, so it is accessed via technology such as a PC, tablet or smartphone. Visitors can view what is conceptually a stand via multimedia presentations. There are no venue or time availability constraints, and so early research on the potential of VEs in the Middle Eastern exhibition market by Lee-Kelley et al. (2004) found that marketers felt it would be good for promotion, price and product, but not for place. The reason was that VEs would be better at conveying information than encouraging and facilitating sales.

Looking at our definition of exhibitions, VEs have a place (cyberspace), a time frame (unlimited) and a potential audience (at their computer), which would appear to make it a

Selling at exhibitions

Jewelsangel (see www.facebook.com/saltashpopup/?hc_ref=SEARCH&fref=nf) is a jewellery business selling a range of local and imported jewellery and accessories. It provides a range of contemporary costume jewellery, and a range of sterling silver rings, earrings, pendants and bracelets, often set with semi-precious stones.

Owner Julie Angel explains how she uses consumer and trade fairs: 'I sell at a variety of events, some regular and some monthly or annually. Jewellery is popular at many different types of event and as I stock a good range of styles and price ranges it is possible to go to some quite diverse fairs. I usually amend my stock depending on my destination, will there be a more affluent crowd in which case it's likely I will sell higher-end pieces or do I need to have a lot more product in the lower range? The types of fair and the stock on offer has to reflect the season and whether customers are predominantly buying for themselves or mainly gifts for others (for example, I sell more earrings on the run-up to Christmas than rings, as customers are reluctant to guess a finger size). Fairs are often chosen on recommendation from other traders, the network of traders is far-reaching and on the whole a helpful community. Some fairs or shows I am invited to attend and some I find online, but usually it's word of mouth.

As a sole trader immediate sales are important to me, especially as I don't sell online, so my intention is always to sell, sell, sell but my long-term reputation is as important as I attend many regular show where I have a lot of repeat business.

I will always give an event a second chance if unsuccessful initially as there are so many factors that affect sales on a particular day, for example weather conditions, school holidays, access to site, cost of getting in for customers, degree of quality of other traders and display, and another event running on the same day.

I always hope that the cost of a fair is no more than 10–20% of the takings, so if I have paid £20 for my pitch I hope to take £200 at that event.

Having worked the circuit for about 12 years I usually only attend events that are profitable. I also find that buying jewellery is a very personal activity and having a good selling technique, always engaging with your customer and remembering regular customers and their preferences helps build a good business relationship. I never quibble about returns and stock good-quality pieces that are reasonably priced and that helps build a customer base.

For those thinking of using fairs as a means of selling products I would suggest that they do some research about the type of fair, footfall, whether your items will allow all costs to be covered and a profit likely. Make sure that you don't clash with other traders. It's always advisable to ask the organiser if they have another trader stocking the same product as you. Do you need to factor in excessive fuel or overnight costs? Is the event likely to have your type of customer? Do you need to provide your own gazebo or will you be in a marquee?

Always check the amount of space your money is buying, will you be able to fit everything in? I think fairs are a great way of starting a business, you get to test your product, check your pricing is right, get ideas about display from other traders and learn about other events and contacts. It gives you the chance to meet your customers and listen to what they are saying so you can offer new lines or styles.'

very attractive proposition. However, VEs in the commercial sector are not a major part of this market. Where we do tend to see VEs is in the not-for-profit sector where libraries, art galleries and museums use them as a means of permanently displaying what are temporary physical exhibitions. They are a supplementary tool used not so much to generate sales, as to maintain the reputation of a venue, such as a museum and a particular display.

CASE STUDY

iVent virtual event

iVent (www.ivent-uk.com/) specialises in the design, management and delivery of online virtual events utilising its own virtual event and webcasting platform. One of its departments specialises in University Open Days. They come from a traditional live events background rather than a technical platform context.

Gavin Newman, Commercial Director, explains how virtual events work: 'Virtual means remote, so a virtual event is any event that is held remotely. Originally many people struggled to understand what it meant, but nowadays enough people are able to get their head around the concept.

The reason why organisations should consider a virtual event is that an event is about communicating with an audience, delivering content or whatever. Virtual events allow you to communicate with a wider audience, more cheaply and for a longer period of time. Some organisations have virtual events because it can save them money, we have had clients save from £500,000 to £2.5 million. However, we would suggest that you do not have a virtual event just to save money; rather, it must add value by creating a good experience.

Some events are better suited to virtual events than others. There are two requirements for successful virtual events:

1 An ever refreshing audience, so not just the same audience.
2 A highly motivated audience, they want to visit.

For example, we organise a number of university recruitment open days, where there is always a new audience each year, and they are very interested in what they see.

When we have a new client come to us we approach this as we would a live event. We start by asking what they want to achieve, so we identify their objectives. Then we look at what we can do to help them – we are trying to open them up to a new way of thinking. Very often clients think as they do for live events, and want to provide it in one day. However, we often suggest that the event, such as a conference, takes much longer. So we help clients develop a new style of event, one which is spanned over a longer period of time.

It is possible to have a physical event supported by virtual events. For example, many of our university clients have live recruitment events, and then support them with virtual events later. This helps those people who attended the live event but missed something, or those who did not attend at all. It is a way of mopping up all the people, so that virtual events gather a bigger audience.

Originally we saw virtual events as a good way of reaching international audiences that could not attend a live event, but now they are equally good for national audiences too.

The technical challenges are fairly easy because we use files and folders; the issue is when there is live screening via a webcast. We have to anticipate what can go wrong, and explain to clients what can go wrong to lower their expectations and test the screening.

Live events are seen to be occurring on a single date, whereas with virtual events we are creating an environment, and as such we can add new material. Commercial organisations increasingly see virtual events as the way forward if their event is relevant and meaningful.

Evaluation of live events depends on what sector they are in. Live events have been around a long time, virtual events have not – you cannot apply the same principles to virtual events because they are different. For example, the thought process as to why a person attends a virtual or a physical event is different. If you have bought the rail ticket and booked the accommodation you are likely to attend a live event, the same issues do not apply for virtual events. We have also noticed cultural differences as to how, for example, Americans, Europeans and Asians behave online. For example, one event attracted people from 48 countries and they asked different questions.

With virtual events you have easy access to the data capture and analytics at each component of the event, compiled in digital format that is quantitative.

Feedback from attendees is also important, and non-requested qualitative feedback is the best.'

The concept was originally conceived as an alternative to physical exhibitions, but is now also being used as a supplement to physical events in the not-for-profit sector. For example, the Smithsonian National Museum of Natural History (wwwmnh.si.edu) currently provides 34 virtual exhibitions such as *Sustainable Seafood*; *Lakota Winter Counts*; and *Dinosaurs*.

	Trade	Consumer	Virtual
Hedonistic		X	
Functional	X		X
Informational	X	X	X

Figure 13.1 Typology for why attend an exhibition?

Typical of these is *Dig It! The Secrets of Soil* exhibition which ran from 2008 to 2010, but can now be accessed online. There is a curator-led tour of the exhibit, so that even though it ended years ago you can still enjoy the exhibition. VEs provide a means of continuing to exhibit ideas, stories and art which do not have a limited time-span.

Figure 13.1 outlines a typology for understanding exhibition attendance, which suggests that trade, consumer and VEs can be categorised as hedonistic, functional or informational. Hedonistic exhibitions are where attendees want to gain pleasure, such as tasting foods and playing computer games. Functional exhibitions are those where an attendee's motivation is to help them achieve their work/career goals, such as to buy appropriate technology or develop skills. With informational exhibitions, the aim of the attendee is to gain information about a topic. A hedonistic motivation is more likely with consumer shows, functional with trade shows and informational could be either.

What often drives the exhibition market, or at least can give an indication of which countries have invested most in exhibitions, is where the largest venues are. According to Statica (www.statista.com/statistics/264240/largest-exhibition-halls-in-the-world-by-hall-capacity/) the largest exhibition hall by capacity in 2016 was Hannover Messegelande. Indeed, of the top ten by capacity, four were in Germany, two in Spain and one each for Italy, France, China and the US. This might imply that the largest exhibitions are still dominated by Europe, though if we look at the top 25, while Germany still dominates, China is the next largest provider, suggesting a possible shift eastwards of the exhibitions' infrastructure. Indeed, the market does seem to be shifting. The 6th Globex Report (2013) found that while Germany and the US are the first and second largest exhibition markets, China had leapfrogged the UK and France to become the third largest (www.amrinternational.com/globex-report). Like the CES example earlier, you may need to consider new geographical markets for your show.

Why attend an exhibition?

The first general reason put forward for attending exhibitions is that worldwide this is a significant and growing industry. The Global Association of the Exhibition Industry's (UFI) 2015 Global Exhibition Barometer found that of the 55 country responses, over 60 per cent declared growth in 2015 and early 2016 (www.ufi.org). The strongest growth was in the US and China, and the weakest in Europe was in Germany and Russia. Similar research by the Center for Exhibition Industry Research (CEIR) found that the US exhibition industry recorded its highest growth rate, 3.8 per cent, for eight years in 2015 (www.ceir.org). GLOBEX supported this general trend where they noted the exhibitions industry grew in 2014, especially in emerging markets such as Mexico (www.amrinternational.com). This may indicate the markets you should be getting into.

Such growth rates represent significant sums of income. According to the Association of Event Organisers (AEO) the UK exhibitions sector contributed £5.4 billion added value to the UK economy in 2010 (www.aeo.org.uk). This figure equates to 0.4 per cent of the total GDP of the economy, and supported 148,000 jobs; 0.5 per cent of the total employed in the UK. In 2010 this equated to 1,600 exhibitions, attracting 265,000 exhibitors of which 20 per cent came from outside the UK. This resulted in 13.1 million people attending these exhibitions.

Figures from the 'Events are Great Britain Report 2014' (www.businessvisitsandeventspartnership.com) are that direct spend on exhibitions and trade shows was £11 billion, and attracted over 13 million visitors to the UK.

A US-based campaign launched in 2011, Exhibitions Mean Business (www.exhibitionsmeanbusiness.org), seeks to educate businesses, the media and policymakers of the value of exhibitions. They note that in 2014, 5.2 million people attended conventions in Las Vegas alone, and that overall there are more than 11,000 exhibitions each year in the US.

While current trends are impressive, we suggest that you have two initial decisions to make: should your organisation exhibit; and if so, at which exhibitions? One of the authors was once employed in a senior communications role at a top 200 UK charity and, as with most such organisations, had a very limited marketing budget. When they first joined it was obvious that an organisation that was a cause in health and safety had a clear message to promote, and exhibitions were a perfectly reasonable route to market. They then asked which exhibitions had been previously attended and why, and from the answers they devised a completely new strategy for attendance. First, most of the exhibitions chosen previously had been national ones at which the audience was primarily professionals with an interest in the field of safety. These were a key audience, but they could be reached more cost-efficiently and effectively by other means such as one-to-one meetings and joint projects. Second, the reason given was to maintain a profile within the safety field. When the budget was explored this motivation did not suggest a high return on investment (ROI). This exhibition strategy was completely changed. The charity sought to raise awareness and change citizen behaviour, and exhibitions were selected on the basis of reaching key audiences, from children through to selected interests/hobbies. In addition, rather than be a general flag waver, exhibitions were used to launch or support campaigns of activity, not just the charity in general. A third component of the strategy was to focus not just on national-level exhibitions, but where they fitted with specific campaigns, including local ones. This meant that if the organisation attended the previous exhibitions it did so with a clearer purpose, but several were immediately dropped and the money spent elsewhere. This strategy encouraged the development of objectives that could be much more easily measured.

We noted above that an exhibition is the happy combination of someone with something to exhibit with an audience that is interested in it, and this is the first key to deciding whether to exhibit. An exhibition can be an effective means of reaching either a mass number or a smaller number of high 'quality' (the right) buyers in one physical space in a short space of time. The exhibition needs to deliver audiences you want to reach to achieve your organisational objectives.

Having decided that exhibitions may provide a means of reaching a desirable audience we suggest that you need to identify what specific purpose exhibitions provide for you. These can include to:

- Launch new products;
- Promote new information on existing products;
- Reach new people/markets;
- Support sales.

Indeed, research of 104 exhibitors at two UK exhibitions by Blythe (1999a) found that the three most popular reasons for attending were to:

1   Meet new customers.
2   Launch new products.
3   Take sales orders.

Blythe questioned the salience of sales because he found that most of the visitors were information gathering, and not decision makers. Therefore, the advice is to question very closely what the size and nature of attendees are likely to be according to the organisers. If decision makers will be present, then to generate sales leads may be a worthwhile purpose. The most obvious lesson is to identify very clear, and ideally measurable, objectives for attending exhibitions in general, and a specific exhibition.

Slightly different motivations for exhibition attendance were identified by Situme (2012) who asked exhibitors in Mombasa (Kenya) how important trade shows were as marketing tools. On a scale of 1–5, with 1 being very important and 5 not important at all, the mean was 1.84, implying that there was considerable importance attached to exhibitions. The three most popular objectives for attending were: PR/publicity; to re-establish links with clients; and to secure feedback on new products. This might suggest that in different countries/cultures the motivations for attending exhibitions may differ a little.

Figure 13.2 is a tool you can use to identify what is the purpose of exhibiting, which helps you decide whether to attend an exhibition, what you will do at it, your key messages and what the objectives might be. We construct the figure by identifying two axes; an exhibition that is primarily a means of enhancing your brand or to generate sales. It is obviously possible to attempt both. Looking at Figure 13.2, position A implies that both reputation and sales are important, but the weighting is towards branding. Equally, position B suggests both are important, but this time the weighting is towards sales. With position C branding is the main purpose for attending, and with D it is primarily sales-focused. This tool helps marketers to decide why they should attend exhibitions.

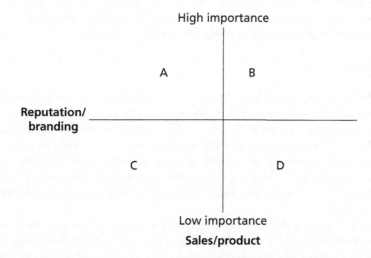

Figure 13.2 Deciding the purpose for an exhibition

Research suggests that the decision to exhibit is not just determined by an internal assessment of why, but it is also shaped by the very nature of your organisation. Herbig et al. (1997) surveyed 204 exhibitors and found why some companies were more likely to use exhibitions than others. They identified that two factors determined which type of companies decided to use exhibitions: product and organisation size. Exhibitions were used by companies with high-price, complex, technically sophisticated or infrequently bought products. Such organisations tended to be older, more global in outlook and have more customers and product lines. Exhibitions were more likely to be used by mature organisations. Irrespective of the likely audience an exhibition may attract, some organisations are simply more likely to attend than others.

We have noted above that exhibitions are a marketing tool, and experiential marketing may help to explain why exhibitions are becoming more popular. As a strategy, experiential marketing (Pine and Gilmore 2011; Schmitt 1999) assumes that buying behaviour is changing, that for many price alone is no longer the prime factor. Rather, the assumption is that consumers want a product or service that also offers an experience. Consumers do not just want a rational explanation of the features and benefits of a product, they also want an emotional connection with it. Exhibitions provide a means by which products and services can connect with consumers by providing a pleasurable experience. Such experiences are easy to achieve at some exhibitions such as food shows, where attendees can sample the delights on offer. Presenting an experience within a technology show might appear more difficult, but the same principle applies, so you will often find that attendees get to 'play' with new products. Understanding the importance of providing an experience will help you to decide whether an exhibition is right for you, and indeed what you might do at your stand.

Some exhibitions are experiential in nature. One example is Game On 2.0 (www.life.org. uk/whats-on/game-on#.VkRk9GBi_IV), where attendees can play on more than 100 games. These include both popular up-to-date games and vintage ones on 1970s/1980s consoles. The whole exhibition is about experiencing these games by using them.

Making the most out of an exhibition

Having decided that an exhibition is right for you, we suggest that there are seven key areas you need to address to maximise the return that you can get from attending: clarity on audience; objectives; plan; assess costs; staffing; promotion; and follow-up.

1 The audience

We have alluded to this above, but you need to be very clear that the promised audience is who you wish to reach. For example, Mwanyumba (2009) found that the number and quality of visitors to agricultural shows in Kenya did not meet the exhibitors' target audience. As a result, exhibitors did not perceive the trade shows to be effective marketing tools. Therefore, it is important to look carefully at the attendance of previous years, and if need be question the organisers. For example, the press release cited earlier of the Consumer Electronics Show (CES) suggested 170,000 attended, which you might expect means only visitors, but it also included exhibitors.

While you can assume that anyone attending a consumer show may be a potential purchaser, this is not necessarily the case with a trade show. Blythe (1999b) stresses that what is important is that visitors to your stand will be decision makers and not just browsers. Thus if you are trying to sell industrial cleaning products the caretaker (janitor) you are speaking to may use the product, but the decision to buy might be made by the estates manager.

2 Objectives

There need to be clear measurable objectives of what you are trying to achieve. Moreover, these should be consistent with the organisation's overall marketing plan.

3 Plan

Attending an exhibition is not normally an impulse decision and is usually taken some months before. It is important, therefore, that you plan your presence in detail. Yet Pitta et al. (2006) suggest that 70 per cent of exhibitors have no plan for their event participation, so they do not have a clear purpose of why they are attending and what they want to achieve. The starting point is our objectives, but our plan should also include how we are going to get there. Table 13.1 identifies the key components of a plan. So, for example, say you have decided that in the past you have not been very good at generating sales leads, but that this is the main outcome for the next exhibition you wish to attend, what do you do? You might, for instance, decide to have an attractive competition where you collect details. You would probably identify who you want on your stand with sales skills, and after the event you will want to set your sales team clear deadlines for follow-up. Any weaknesses identified will affect the components of your plan.

4 Assess costs

You need to calculate all the likely costs you will face (and within which budget they will be allocated). The very last thing you want a couple of weeks before the exhibition is to realise that there is an unexpected bill. The sort of things that might be relevant include:

Table 13.1 Exhibition plan

Component	Possible outcomes
Identify previous lessons	Make sure that the lessons are discussed and written down after every exhibition. What has worked? What has not?
Objectives	Are they clear and measurable? Do they need to change for each exhibition?
Assess current exhibition capability	How fit for purpose is our equipment? Do we have the right team?
Budget	What is it? How much can be spent on each component? What does it cover, for example do travel and accommodation have to be covered, or can this be charged to other budgets?
Strategic approach	How important to you is this exhibition? What is your overall approach – to be loud and visible, or quiet and professional? Are you throwing resources at it, or is this low key?
Message	What do want to say about the organisation, its brand and products?
Follow-up	Will there be any? Who will do it? How? What is the measurement of success?

- Exhibition fees;
- Exhibition design (including designers' fees);
- Your stand (including printing costs);
- Flyer/brochure design and printing;
- Equipment such as tablets, microphones;
- Courier costs;
- Setup and take-down costs (are your staff setting up your stand or are you hiring a company to do it for you, such as www.amcexhibitions.co.uk/set-up-dismantling-and-storage-gallery.html), and will you be providing food and accommodation?
- Equipment storage;
- Insurance;
- Taxes;
- Utilities (electricity, generator etc.);
- Travel;
- Accommodation;
- Food;
- Product line/giveaways;
- Uniforms;
- Staff;
- Contingency (typically 10 per cent of the total).

5   Staffing

This is often a part of the plan that marketers forget. Have you got the right team involved in the preparation, so that all the details are covered? Perhaps more importantly, who will be on the stand, and are they the right people for what you want to achieve? So if your main objective is sales, then you need people who are experienced at this; if you want a more profile-raising presence, then probably people who can talk about your products/services. Having identified what skills and which individuals you need, you might need to fill any gaps by providing appropriate training.

You should also brief all of your team to tell them what you expect. Typically, this might include:

- No eating or drinking on the stand (this presents an unprofessional image);
- No sitting at seats (this creates a perception of not wanting to talk to visitors);
- Smart and appropriate clothing;
- What you are trying to achieve;
- Product information;
- The need for regular breaks away from the stand;
- Everyone's roles (including reporting structures).

As the manager, it is your role to make sure that everyone knows what to do, and to manage the team so they get frequent breaks.

6   Promote your presence

You need to market your presence prior to the exhibition to support your objectives. This might include invites (with a properly written personal invite) to key potential and actual customers, partners or other influential stakeholders to visit your stand. Produce press releases of key stories which you need to put on your website, send to key target journalists and provide a copy for the organisers' press office.

You might also enhance your presence by providing easily visible merchandise that people carry around so that others can see, such as tote bags. You should also use your social media presence using the exhibitions hashtag# telling people where you are/what you are doing and to come and find you. You should provide a reason for people to visit you, for example, promote a competition or other feature you are running from your stand.

7   Follow-up

Obviously this depends on your exact objectives, but after the exhibition contact all those you met. This is primarily going to be visitors to your stand, but it could also include other exhibitors who might be of use to your organisation. You could continue your promotion post-event. For example, if you had a competition you could produce a press release, with a picture of the lucky winner.

Driving traffic to your stand

There is of course another key factor, namely your presence: how visitors view your stand. When attending exhibitions you will be allocated a set amount of space, and it is up to your organisation to use this space appropriately in order to attract your target. Your objectives shape your stand, so Rayner (2004) suggests if you are launching products you should focus on demonstration and display, and for brand development the graphics and staff are key.

You need to be aware that the behavioural patterns of people who attend an exhibition tend to be:

- Those who decide which stands to visit by looking at the brochure and going straight to them;
- Those who wander around several times deciding which one(s) they will visit;
- Those who look at the stands from a distance – they are hard to attract closer.

Your stand must be attractive to all of these.

As Rayner (2004) suggests, we can identify two different types of exhibition visitor:

1   Browsers who look at stands from afar;
2   Participants who probe for information and interactivity.

Your stand needs to be set up to attract the second group.

There are clear design factors that shape what you can and should do:

- The size of the stand;
- Assess how much space your display/banners, staff and visitors need – do not make it feel too cramped nor empty;
- Create a theme – what do you want your stand to look like – funky, functional, traditional, fun?
- Remove barriers – do not put physical barriers such as tables at the front of your stand;
- Use appropriate lighting to highlight what you have to offer – avoid dark or shaded areas;

- Think about whether you offer something – giveaways or refreshments – but will you only be attracting those who want a freebie and are not serious buyers?
- Consider whether technology attracts people and adds to their experience or distracts from your message;
- Do you need signage, if so what? And remember, keep it clear, easy to read (from a distance) and simple.

First impressions of your stand matter. Experienced exhibitors suggest that you need to apply the three-second rule – you have three seconds in which to grab a potential client's attention, and get them to visit your stand. However, being the biggest, loudest, brashest or most colourful is not automatically a good thing. You want to stand out, but for the right reasons.

To assess whether your stand will meet the three-second rule we suggest you do two things. First, before the exhibition is open you (and some colleagues) should visit your stand as if you were visitors, and see what you think, and make changes accordingly. Second, once the exhibition has started take time off from your stand and observe the reactions of visitors when they come past your stand. This may give you an insight as to whether they see it or not. We would also suggest that you wander around the exhibition a few times and look at other stands, and how visitors react to them. Attending exhibitions is all about learning what works for that audience in that venue.

Lee and Palakurthi (2015) suggest that interesting activities attract people to an exhibition: can they see and experience something new, different or fun? This clearly supports an experiential marketing approach, and can help determine what you do on your stand to attract visitors. Stands that encourage people to 'have a go' are often the most successful (if queues are not too long).

To help you assess your stand further, Whiteling (2003) suggests that you need to address:

- What the stand looks like – look at it from the perspective of a visitor;
- Your stand should reflect your product and what it does;
- Consider the look, body language and personality of your stand personnel.

In order to choose what type of stand you will have, you need to be aware of the different types:

1 Custom-built – created from scratch to meet your needs. Tend to be for larger spaces, often have the wow factor but cost the most.
2 Modular – tend to be lightweight aluminium frames with a range of graphics.
3 Portable stands – probably the cheapest and very easy to transport.

To a large degree these will be shaped by your budget, how often you use exhibitions and what you want to achieve.

Did it work? – Evaluating an exhibition

When the authors were responsible for an organisation's exhibition presence and we evaluated attendance, especially return on investment (ROI), we would focus on:

- Clear questions – for example, how well did we do, what worked/what did not and should we return?

- How will the process of evaluation work?
- What measurements/metrics do we value?

There is an inevitability that when evaluating your exhibition presence you hold a 'wash up' or 'wash and brush up', where the team involved have a meeting and discuss how things went. Such a meeting is important, but we do have a health warning, namely that we are humans and most of us are unlikely to be too critical of ourselves or colleagues. That said, it is important to discuss whether you achieved your objectives. We strongly advise you to write down the lessons learnt, and the next time you are planning for an exhibition look at what your recommendations were and implement them if appropriate.

We suggest that any meeting should divide your evaluation into the time frame and the activity. The time frame should be divided into what happened before, during and after the exhibition. Looking at before, you might focus on the marketing, logistics and planning process. During the event you might focus on setup/breakdown, number of visitors and competitors. Afterwards we are more likely to be looking at the impact, such as costs and sales. The activity could be broken down to things such as the stand and processes. This reminds us that people are key to our exhibition presence, a factor sometimes ignored, so how well did our team work together?

In terms of assessing the event it is possible to construct a measurement based on a scale, say 1–5, and you mark how well you (and possibly your competitors) did on for example your stand, message and quality of visitors. As noted earlier, you might well consider participant observation of visitor behaviour to assess their response to your stand. You would also be advised to develop some statistical matrix. These will depend on your exact objectives but might include number of visitors, number of details collected, job title of attendees and spend/orders/sales. You should also analyse what is said about the show and your stand on social media. If your objectives were more sales-oriented, this may be easier to measure by metrics; if your aim was more reputational, then you need to assess what people say to you at your stand, in the media and on the internet.

One thing you can consider is using your presence as a means of conducting market research – what do visitors think of particular ideas, and should you now actively develop them?

Blythe (1999b) found that the methods used to evaluate the impact varied in quality and type. The factor that shaped this was frequency of exhibiting; those who exhibited most had the best measurement tools, reflecting a learning process.

CASE STUDY

Exhibitions and trade shows

Closer Still Media (www.closerstillmedia.com/) specialises in B2B events and has a portfolio of medical and technology shows. Gayle Trott, Business Development Manager for Best Practice & Best Practice in Nursing, explains that the benefits that companies gain from exhibiting at their shows are:

- Face-to-face communication/direct client contact;
- Exposure to potential clients and industry;
- Product showcase to clients;
- Speaker opportunities to address audience;
- Brand awareness to create recognition in sector.

'We promote our exhibitions through a range of external promotion such as sales calls, social media, sales meetings, e-shots, brochures, adverts and stands at sister shows with similar delegate audiences. We also have dedicated delegate teams calling our potential visitors, getting them to register. We then do a courtesy call closer to the show to ensure our delegates have all the information they need. The more visual promotion is through newspapers, e-shots and postcards.

The main ways in which we communicate with our audiences at the show are show guides, a branded floorplan board, branded speaker boards per theatre, workshops/speaker sessions and the programme.

When companies decide to exhibit we want to know their aims and objectives so we can create the correct package for them, and their company name, trading name and all company contacts and details.

Our advice to someone thinking of exhibiting at one of your shows is book your stand or speaker session earlier rather than later, because it will allow you to secure a preferred location and speaker time slot. The earlier you book the more marketing you can do around the exhibition; perhaps build a campaign around it. You will also have more time to set up meetings on-site. You should place very engaging and knowledgeable people on your stand to sell your solutions to the audience. Use visual aids on the stand, allowing it to be as engaging and inviting as possible. Stand staff should be approachable and knowledgeable, and proactively networking with attendees.

We find that companies attending our shows measure their success of attending by:

- Number of leads;
- Number of quality leads;
- Incoming business on-site and post-show;
- Building business pipelines.

The way we measure the success of our shows is by the delegate numbers, the total sponsorship and exhibitor revenues, on-site rebook percentage, positive feedback from delegates, minimal negative feedback and show profile in industry media pre- and post-show.'

Discussion questions

1   We have looked at how marketers should use exhibition stands. Consider that you are organising a whole exhibition, what should you do to attract people to exhibit at your event?
2   Design is important to a stand. However, there is sometimes a danger that the stand focuses on how it looks and not the substance of your message/products. How do you ensure that the look and feel of your stand does not distract from your key messages?
3   If you are a marketer considering how best to spend your budget, it is not sufficient to look at each exhibition one at a time. Rather you require a strategy that assesses exhibitions as an overall tool, as well as each one you might attend. What would be the key components of any exhibition strategy?
4   Your boss asks you to explain how worthwhile attending a particular exhibition was, what are the key components your evaluation would cover? Think about hard and soft aspects of your exhibition presence.

Further information

Websites

What makes a good brief:

http://mpdcreative.co.uk/what-makes-a-good-exhibition-stand-design-brief/

Skills for highly effective trade shows:

www.forbes.com/sites/kenkrogue/2013/06/10/17-skills-for-highly-effective-tradeshow-events/
www.forbes.com/sites/kenkrogue/2013/04/05/the-12-commandments-of-incredibly-successful-
    tradeshows/

Comprehensive guide from the Association of Event Venues which covers a lot of detailed information relevant to trade and consumer shows:

www.aev.org.uk/files/eguide_august_2015_clean_copy__with_new_logos.pdf
www.tradeshowguyblog.com/
www.skylinetradeshowtips.com/
www.tsnn.com/blogs

Trade bodies

Association of Event Organisers (AEO) represents UK companies which conceive, develop or manage trade shows and consumer events: www.aeo.org.uk/

Event Supplier and Services Association (ESSA) represents contractors and suppliers of goods and services in the UK exhibition industry: www.essa.uk.com/

International Association of Exhibitions and Events (IAEE) represents the global exhibition industry in over 50 countries: www.iaee.com/

Multimedia

UFI represents tradeshow organisers and exhibition centre operators in 85 countries: www.ufi.org/

Magazines

There are some online magazines which may give you access to the latest news:

http://exhibitionnews.co.uk/featuredetails/189/show-by-association-uk-trade-association-exhibitions
www.exhibitionworld.co.uk/

Chapter 14

Conclusion

Introduction

In the previous chapters we first set up how best to promote an event by addressing some core communication concepts. We then grouped together the remaining chapters into three different sections: written materials; the application of online tools; and visual techniques. This final chapter will first sum up some key points from across the chapters: we will then identify some core themes that cross individual topics. We shall finish by looking ahead to where events promotion may be moving, especially concerning the application of technology.

Summary

The importance of communication

This book is about the routes to market that you will be using, what are available and which is the best for your event and why? We suggest that you should not limit yourself to just one channel; rather, you will need to master a range. These routes can be codified as written (such as flyers), broadcast media (typically but not only advertising-based such as local radio) and the internet. It is rare for an event manager to be able to use just one of these three approaches.

The starting point to promoting your event is to identify what the problem is, that communication is the solution to. This could be of a logistical matter, and so the focus is more internal, whereas when we are looking to get 'bums on seats' we are looking externally. Whichever is the case, it will help to decide how you communicate. However, communication is not just about what you want, you also need to understand what the audience wants or the effect your message has on them. Being able to understand how people read your promotional material will help you to present your argument to best effect. If you are constructing something like a newspaper advert, then applying the Gutenberg diagram will help you know where to put your key messages. Similarly, if you are producing a flyer, the Z-pattern may help you decide how to structure it. The purpose of understanding how to communicate is that not only do you want to impart information, more importantly you want to change behaviour: to get people to attend.

You may well interpret communication to be primarily about the written or spoken word, but in order for you to market your event effectively we want you to think continually about the design of your materials. A leaflet, website or video is not put together haphazardly; you need to think about the use of colour, fonts and layout. These design features can make the difference between success and failure.

Producing written materials

Semiotics helps us understand whether your written materials will get across your messages. Your adverts, mugs and posters are full of signs such as your logos and use of colour, but will your audience interpret them correctly and respond in the desired way? The nature of the promotional material will decide what we say on it. For example, adverts, posters and merchandising offer very limited physical space, and so the message – both the words and the branding – has to be short, simple and to the point and often relies on images. Whereas with direct mail and feature articles you can get across more complex messages, and can be more text heavy.

You need to be aware of whether you can directly reach people, or will you have no idea who is receiving your message? If you know the audience, as with direct mail, then you can narrowcast your message and have more than one version for different audiences. This can be very effective, but is labour-intensive. Broadcasting on the other hand, such as with adverts and press releases, means you reach more people, but most may not actually be interested in your event. Moreover, you do not necessarily get to know who they are. Some channels such as flyers and leaflets could be either narrowcast or broadcast, what matters here is whether you know who they are being delivered to.

When using the primarily written channels we highlight key issues that need to be addressed with each. For advertising you need to choose the correct publication to reach your audience. For direct communication the mailing list is king: if you buy one in, is it the right one, and if you construct your own, how will this be managed? If you are going to invest the resources to use media relations, then the starting point is to construct a means of identifying news, and planning when you will release it. With merchandising, the ever-moving question is what to stock to maximise the branding or revenue-generating opportunities, and how to avoid being left with unused stock.

Online channels

The internet is inherently different to other print publications, partly because of how it is accessed and how quickly it can be updated but also why, when and how people visit it. We therefore suggest that if you are going to use an online channel, then it is important that you know clearly why you want to, but also that you understand why others might want to visit it. Whether you are considering a website, social networking site or email, you need to assess its characteristics: and what this means for how you present your message. Possibly the biggest contrast with print publications and online media is that there is the potential for co-production of content. You may set up the site, but others may offer material, such as photographs of themselves at your event. Another key difference is how the page is read online; the F-pattern may help you to construct your website so that the key information is in the right places.

We suggest, therefore, that there is a conflict when using the internet, especially social media, between the event wanting to control its message and possible attendees who want to have an input. We recommend that conceptually this can best be understood by the term Web 1.5. Many organisations put their effort into their website, often because they control the content, whereas many event attendees may be more interested in social media. We make an appeal for email, the Cinderella of the internet, such that if you are looking to build up long-term relationships, especially in a B2B market, this may be your most persuasive tool.

Multimedia

For many years commentators have suggested that video may become the marketers' strongest tool. The development of easy-to-use and affordable technology, such as smartphones, means that this prediction is now becoming a reality. Moreover, many events are an ideal subject for utilising video, and you can produce video of past events with action that supports your key messages fairly easily.

When you are considering using AV to create the atmosphere and enhance the experience of your event you need to be clear what you want to achieve, the impact of the venue on your ability to achieve this, the nature of the event and your budget. Key to this is building up the relationship with your supplier, viewing them as part of your team.

With visuals there is a wide range of technical terminology, and so you may need to seek advice on what it means. Always remember what you want to get across, and how visuals support this. We suggest that mastering the use of photography will support all your print and online promotions. Infographics is the latest buzzword, and they can be useful, but we suggest that for the event marketer photography and video are what you need to focus on first. So think how you will construct photographs and how they will be used.

Many of you will at some point take a stand to an exhibition. It is important for you to understand the importance of the design of your space. Start by seeing your presence through the eye of an attendee. When you are assessing whether your multimedia has had the desired effect, make sure that you consider not just the physical side of the equipment and message delivery, but also how well your team worked.

The future

CASE STUDY

The future of events management

Simon Walton from Silverstream TV (www.silverstream.tv), who spoke about creating a video in Chapter 11, looks ahead to the possible impact of technology on events management in the next few years.

'When we are looking at the current trends in events management that shape the technology we use, the big thing is that events are keen to build their community. An event is a landmark for a community, and technology such as video is being used to spread the reach of the event. The key to this is trying to become the place where your niche/interest group comes to, and recognises this as the place for insight and innovation. An event's online presence needs to become the place for authentic and reliable information about their interest or profession. So six months prior to the event, it may tweet about a current issue, host workshops or create a launch event.

One of the big things currently is that because of social media, event organisers are recognising that via online communities they are able to build up audiences in different geographical locations and so push the brand into new territories.

One of the new technologies being considered at present is 360 video (Virtual Reality). We see a lot of Virtual Reality (VR) headsets at exhibitions to bring the experience to the event, so that you can see what it's like on board a cruise ship, for example. But we are also looking at the other side, videoing the event through a 360 camera. The advantage of 360 is that because the person has control of what they are looking at they are more likely to trust what they see. The next stage is to deliver the event live in 360 so that people elsewhere in the world can experience it and join in. Events are largely two-dimensional. With 360 cameras we think it's going to be possible to invent a totally a new type of three-dimensional online event.

For event managers to make best use of technology we need to come back to the core objectives of the event, and to not stray too far from them because of a technological gimmick. A good tip is that ideas can be discussed for months in meetings, but in the heat of battle at the event will those there have time to make use of the technology? We have discussed plenty of ideas that seemed good, but at the event everyone was too busy to use them. Similarly, do your visitors have time to use them, or are they too complicated to get to grips with in the middle of an event?

One of the main purposes of a trade event is the exchange of data, networking, reaching new people and learning new things. We're always looking for ways to link video to the new technologies that are powering this process, from barcode readers to proximity marketing tools such as Apple Beacon. Looking at the near future, we should expect this exchange of data to become more developed, so there will be more intelligence in the exchange of data. We may also see the use of proximity technology, so that you can look for people near you at the event who have a similar interest. Another new technology that's creating a lot of buzz is the use of holograms to bring in people to an event who are not there or even alive!'

In 2013 the International Association of Exhibitors and Events (IAEE) published a white paper: 'Future Trends Impacting the Exhibitions and Events Industry' (Friedman 2013). The IAEE sought to identify the major trends that they felt would have greatest impact on the exhibitions and events industry. Friedman identified 13 trends; 11 of these were based on the impact of technology such as 'Big data' – collecting every bit of data about the event and its customers. Reading through these 11 trends it is obvious that the IAEE believes that technology changes the nature of events, how customers engage with them or how they communicate messages about them. We suggest, therefore, that as you prepare to promote your events in the future, one of the key areas you will need to grapple with is to assess what is happening with technology, and how it can help you. We are not suggesting that you must adopt all new technologies, indeed this would be unwise and lead to wasted resources, rather we suggest that you look ahead by assessing what technology is being used well by events now, and what new technologies are evolving that might have an events application.

When we are looking at how technology might affect how we communicate at events we need to consider what is happening in our country, audience market or event sector:

- What technological innovations are likely to have an impact on market conditions?
- What is the rate of new innovations?
- How supportive to technological development is a society/country?
- How technologically aware is your audience?
- How do we communicate and exchange information?
- Are there technological barriers to entry to market?

These questions are especially important if you are looking to enter into a new market, for example in another country.

New technology is not just about finding a way of doing an existing task more cheaply or better, often the event has to respond to popular demand, so that smartphones, apps and social media are consumer-led, and hence imply the need for more interactivity as events use them. The implications of such bottom-up pressure is that the messages about, and even the delivery of, events are likely to be increasingly customised.

Hudson and Hudson (2013) conducted a study of the use of social media and technology (such as radio-frequency identification (RFID)) at music festivals. They found that social media influenced consumer buying. The three American festivals they studied all used social media actively to engage with consumers. They noted that consumers have different stages in the buying process, and that social media should be used to help the consumer's journey, and is of particular use at the later stages of the process. This suggests that social media can be a sales as well as an experiential tool.

We noted in earlier chapters the development of hybrid events, where technology such as the web is used to enhance a physical event. You may have realised throughout this book that while we think technology is having a major impact on events and how they are communicated, we are less sure that virtual events will dominate in the future. Rather, we think that they will be a niche, though one growing in importance, to select event industries. However, we do note that there is evidence that they are growing in importance. Market Research Media (2016) forecast that in each year from 2013 until 2018 this market will have a compound annual growth of 56 per cent.

Not unsurprisingly, the data suggest that event managers believe that technology is going to be ever more important. For example, Julius Solaris (eventmanagerblog.com 2015) conducted research of event professionals with 6,000 respondents. The key findings of his research are:

- 94 per cent of event professionals will buy technology to boost engagement;
- 75 per cent of event professionals will buy apps to increase engagement;
- 1 in 4 event professionals use tablets to manage registration;
- 1 in 2 event professionals have tried apps, projection mapping, digital touch screens, photo-booths or audience response systems.

This suggests that thus far technology has been more about engagement, but that the potential exists for technology to become embedded within event production and not just one component part. This implies that technology may well lead to a change in the mindset of event managers, who will no longer compartmentalise technology as just one separate part of the event.

Many new technologies are being created each year: we suggest that possible technologies to consider in the next few years are:

- Contactless payment;
- Drones;
- 3D technology;

- Live streaming (such as Periscope);
- Online goody bags;
- Online voting.

One of the technologies that has secured some interest is Augmented Reality, generally known as AR. While this term covers a multitude of different technologies and equipment, put simply AR seeks to add sound, visuals and sometimes smell and touch to enhance an experience. The idea is to bring experiences alive. Typically, it involves wearing smart glasses, effectively wearable technology, which display graphics or information. Thus, you might be looking at a piece of machinery and the glasses offer you a vision of what the machinery looks like on the inside. Other applications of AR use smartphones, which you can point at the subject and get additional information. AR therefore is using existing technology such as 3D, 360 vision, videos, graphics and sound to enhance the experience.

One of the popular areas of the use of AR, tourism, offers lessons for events managers. Here AR has been used especially in heritage and cultural tourist sites to enhance the visitor experience. Yovcheva et al. (2012) found that AR provided variable content for tourists, they suggested that it was especially suited to adding location-based information. It is precisely this aspect that makes this technology interesting for events. Obvious areas include exhibitions where AR could present your products in an 'experience' format, or add 'reality' to a corporate event such as an annual conference. It is possible that AR could revitalise the concept of virtual events by providing a level of detail. We suggest that AR is a likely area of development, so look out for affordable glasses that may make this technology more accessible.

Lessons learnt

This book has covered a wide range of communication tools, and you will need to experiment and learn lessons as you try them. What works for one event may not work for another. However, we suggest that there is a lot of advice out there and you should regularly consult it, especially if faced with a new problem. For example, you might use your own networks to talk to people, but there are also resources such as trade associations, blogs, websites and forums, some of which we have highlighted, which could provide a range of advice, expertise and information.

One of the key points we have tried to convey is that there is rarely a one-size-fits-all approach. However, we do suggest that there are seven core themes contained within this book which provide a framework for learning how best to promote your event:

1 Type of event;
2 Size of event;
3 Event history;
4 Budget;
5 Audience;
6 Timescale to event;
7 Culture.

1 The type of event is the first factor that shapes promotion. Not surprisingly the nature of an entertainment-based event implies a very different approach from a corporate event.
2 Irrespective of type of event, the size/length and duration of an event shape the promotional decisions taken. A larger event has to grapple with more complex communication issues.

Moreover, with a smaller event more personal face-to-face communication is possible than in a larger event.

3 The event history refers to an event's longevity. A long-standing event will have access to more links with past customers, with data and testimonials, case studies and images that can be used. Whereas a new event has little past history of promotional content to use.

4 Related to size and possibly event history is the budget. We have spoken throughout about choosing the channels that fit what your event can afford. This is especially the case since advertising and direct marketing require significant financial backing. Whereas those with a small budget or no budget will probably rely on flyers and media relations.

5 The nature of the audience heavily influences event communication. In very general terms, this would include whether the event is B2B or B2C, but also includes other forms of segmentation, such as demographics.

6 Event timescale refers to when the event will be, and how long the planning process is. Some events require a drip, drip of communication over a long time, others may require a more burst approach where communication happens over a short, concentrated period.

7 Cultural factors of the audience such as religion, ethnicity, language or country characteristics can also typically, but not exclusively, drive the nature of promotional material.

Further information

Article

Flowers, A. and Gregson, K. (2012) 'Decision-making factors in selecting virtual worlds for events: advocacy, computer efficacy, perceived risks and collaborative benefits', *Event Management* 16 (4): 319–334.

Websites

Festival Insights (2015) 'The cashless festival: why 2015 will be the tipping point for the UK'. Online. Available: www.festivalinsights.com/2015/02/cashless-festival-2015-tipping-point-uk/ (accessed on 12 February 2017).

http://publications.arup.com/publications/t/technology_in_sport (accessed on 6 May 2016) – details how technology is transforming the experience in one event field.

Conferences

http://armarketingconference.com/
http://www.augmentedworldexpo.com/

References

Abbate, J. (1999) *Inventing the Internet,* Cambridge, MA: MIT.

Accenture (2014) *Archtypes: winning in a geographically diverse and digital world.* Online. Available: <www.accenture.com/gb-en/insight-market-and-consumer-archetypes-winning-geographically> (accessed on 1 November 2015).

Allen, J. O'Toole, W., Harris, R. and McDonnell, I. (2011) *Festival and Special Event Management,* Milton, QLD: John Wiley.

Black, R. (1986) *The Trade Show Industry: management and marketing career opportunities,* East Orleans, MA: Trade Show Bureau.

Blythe, J. (1999a) 'Visitor and exhibitor expectations and outcomes at trade exhibitions', *Marketing Intelligence and Planning,* 14 (5): 20–24.

— (1999b) 'Learning by doing – frequency of exhibiting at UK trade exhibitions', *Journal of Marketing Communications,* 5 (4): 207–221.

— (2000) 'Objectives and measures at UK trade exhibitions', *Journal of Marketing Management,* 16 (1–3): 203–222.

Boorstein, D. (1962) *The Image: a guide to pseudo-events in America,* New York: Atheneum.

Booz & Co. (2010) *Getting Routes to Market Right: designing profitable go-to-market models in consumer goods.* Online. Available: <www.strategyand.pwc.com/de/studien/getting-routes-market-right-designing> (accessed on 16 February 2015).

Boris, C. (2013) 'Social media referrals: Facebook and Pinterest leave Google+ in the dust', 16 October 2013. Online. Available: <www.marketingpilgrim.com/2013/10/social-media-referrals-facebook-and-pinterest-leave-google-in-the-dust.html> (accessed on 9 June 2015).

British Promotional Merchandise Association (2012) *Research 2012.* Online. Available: <http://bpma.co.uk/bpma-research-2012> (accessed on 7 July 2015).

British Promotional Merchandise Association (2013) *Research 2013.* Online. Available: <http://bpma.co.uk/bpma-research-2013> (accessed on 7 July 2015).

Byrne, J. (2002) *Face the Media: the complete guide to getting publicity and handling media opportunities,* How To Books.

Byrne, M. and Hilbert, D. (2003) 'Colour realism and colour science: evolution and animal colour vision', *Behavioural and Brain Sciences,* 26: 791–794.

Cameron, G. and Ju-Pak, H.-K. (2000) 'Information pollution?: labelling and format of advertorials', *Newspaper Research Journal,* 21 (1): 65–77.

Castells, M. (1996) *The Rise of the Network Society,* Oxford: Blackwell.

Chaiken, S. (1980). 'Heuristic versus systematic information processing and the use of source versus message cues in persuasion', *Journal of Personality & Social Psychology,* 39 (5): 752–766.

Cialdini, R. (1999) *Influence: science and practice,* Boston, MA: Allyn & Bacon.

CMO Council (2015) 'From content to creativity: the role of visual media in impactful brand storytelling', 4 August. Online. Available: <www.cmocouncil.org/press-detail.php?id=5084> (accessed on 10 October 2015).

Curran, J. and Seaton, J. (1997) *Power without Responsibility: press, broadcasting and the internet in Britain*, Oxford: Routledge.

Cyr, D., Head, M. and Larios, H. (2010) 'Colour appeal in website design within and across cultures: a multimethod evaluation', *International Journal of Human-Computer Studies*, 68 (1): 1–21.

Davis, F., Bagozzi, R. and Warshaw, P. (1989) 'Use acceptance of computer technology: a comparison of two models', *Management Science*, 35 (8): 982–1003.

De Bortoli, M. and Maroto, J. (2001) 'Colours across cultures: translating colours in interactive marketing communication'. Online. Available: <www.globalpropaganda.com> (accessed on 1 June 2015).

Diemand-Yauman, C., Oppenheimer, D.M. and Vaughan, E.B. (2010). 'Fortune favors the **bold** (*and italicized*): effects of disfluency on educational outcomes', *Cognition*, 118 (1): 111–115.

Downes, L. and Mui, C. (2000) *Unleashing the Killer App*, Boston, MA: Harvard University Press.

Elliott, A., Maier, M., Moller, A., Friedman, R. and Meinhardt, J. (2007) 'Colour and psychological functioning: the effect of red on performance attainment', *Journal of Experimental Psychology: General*, 136 (1): 154–168.

Eventmanagerblog.com (2015) '10 event trends for 2016', 1 December. Online. Available: <www.eventmanagerblog.com/10-event-trends-2016> (accessed on 2 March 2016).

Fleming, N. (1995) 'I'm different; not dumb, modes of presentation (VARK) in the tertiary classroom', in A. Zelmer (ed.) *Research and Development in Higher Education*, Proceedings of the 1995 Annual Conference of the Higher Education and Research Development Society of Australasia, 18: 308–313.

Frankly, B (1738) *Poor Richard: an almanac,* Philadelphia, Pennsylvania: Benjamin Franklyn.

Friedman, F. (2013) 'Future trends impacting the exhibitions and events industry', IAEE white paper. Online. Available: <www.iaee.com/downloads/1463999507.41069900_1eb8041bd7/2013%20IAEE%20Future%20Trends%20Impacting%20the%20Exhibitions%20and%20Events%20Industry%20White%20Paper.pdf> (accessed on 23 May 2016).

Frost, W. and Laing, J. (2013) 'Communicating persuasive messages through slow food Festivals', *Journal of Vacation Marketing,* 19 (1): 67–74.

Galfano, G., Dalmaso, M., Marzoli, D., Pavan, G., Coricelli, C. and Castelli, L. (2012) 'Eye gaze cannot be ignored (but neither can arrows)', *Quarterly Journal of Experimental Psychology,* 65 (10): 1895–1910.

Gehrle, D. and Turban, E. (1999) 'Determinants of successful website design: relative importance and recommendations for effectiveness', Proceedings of the 32nd Hawaii International Conference on System Sciences, Marui Island, January.

Getz, D. (2008) *Event Studies: theory, research and policy for planned events*, London: Butterworth Heinemann.

Gangeshwer, D. (2013) 'E-commerce or internet marketing: a business review from Indian context', *International Journal of u- and e- Service, Science and Technology*, 6 (6): 187–194.

Gronroos, C. (1994) 'From marketing mix to relationship marketing: towards a paradigm shift in marketing', *Management Decision*, 34 (3): 5–14.

Gupta, A. (2013) 'The shift from words to pictures and implications for digital marketers', 2 July 2013. Online. Available: <www.forbes.com/sites/onmarketing/2013/07/02/the-shift-from-words-to-pictures-and-implications-for-digital-marketers/#4d55b4ac2549> (accessed on 1 May 2016).

References

Harrison-Hill, T. and Chalip, L. (2005) 'Marketing sport tourism: creating synergy between sport and destination', *Sport in Society: Cultures, Commerce, Media, Politics*, 8 (2): 302–320.

Hendy, D. (2013) *Noise: a human history of sound and listening*, London: Profile.

Herbig, P., O'Hara, B. and Palumbo, F. (1997) 'Differences between trade show exhibitors and non-exhibitors', *Journal of Business & Industrial Marketing*, 12 (6): 368–382.

Holzner, S. (2008) *Facebook Marketing: designing your next marketing campaign*, Indianapolis, IN: Que Publishing.

Hudson, S. and Hudson, R. (2013) 'Engaging with consumers using social media: a case study of music festivals', *International Journal of Event & Festival Management*, 4 (3): 206–223.

Jackson, N. (2008a) 'Online political communication: the impact of the internet on MPs 1994–2005', unpublished PhD thesis, University of Bournemouth.

__ (2008b) 'MPs and their e-newsletters: winning votes by promoting constituency service', *Journal of Legislative Studies*, 14 (4): 488–499.

— (2009) 'All the fun of the seaside – the British party conference season', *E.Pol*, 2 (1): 8–10.

— (2013) *Promoting and Marketing Events: theory and practice*, London: Routledge.

Jackson, N. and Lilleker, D. (2009) 'Building an architecture of participation?: political parties and Web 2.0 in Britain, *Journal of Information Technology and Politics*, 6 (3/4): 232–250.

Jenkins, O. (2003) 'Photography and travel brochures: the circle of representation', *Tourism Geographies: An International Journal of Tourism Space, Place and Environment*, 5 (3): 303–328.

Karr, D. (2014) 'Seven deadly sins of SMS marketing', 8 January. Online. Available: <www.marketingtechblog.com/text-message-mistakes/> (accessed on 20 January 2014).

Keshaven, V. and Tandon, N. (2012) 'How to give an effective presentation', *Asian Journal of Psychiatry*, 5 (4): 360–361.

Kim, S.-E. Shaw, T. and Schneider, H. (2003) 'Web site design benchmarking within industry groups', *Internet Research: Electronic Networking Applications and Policy*, 13 (1): 17–26.

Langton, D. and Campbell, A. (2011) *Visual Marketing: 99 proven ways for small businesses to market images and design*, Hoboken, NJ: Wiley.

Lee, D. and Palakurthi, R. (2013) 'Marketing strategy to increase exhibition attendance through controlling and eliminating leisure constraints', *Event Management*, 17 (4): 323–336.

Lee-Kelley, L., Gilbert, D. and Al-Shehadi, A. (2004) 'Virtual exhibitions: an exploratory study of Middle East exhibitors' dispositions', *International Marketing Review*, 21 (6): 634–644.

Loss, J. Lindacher and V. Curbach, J. (2014) 'Online social networking sites – a novel setting for health promotion?', *Health and Place*, 26 (March): 161–170.

Luo, X. and Donthu, N. (2005) 'Assessing advertising media spending inefficiencies in generating sales', *Journal of Business Research*, 58 (1): 28–36.

MacArthur, A. (2016) 'The 17 best email subject lines for increasing open rates', 3 February 2016. Online. Available: <www.mequoda.com/articles/audience-development/best-email-subject-lines> (accessed on 9 March 2016).

McCarthy, E.J. (1964) *Basic Marketing*, Homewood, IL: Richard D. Irwin.

Mackay, K. (2015) 'My favourite colour was yellow'. Online. Available: <https://kirstymackay.wordpress.com/category/generation-pink/my-favourite-colour-was-yellow/> (accessed on 10 May 2016).

Manjoo, F. (2013) 'You won't finish this article', *Slate*. Online. Available: <www.slate.com/articles/technology/technology/2013/06/how_people_read_online> (accessed on 15 July 2015).

Market Media Research (2016) 'Virtual conference and trade show market forecast 2013–2018', 7 January 2016. Online. Available: <www.marketresearchmedia.com/?p=421> (accessed on 23 May 2016).

Mazereeuw, A. (2015) 'Why infographics work', 12 May 2015. Online. Available: <www.lifelearn.com/2015/05/12/why-infograhics-work> (accessed on 20 January 2016).

Mehrabian, A. (1972) *Nonverbal Communication*, New Brunswick, NJ: Aldine Transaction.

Miller, B. and Barnett, B. (2010) 'Understanding of health risks aided by graphs with text', *Newspaper Research Journal*, 31 (1): 58–68.

Morrow, S. (2001) *The Art of the Show*, Dallas, TX: IAEM Education.

Mwanyumba, J. (2009) 'Managers' perception towards effectiveness of trade shows and exhibitions as a method of promotion: a case of Mombasa agricultural society of Kenya show', MBA, University of Nairobi, Kenya.

Nielsen Group (2014) 'Super Bowl XLViii draws 111.5 million viewers, 25.3 million tweets,' 2 March 2014. Online. Available: <www.nielsen.com/us/en/insights/news/2014/super-bowl-xlviii-draws-111-5-million-viewers-25-3-million-tweets.html> (accessed on 5 January 2015).

Nielsen, J. (2006) 'F-shaped pattern for reading web content', Nielsen Norman Group, 17 April. Online. Available: <www.nngroup.com/articles/f-shaped-pattern-reading-web-content/> (accessed on 10 June 2013).

— (2008) *How Little Do Users Read?* Nielsen Norman Group. Online. Available: <www.nngroup.com/articles/how-little-do-users-read> (accessed on 15 July 2015).

— (2010) 'Photos are web content', Nielsen Norman Group, 1 November 2010. Online. Available: <www.nngroup.com/articles/photos-as-web-content> (accessed on 20 January 2016).

Norris, P. (2000) *A Virtuous Circle: political communications in post-industrialised societies*, Cambridge: Cambridge University Press.

O'Keefe, D. (1997) 'Standpoint explicitness and persuasive effect: a meta-analytic review of the effects of varying conclusion articulation in persuasive messages', *Argumentation and Advocacy*, 34 (1): 1–12.

— (1999) *Persuasion: theory and research*, London: Sage.

Oppenheimer, D. (2012) 'Hard-to-read fonts promote better recall', *Harvard Business Review*, March. Online. Available: <https://hbr.org/2012/03/hard-to-read-fonts-promote-better-recall> (accessed on 10 May 2016).

Outsourced Events (undated) 'Mobile World Congress 2015. Gaga over Google's Android pins'. Online. Available: <www.outsourcedevents.com/tag/best-exhibition-stands> (accessed on 3 July 2015).

Pease, E. and Dennis, E. (1995) (eds) *Radio: the forgotten medium*, New Brunswick, NJ: Transaction.

Perloff, R. (2008) *The Dynamics of Persuasion: communication and attitudes in the twenty-first century*, New York: Lawrence Erlbaum Associates.

Pine, B.J. and Gilmore, J. (2011) *The Experience Economy*, Boston, MA: Harvard Business Review Press.

Pincas, S. and Loiseau, M. (2008) *A History of Advertising*, Cologne: Taschen.

Pitta, D., Weisgal, M. and Lynagh, P. (2006) 'Integrating exhibit marketing into integrated marketing communications', *Journal of Consumer Marketing*, 23 (3): 156–166.

Preston, C. (2012) *Event Marketing: how to successfully promote events, festivals, conventions and expositions*, Hoboken, NJ: John Wiley.

Printperfection.com (2010) 'What is merchandise marketing?', 6 August 2010. Online. Available: <http://blog.printfection.com/what-is-merchandise-marketing/> (accessed on 1 August 2014).

Promotional Products Business (2013) 'Reasons to use promotional merchandise'. Online. Available: <https://promotionalproductsbusiness.wordpress.com> (accessed on 4 July 2015).

References

The Radacati Group, Inc. (2015) 'Key statistics on business and consumer email 2015–2019', 2 March 2015. Online. Available: <www.radicati.com/?p=12964> (accessed on 11 August 2015).

Rayner, S. (2004) 'Getting yourself noticed', *Marketing Week*, July 8: 37–38.

Reuters (2010) 'Paris police ban mass "Facebook aperitif" party', 20 May 2010. Online. Available: <www.reuters.com/article/us-france-party-ban-idUSTRE64J5A420100520> (accessed on 4 February 2016).

Robinson, A. (2002) 'Examining advertorials: an application of the elaboration likelihood model', Unpublished thesis, Lincoln University, Auckland, New Zealand.

Rodriguez, J. (2011) *Direct Marketing 234 Success Secrets – 234 Most Asked Questions On Direct Marketing – What You Need To Know*, Emereo Publishing, eBook.

Schaie, K. and Heiss, R. (1964) *Colour and Personality*, New York: Huber, Grune and Stratton.

Schmitt, B. (1999) *Experiential Marketing: how to get customers to sense, feel, think, act and relate to your company and brands*, New York: The Free Press.

Schneider, S. (2013) 'The trick to designing a great layout', 10 June 2013. Online. Available: <www.webdesignerdepot.com/2013/06/the-trick-to-designing-a-great-layout/> (accessed on 1 February 2016).

Serrano, I. (2015) 'How to use Pinterest and Instagram to promote your next event', *We Think*. 12 March 2015. Online. Available: <http://blog.etouches.com/tips-and-tools/how-to-use-pinterest-and-instagram-to-promote-your-next-event/> (accessed on 13 May 2016).

Simons, H. (2001) *Persuasion in Society*, London: Sage.

Situma, S. (2012) 'The effectiveness of trade shows and exhibitions as organisational marketing tools (analysis of selected companies in Mombasa)', *International Journal of Business and Social Science*, 3 (22): 219–230.

Solaris, J. (2014) 'How to win and influence attendees', 5 May. Online. Available: <www.eventmanagerblog.com/influence-persuasion-events> (accessed on 11 November 2014).

Sporting Charts (2014) 'Super Bowl attendance by numbers'. Online. Available: <www.sportingcharts.com/articles/nfl/super-bowl-attendance-by-the-numbers.aspx> (accessed on 8 January 2015).

Tan, G. and Wei, K. (2006) 'An empirical study of web browsing behaviour: towards an effective website design', *Electronic Commerce Research and Applications*, 5 (4): 261–271.

Thaler, R. and Sunstein, C. (2008) *Nudge: improving decisions about health, wealth and happiness*, London: Penguin.

Urry, J. (1990) *The Tourist Gaze*, London: Sage.

Von Rosen, V. (2012) *LinkedIn Marketing: an hour a day*, Hoboken, NJ: Wiley/Sybex.

Whitfield, T. and Wiltshire, T. (1990) 'Colour psychology: a critical review', *Generic, Social and General Psychology Monographs*, 116 (4): 387–412.

Williams, G. (2010) 'Big marketing stunts, small business style', 3 August 2010. Online. Available: <www.entrepreneur.com/article/207690> (accessed on 5 October 2015).

Wiscombe, C. (2010) 'Funding, sponsorship and financial management', in D. Wale, P. Robinson and G. Dickson (eds) *Events Management*, Oxfordshire: CABI: 46–71.

Whiteling, I. (2003) 'Taking a stand', *Marketing Week*, February 20: 47–48.

Yovcheva, Z., Buhalis, D. and Gatzidis, C. (2012) 'Overview of smartphone augmented reality applications for tourism', *e-Review of Tourism Research*, 10 (2): 63–66.

Zaller, J. and Hunt, M. (1994) 'The rise and fall of candidate Perot: unmediated versus mediated politics', *Political Communication*, 11 (4): 357–390.

Index